This book demonstrates that truth and trust have never been more important for brands and that there is a close link for customers in what you say and where you say it - this is crucial reading for all those planning marketing communications in a programmatic and algorithmic world
Jonathan Allan, Interim CEO, Channel 4

You can't see it, or smell it or touch it, but trust, along with creativity, is the most valuable quality of effective advertising. This fascinating and comprehensive book shares all the insight that the industry has amassed over the years on the subject of trust. It lists the achievements but is honest about the ongoing challenges that an evolving media landscape inevitably brings.
Tess Alps, Mac Medal, Founding CEO of Thinkbox, NED at Channel 4 and Comic Relief Trustee

If an advertiser is not trusted, everything else is academic. This timely book reminds us of the key components of trust in an age where trust is in short supply.
Paul Bainsfair, Director General, Institute for Practitioners of Advertising

Every brand wants to be trusted; however it is a dense and multifaceted topic. This book turns trust into something easily accessible and relevant for any advertising practitioner, helping them with ways to make it stronger, more competitive and, ultimately, more successful.
Alessandra Bellini, NED, Executive Coach, Adviser

Many valuable things in life are intangible. Trust is one. But it's an essential element in building brand preference and customer loyalty, and this excellent book will help you turn trust into a real and tangible asset.
Kathryn Jacob, CEO, Pearl & Dean and co-author of *Belonging*, *The Glass Wall* and *A Year Of Creativity*

Trust is central to a healthy democratic society and our need for trustworthy sources of news and information has never been more vital. If you're responsible for any kind of brand, this book is a timely and necessary read. It will equip you with everything you need to know to put trust at the heart of your advertising campaigns.
Owen Meredith, CEO, News Media Association

Every marketer is passionate about their brand and the best marketers know that building brand trust can be a powerful differentiator and source of competitive advantage. This comprehensive book is a guide to how to leverage advertising as means of building trust amongst both customers and stakeholders, ensuring both soft and hard return on investment and strengthening advertising's role as a vital part of the marketing mix.
Simon Michaelides, Director General, ISBA

James and Matt have a lifetime's experience in the advertising sector – so their book on why trust in advertising matters, full of insights and written for everyone working at the frontline of modern advertising and dealing with new platforms and technology, is both timely and thought-provoking.
Baroness Nicky Morgan

Without trust, the brands we are building amount to nothing more than their base transactional value. Trust is the most alchemic and value adding element of any marketeers armoury. What James Best and Matt Bourn don't know about the subject isn't worth trusting.
James Murphy, CEO, Ogilvy Group UK

One thing that always fascinates me from the annals of true-life crime are the convoluted mechanisms people must resort to when they pay a bribe, buy off a blackmailer or deliver a ransom payment (think of *Strangers on a Train*). These devices are emblematic of the extraordinary high transaction costs involved in any economic activity when trust is completely absent. Perhaps the greater part of economic activity cannot take place at all in the absence of a high level of trust, and without the assurance of some kind of reputational skin in the game. And yet until recently the whole of economics ducked this question entirely. Thankfully two of the most reputable (an interesting word that, when you think about it) names in advertising have now come together to set the record straight.
Rory Sutherland, Vice Chairman, Ogilvy Consulting

This book is a great resource for anyone in the ad field or interested in advertising. The perspective on ethics provided is valuable as advertising clearly has the potential to have positive societal impacts, but if left unchecked, problematic practices can undermine trust in the industry and limit its effectiveness. The book is also a valuable resource for understanding what helps make an advertiser earn trust—while this issue has always been important, it is more critical than ever in today's competitive marketplace.

Charles R Taylor, Editor-in-Chief, *International Journal of Advertising*

A very wise, well-researched and timely book. Trust is more elusive than ever, and this is your self-help handbook on how it can be earned.

Charles Vallance, Chairman, VCCP

Trust is essential for any brand, and as a CEO, I recognize the central role advertising plays in building it. *Trusted Advertising* is timely, given the current challenges to trust in society. James and Matt offer valuable insights on how advertising can remain credible now and in the future. By applying their recommended principles, your brand can gain the benefits that come with genuine trust

Andria Vidler, CEO, Allwyn UK and President, Advertising Association

Trusted Advertising

How to harness the value of trust in your brand

Matt Bourn and James Best

KoganPage

First published in Great Britain and the United States in 2026

Kogan Page
Kogan Page Ltd, 2nd Floor, 45 Gee Street, London EC1V 3RS, United Kingdom
Kogan Page Inc, 8 W 38th Street, Suite 902, New York, NY 10018, USA
www.koganpage.com

EU Representative (GPSR)
eucomply OÜ, Pärnu mnt 139b -14 11317, Tallinn, Estonia
www.eucompliancepartner.com

Kogan Page books are printed on paper from sustainable forests.

© Matt Bourn and James Best 2026

The moral rights of the authors have been asserted in accordance with the Copyright, Designs and Patents Act 1988.

ISBNs
Hardback   978 1 3986 2357 6
Paperback   978 1 3986 2355 2
Ebook   978 1 3986 2356 9

British Library Cataloguing-in-Publication Data
A CIP record for this book is available from the British Library.

Library of Congress Cataloging in Publication Data
A CIP record for this book is available from the Library of Congress.

Typeset by Integra Software Services, Pondicherry
Print production managed by Jellyfish
Printed and bound by CPI Group (UK) Ltd, Croydon CR0 4YY

CONTENTS

07 Trust in the age of the influencer: Part 2 119

08 Can advertising generated by AI be trusted? 138

09 Does it matter where you show up? Part 1 161

ABOUT THE AUTHORS

James Best CBE is Chair of the Committees of Advertising Practice (CAP, UK advertising's rule-making body) and of Credos, the advertising industry-funded thinktank. James was Chair of the Advertising Association 1997–2003, President of the EACA (the European advertising agencies representative body) 2003–06, a member of the Advertising Standards Authority Council 2007–11, vice-chair of the History of Advertising Trust 2016–24, Visiting Professor of Advertising at Richmond International University 2016–20, and is a Fellow of the IPA. In his executive career, he was Chair of BMP DDB from 1990–2000, during which time it became one the UK's most successful and most admired top agencies, and then a board director of DDB Worldwide as VP Northern Europe and later Chief Strategy & People Officer, retiring from DDB in 2007. He started as a planner at BMP in 1975, so has been in and around the industry for 50 years. James was awarded a CBE in The King's Birthday Honours List 2025 for services to advertising.

Matt Bourn is Director of Communications for the Advertising Association, the trade body that brings together advertisers, agencies, media owners and tech companies from across the UK advertising industry. He oversees the association's communications on key policy areas and helps to steer the industry's work around Public Trust, Talent & Inclusion and Climate Action, including the formation of Ad Net Zero. With 25 years' experience, previously he was Managing Director of Braben, working for companies such as Sky, Channel 4, Disney and Sony. In 2024, Kogan Page published *Sustainable Advertising* which Matt co-authored with Ad Net Zero Chair Sebastian Munden, which sets out a manifesto for the world's advertising industry to help build a sustainable economy and support a better future.

PREFACE

'Trust me, I'm in advertising.' Really? Why should we trust a salesman?

But trust in advertising matters, especially to the advertisers who pay for it. If you don't trust the messenger, can you believe the message?

So, for over a century the companies involved in the advertising industry, meaning brand owners, the media they use and the agencies they employ, have worked to engender trust in what they do amongst their customers and audiences.

A key objective of the Advertising Association back in 1926 was 'to promote public confidence in Advertising and advertised products'.

Trust mattered. Both in advertising as a discipline and in the products it promoted – an important distinction. Distrust undermined the very foundations of brands' appeal and the worth of their advertising. It still does.

In this book we set out to explain what trust is, its value, how it is won and lost, and what to do about it to make your advertising more effective. It's a practitioners' guide, bringing together research past and present, the thinking of experts and the experiences of current advertisers large and small to show how trusted advertising that enhances business performance can best be achieved in the 21st century. A century that has already seen a 'crisis of trust', with fundamental changes in who, what and how people trust.

We do not claim that trust is everything – some businesses may possess such compelling appeal that they can afford to risk their reputations, at least for a while, but they are few and far between. We do claim that a trusted messenger will convey a more credible message, and that credibility – and, indeed, precious qualities of trust that go beyond simple credibility – are assets companies and brands should nurture, with the full engagement of their partners in the advertising industry, media owners and agencies alike. We claim this because we believe trust can be a competitive differentiator for you and your brand.

A hundred years on from the Advertising Association's first commitment 'to promote public confidence', we aim to show how central it remains to every advertiser's success, every agency's work, every media channel that carries advertising, for all companies, large and small, involved in advertising's technology evolution, and to anyone interested in advertising.

London, July 2025

ACKNOWLEDGEMENTS

First, a big thank you to the Credos team, led by Dan Wilks with the able support of George Grant, whose work to consistently track and understand why the public trust advertising, building on work originally developed by Karen Fraser.

The work to protect and build public trust in advertising has been supported by many people from across the industry. They include Stephen Woodford, the current Chief Executive of the Advertising Association, and his predecessor, Tim Lefroy, but also two Director Generals of ISBA and the IPA respectively, Phil Smith and Paul Bainsfair, who have chaired the Trust Working Group since its inception. Support has also come from Advertising Association Presidents, Andria Vidler, Alessandra Bellini and Keith Weed, and Front Foot Chairs, Pete Markey and Mark Evans, as well as the many AA members who have participated in the group and on the board of Front Foot.

Many people gave us their time and support to help inform the content in this book, so our thanks to Laurence Green, Fran Cassidy, Carlos Grande and Maria Grey at the IPA; Abi Slater at ISBA; the team at the ASA including Guy Parker, Shahriar Coupal, Donna Castle, Matt Wilson, Kam Atwal and Kim Martinez, and the ASA's Chair, Baroness Nicky Morgan; Lynne Deason and Dom Boyd at Kantar, as well as Russell Parsons of Marketing Week for their support for The Works; the team at Edelman including Tonia Ries, Caitlin Semo and Francesca Woodhouse for insights about their work with the Trust Barometer; Professor Charles (Ray) Taylor, editor of the *International Journal of Advertising*; Samira Brophy, Sara Gundry and Ben Page at Ipsos; former DCMS Minister, Sir Chris Bryant MP; Gideon Spanier at Campaign; Ian Murray at everyday people; Sam Smith at Clearcast; Rachel Barber-Mack at Media Smart; Scott Guthrie at the Influencer Marketing Trade Body; Lindsey Clay and Simon Tunstill at Thinkbox; Jon Mew and Jessie Sampson at IAB UK; Rachel Aldighieri at the Data Marketing Association; Karen Stacey at Digital Cinema Media; Heather Dansie at Newsworks; Damon Reeve at Ozone; Douglas McCabe, formerly of Enders Analysis; Nick Manning at Advertising: Who Cares?; Amanda Griffiths and Eve Stansell at Royal Mail Marketreach; Dyana Najdi, Yves Schwarzbart and Jo Ogunleye at Google; Isabelle Quevilly and Sophie Cartwright at Meta; and Rob Ryan at TikTok.

Also, marketing and communications leads including Katie Jackson at Channel 4; Steve Parkinson at Allwyn; Georgina Bramall and Lisa Boyles at giffgaff; Murray Bisschop at Tesco; Marg Jobling and Petra Cameron at NatWest; Richard Warren at Nationwide; Hayley Shortman at TUI; and Simon Baugh and Conrad Bird at the Government Communications Services. And agency leads including James Murphy, Dan Bennett, Rahul Titus and Hugo Eyre-Varnier at Ogilvy; Charles Vallance, Alex Dalman and Georgia Wright at VCCP; Lucy Jameson at Uncommon; Jessica Tamsedge at dentsu creative; the team at Billion Dollar Boy including Thomas Walters, Sophie Crowther and Erin Pugh and the content creators Em Wallbank and Keith Afadi; Dafydd Woodward at Goat; Emma Harman at Whalar; Sean Betts at OMG; Dr Daniel Hulme at WPP; Jenny Biggam at the7stars; Luke Bozeat at WPP Media; Venya Wijegoonewardene at Spark Foundry; Natalie Bell and Kat Bozicevich at MG OMD; and Charlie Ebdy at OMG. And finally, comms and policy leads including Jo Tomlin at the Professional Publishers Association; Michael Ireland at Radiocentre; Bryan Scott at Ozone; Rupert Smith at Newsworks; Tristan O'Carroll at Channel 4; Eva Dvorak at Bauer Media Outdoor; Janet Guest at JCDecaux; Rebecca Khan, formerly of Publicis Media; Jennie Rock at WPP Media; and Louise Lacourarie at WPP.

Finally, a special thanks to Advertising Association colleagues for all their support including Grace Hughes, Polly Devaney, Mariella Brown and Maddie Brooks.

01

Trust in the 21st century

Introduction

Imagine you are faced with a choice between two options. There is little to differentiate between the two; they are comparable on many levels and both options are within easy reach. But you have a feeling, a sense of connection, a confidence even, in one choice more than the other; you believe more that it will deliver what you want. So, you make the decision, choose the one you trust and leave the other for someone else.

There, in that moment, is the competitive advantage that comes from, in this loosest sense, being trusted.

If you believe that trust in one choice over another can decide which you select, then this book is for you because it will set out how to deliver the very best, trusted advertising. If you don't, please read on anyway, and let's see if we can make a convincing enough case to change your mind.

Let's be honest (an important facet of trust), 'trust' and the concept of being trusted is a slippery one to pin down, as James is fond of reminding Matt. It's fair to say the word 'trust' is being thrown around a lot at the time of writing in 2025. It's at the heart of claims and counterclaims in the worlds of politics, news and business, as it is in popular culture.

So much so that one of the most successful series on UK TV screens right now is the BBC's *The Traitors*. It first appeared in 2021 as a Dutch reality TV series and is now broadcast or licensed in at least 20 different countries and territories.[1] The show's developer, Marc Pos, shared his inspiration for the series – to create a world where people can't trust each other and put them in a bubble.[2] Millions of people around the world are hooked on a show with the concept of trust and distrust right at its heart.

Many of the ideas we are going on to explore in this book can be seen in practice as the show (and game) unfolds. We've had lots of fun pointing them out to each other – people gravitating towards those like themselves;

our comfort with the known rather than the unknown; the instinct to follow the herd in adopting views; the propensity to trust people we like; the power of feeling over reason or evidence; and a hunger for authenticity and consistency. All aspects of trust that sit at the heart of what we will unpack in this book.

We believe it's important to consider 'trust' in its social context in this opening chapter, because advertising doesn't operate in a vacuum. Far from it: advertising is a window into our society and the way we live our lives, sometimes reflecting the past and sometimes projecting things to come.

To understand how and why advertising must be trusted in order to fulfil its vital economic and social role, we must first consider what is happening to trust in the 21st century...

To trust is a human instinct

Trust is an inherent human emotion. Developmental psychologists have identified it as being hugely important in early-stage development. The ability to trust in caregivers is necessary to survive in the world, to form relationships and to function in society as we grow.[3] All our social relationships, whether we are aware of it or not, are impacted by trust. Even interactions between governments across the world are dictated in large part by trust. Society as a whole depends on mutual trust – without it our social lives, our businesses, our institutions would struggle to function.

A recent meta-analysis of 338 academic papers, titled 'How and why humans trust: A meta-analysis and elaborated model', summarizes its findings that trust determines whether and how individuals interact with others.[4] Trust and trustworthiness underpin social and economic interactions, but more than that, they are fundamental to all types of social and moral behaviours including fairness, honesty and cooperation.

In short, people need to trust others and we all want to be trusted – it matters.

With that fundamental psychological and social importance, it is easy to see why trust should matter in business. Because although trust is first a social, psychological process, successful business practice is often rooted in the social and the psychological.

Marketing and advertising rely on trust as much as any industry, if not more. On one level, we rely on people trusting the advertising they see as honest and truthful – we need to earn that level of trust to have any ability to communicate successfully with them. But on a deeper level, advertising is about winning trust in order to convince, persuade, engender confidence and create a lasting connection between an audience and a brand.

How it does so and how it can be maximized in our work is what we will be exploring with you.

Exploring the meaning(s) of trust

What do we mean when we say 'trust'?

The English word *trust* comes from the Proto-Indo-European word *dreu* (which means to be firm, hard, solid), and then later from the Proto-Germanic word *traustaz* (which means firm, strong).[5] So, something you can rely on, a foundation to build on. Right away, there is a feeling here about how the word trust conveys strength, in that we trust the strong to do what is right.

Trust as a noun can be described as the firm belief in the reliability, truth or ability of someone or something, to have confidence or faith in a person or thing, or in the attribute of a person or thing.

Trust as a verb is to have faith or confidence in a person, quality or thing; to rely on; and trust as an adjective is to feel confident, sure, safe, secure.

If we were to describe you as 'trusted' then we would mean you are some-one that can be relied on; you're dependable.

Better still, you might be 'trustworthy', a word that means you're worthy of trust or confidence; someone we can believe or that is credible.

If you are, then people will go with you when they cannot be sure of the consequences. To trust someone means you are prepared to take a risk because you have confidence in their judgement, skills or knowledge, or in the case of a brand, in its benefits and claims. We can't know everything for sure, so we rely on trust to make our decisions.

Applying the word 'trust'

Trust is a commonly used word, one of the 5,000 most common in modern written English (according to the *Oxford English Dictionary*).

When you consider how it is used now, it has all sorts of roles in our language.

Looking back at how the word evolved in the English language, trust began to be used in a legal and financial sense in the 17th century – as in a trust fund where money is placed, where you have trustees, trust certificates, trust investments and more.

In 1895, the word was given an association with the preservation of places of historic interest or natural beauty in England, Wales and Northern Ireland, with the formation of the National Trust.[6]

In the early decades of the 20th century, the writer Virginia Woolf used the word to convey something with healing properties, implying that trust could, perhaps, be good for us.[7]

In 1932, US presidential candidate Franklin D. Roosevelt was supported during his first campaign by a team of specialist advisers dubbed the Brains Trust by journalist John F. Kieran, a term which quickly became popular, adding the notion of expertise to the word.[8]

Trust is also a word connected to public services, for example, health. It has a direct link to the UK's National Health Service where we talk about NHS Trusts, people entrusted with the future health of the nation.[9] In this sense, trust exists in every sphere. There's even a History of Advertising Trust,[10] preserving the work of our industry for future generations to study and enjoy.

There's quite a lot invested in this one-syllable, five-letter word.

Intellectual prowess, health, finance and investments, value, a promise of something to come, caring for things important to us.

Trust can be founded on faith, reason or experience, with the success (or not) of the major pillars of society critically dependent on it. From the church to the monarchy; from the government to the media. And all of them have been challenged recently by the voice of the individual (or the citizen) shared through the spread of technology, particularly the advent of social media.

Whether personal or societal, emotional or rational, institutional or individual, trust takes many forms. No wonder it's a slippery word to pin down!

What's the opposite of trust?

William Shakespeare, as was his way, played with the word *trust* and highlighted the problems this 'very simple Gentleman' (*The Winter's Tale*) could bring, whether in Othello's blind faith in his 'honest Iago' or the doomed King Duncan's description of the traitorous Macbeth as 'a gentleman on whom I built an absolute trust'.[11]

Maybe he was on to something.

In critiquing the naivety and dangers of trusting too readily, he was opening up the consideration of its opposite: distrust.[12]

This means to dread or doubt something or someone. If we were to say that we 'distrust' you, that would be to communicate to you that we are without confidence in you. We suspect, we question the reality, the validity or the genuineness of what you might say, be or do.

As we will see, there has been a growth of distrust in the institutions we have relied on in society for it to work properly for everyone, in the pillars that society is built on – the government, police and judiciary, the media and business. We need to examine this change and what it means for trust in advertising.

Testing levels of trust in the 21st century

One compelling piece of research which marked its 25th anniversary as we wrote this book is the Edelman Trust Barometer.[13] A look at it helps to explain why we are writing about trust now, and the importance for advertisers of ensuring your work can be trusted.

For context, the Trust Barometer is an annual online survey of more than 33,000 respondents, covering 28 countries with more than 1,150 respondents per country. The nations are a mix, representing western democracies including the US, the UK and many European countries as well as single party states including China and Saudi Arabia.

Matt attended the UK launch event at the Royal Academy in January 2025 and heard from speakers including the President and CEO of Edelman, Richard Edelman.

Edelman opened proceedings by presenting a point of view on how trust had been eroded during the first quarter of the 21st century by a series of different world events. He argues that this began back in 1999 at something called the Battle of Seattle, when the World Trade Organization protests inspired the first Trust Barometer research, which established that NGOs were the most trusted institutions when compared with governments, media and business. This was followed by an erosion of trust in the US government following the decision and evidence presented to justify their invasion of Iraq in 2003.

Then, in 2008, trust in banks slumped during the global financial crash. The timeline moves onto 2016, when a rise in populism powers Brexit, trust in media declines along with a growth in inequality of trust between the wealthy and the poor. The Covid-19 pandemic was cited as a moment when business responded well to the crisis, keeping products on shelves and people in jobs and the barometer results in 2021 showed that business tied with then surpassed NGOs as the most trusted. The invasion of Ukraine in 2022 sparked brand boycotts, caused by geopolitical conflicts. Now, in 2025, the headline theme is that a lack of trust generally has led us to what Edelman describes as 'an Age of Grievance'.

An even more detailed description of this timeline of trust can be seen in Figure 1.1.

Richard Edelman summarized the state of play into six main headlines:

1 There has been a loss of belief in leaders.

2 There is a massive class divide in trust.

3 Single party states fare better with trust than democracies.

4 There is a battle now for truth with no agreed facts and a proliferation of false news.

5 Trust in business is rising, thanks to a 'good' Covid where companies proved competency.

6 Trust has moved local, with many trusting their employer.

Some of the interesting findings of the 2025 Edelman Trust Barometer include an increase to an all-time high in the fear that leaders lie to us; also seen in the fear of being discriminated against. Meanwhile there is a pervasive belief that Hostile Activism is a viable means to drive change, particularly in the young where more than half all 18–34 year olds approve of action ranging from attacking people online, intentionally spreading disinformation, threatening or committing violence, or damaging public or private property. This all indicates a general sense of grievance – and the higher the perceived grievance, the less likely there will be trust in any of the main institutions.

The 2025 Edelman Trust Barometer shows that only business is seen as both competent and ethical, rating almost as high as NGOs on the latter and well above government on competency.

Specifically, Edelman's report recommends that businesses should aim to restore levels of public trust by focusing on four areas of action:

1 **Grievances must be addressed:** The institutional failures of the last 25 years have produced grievances around the world, stifling growth and innovation in turn. To lead through this crisis, understand the economic

FIGURE 1.1 2025 Edelman Trust Barometer: 'Institutional Failures'

A Generation of Institutional Failures Erupts Into Grievance

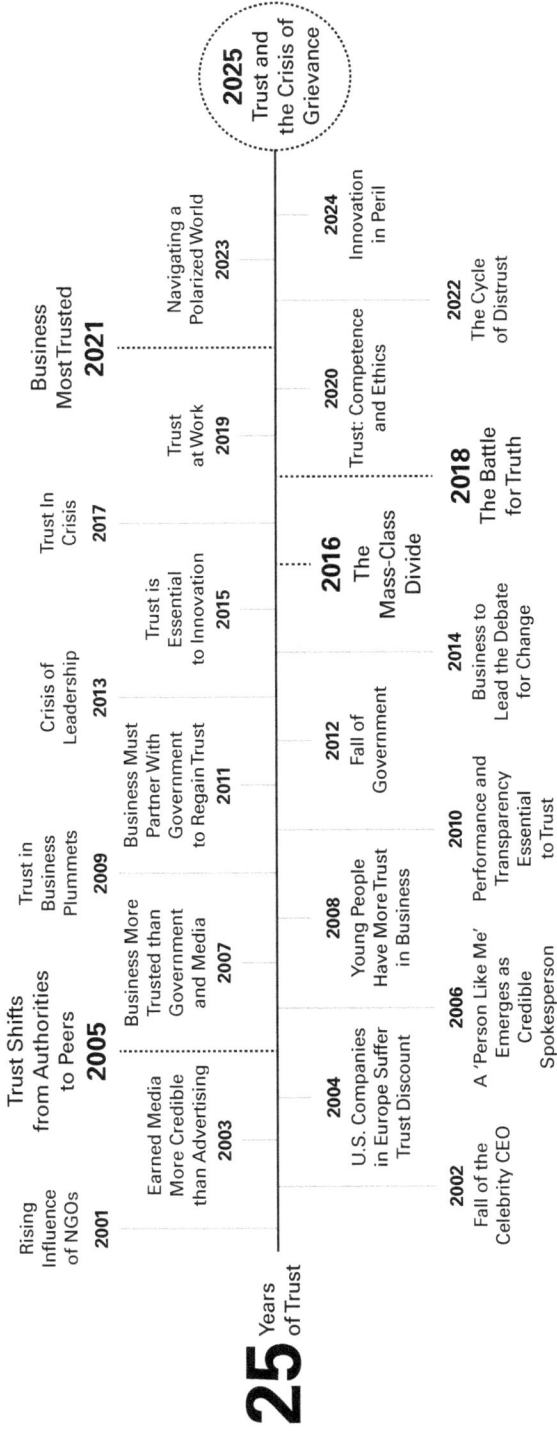

25 Years of Trust

- 2001 — Rising Influence of NGOs
- 2003 — Earned Media More Credible than Advertising
- 2005 — Trust Shifts from Authorities to Peers
- 2007 — Business More Trusted than Government and Media
- 2009 — Trust in Business Plummets
- 2011 — Business Must Partner With Government to Regain Trust
- 2013 — Crisis of Leadership
- 2015 — Trust is Essential to Innovation
- 2017 — Trust In Crisis
- 2019 — Trust at Work
- 2021 — Business Most Trusted
- 2023 — Navigating a Polarized World

- 2002 — Fall of the Celebrity CEO
- 2004 — U.S. Companies in Europe Suffer Trust Discount
- 2006 — A 'Person Like Me' Emerges as Credible Spokesperson
- 2008 — Young People Have More Trust in Business
- 2010 — Performance and Transparency Essential to Trust
- 2012 — Fall of Government
- 2014 — Business to Lead the Debate for Change
- 2016 — The Mass-Class Divide
- 2018 — The Battle for Truth
- 2020 — Trust: Competence and Ethics
- 2022 — The Cycle of Distrust
- 2024 — Innovation in Peril

- 2025 — Trust and the Crisis of Grievance

Courtesy of the Edelman Trust Institute © 2025 Daniel J. Edelman, Inc.

FIGURE 1.2 2025 Edelman Trust Barometer: 'Trust In Business'

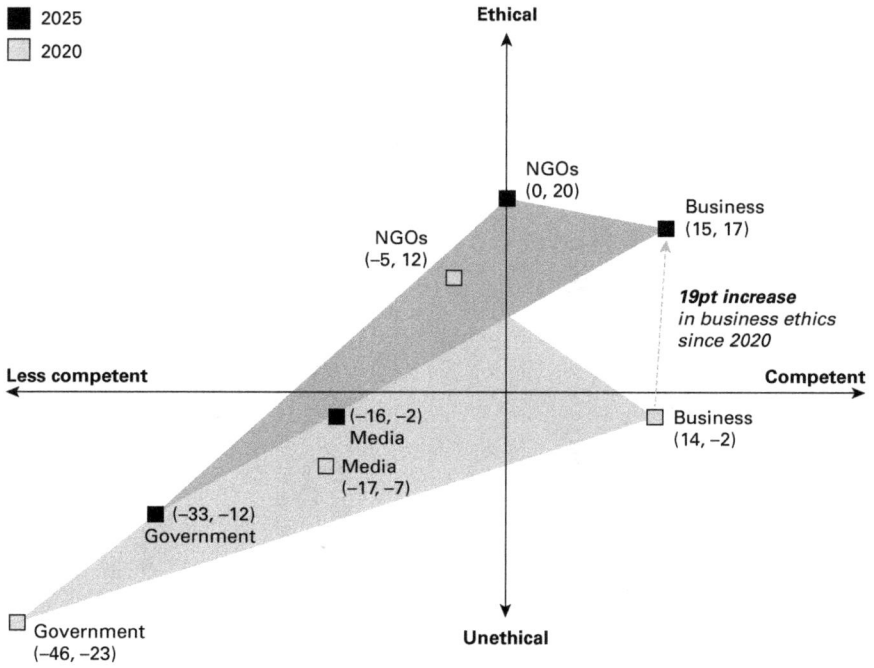

■ 2025
☐ 2020

Ethical

NGOs
(0, 20)

Business
(15, 17)

NGOs
(–5, 12)

19pt increase
in business ethics
since 2020

Less competent

Competent

(–16, –2)
Media

Business
(14, –2)

Media
(–17, –7)

(–33, –12)
Government

Government
(–46, –23)

Unethical

Courtesy of the Edelman Trust Institute © 2025 Daniel J. Edelman, Inc.

realities of your stakeholders, champion shared interests and create opportunities for optimism.

2 **Business has a license to act:** Those with a higher sense of grievance are more likely to believe that business is not doing enough to address societal issues. To navigate these expectations, understand where you have obligations, act on behalf of your stakeholders and advocate for your organization.

3 **Business can't act alone:** Business, government, media, and NGOs must work together to address the root causes of grievance and enable trust, growth and prosperity. Invest in local communities, quality information and job skills. Deliver results that benefit everyone fairly.

4 **With trust, optimism overpowers grievance:** When institutions can't be trusted to do what is right, grievances fester and outlooks darken. To dissipate grievance and increase optimism, prioritize and rebuild trust across your organization and local communities.

SOURCE Courtesy of the Edelman Trust Institute © 2025 Daniel J. Edelman, Inc. For the most up-to-date data, please visit Edelman.com

The way we trust one another has changed

Another important commentator on what's happening to trust in the 21st century is Rachel Botsman, author of *Who Can You Trust?* (2018).[14] Botsman argues that we are at the tipping point of one of the biggest social transformations in human history. Through her book and subsequent interviews, she has shown that we are living through a time when the way trust is built, managed, lost and repaired is undergoing significant change, and the old way of thinking, something she describes as an institutional mindset, is failing to recognize how the dynamics of trust have altered.

Botsman challenges the notion that we are living in an age of distrust, saying rather that we still trust, but whom we trust and how we trust has changed. She points to evidence of the loss of trust in institutions, but at the same time points to how millions of people around the world make decisions and choices every day based on her definition of trust – a confident relationship with the unknown.[15]

Botsman says this new form of trust might be hopping into the back of a car driven by a stranger, trusting them to take us to our destination, or exchanging money in digital forms, or even trusting the advice that comes from a bot on a website handling your customer enquiry. In this world, she says trust is changing direction: whereas it used to flow upward to the leaders we have historically placed our trust in, now the networks, platforms and marketplaces that have been enabled by digital technology means we place our trust sideways in peers, crowds and even strangers.[16] Botsman spoke in London at a Channel 4 event in January 2025, and built on this point further, noting a shift, particularly with a younger audience, to 'feeling over fact'.[17] Meaning trust is built less on who expresses something and more on how they do it, and critically how that makes people feel in the moment, and whether it fits with their own world view.

In 2025, Botsman exhibited a new piece of work called 'Roots of Trust' at the fifth edition of the London Design Biennale at Somerset House.[18] This reimagining of a historical design artefact was based on the first known organizational chart, created in 1855 by Daniel McCallum, Superintendent of the New York and Erie Railroad Company, and rediscovered and restored from the U.S. Library of Congress 170 years later.

What Botsman highlights is the contrast between the pyramid leadership structures we are familiar with today, with a leader at the top, and how, in McCallum's design, the leadership team is at the base – the roots – with frontline workers extending outward along the branches. Her goal with 'Roots of Trust' is to invite people to reconsider the linear and hierarchical ways organizations think about power and trust today and to reimagine the rigid systems and the structures that are collapsing, broken or no longer relevant.

This work, plus that of the Edelman Trust Barometer, points to a systemic change in trust within our society that we need to be aware of, and respond to, as we consider the way advertising can best help build people's trust in brands.

We followed up the UK launch of the Edelman Trust Barometer with an interview with its Executive Director, Tonia E. Ries, who has led the team working on the research initiative for nearly 10 years.[19]

Under her leadership, the Edelman Trust Barometer has expanded into a year-round series of reports and publications that examine trust across society. It seeks to explore the expectations for business and other societal leaders on issues such as employee activism, climate change and the evolving information ecosystem.

INTERVIEW WITH TONIA E. RIES, EXECUTIVE DIRECTOR OF THE EDELMAN TRUST BAROMETER[20]

In your view, just how important is it that businesses make sure that their advertising and communications are trusted by people?

Trust is essential for businesses and brands – and also for governments, NGOs and the media – because there are real consequences when it's lacking. Right now, businesses are more trusted than the other institutions we measure, but that trust brings heightened expectations. It places greater pressure on companies to act responsibly and communicate in ways that are credible and transparent.

This is especially difficult in a polarized political culture. Whatever stance you take, or even if you try to remain neutral, someone will likely be unhappy. That's why your trust strategy must include preparation for backlash, particularly around social issues like DEI and sustainability. Walking back commitments will quickly erode trust and drive customers away, so you have to be intentional and ready to take some heat if you want to be seen as sincere.

What makes this all the more tricky is that businesses may be trusted, but business leaders are not, and CMOs and CEOs no longer control the narrative.

Traditional advertising alone isn't enough; brands are part of an ongoing, real-time public conversation. So it matters if people trust your brand enough to speak up for it or defend it when it's under pressure. Trust enables you to move quickly and engage authentically when a brand-related issue flares up and there's no time for a five-round press release approval cycle. In these moments, trust becomes your most valuable asset.

This is why communications strategies need to shift away from messaging to trust-centred strategies across all activities. Every part of the business should be working toward one question: how are we earning and protecting trust?

Beyond learnings from a 'good' Covid, when else has business managed to improve levels of trust from people and why do you think that is?

The Trust Barometer data shows that while government is seen as 'broken', business is seen as far more creative and effective in solving problems. People believe that business, if it chooses to commit the resources, has the power to create meaningful change. And many businesses have responded to that expectation, finding ways to make a positive difference for their workforce, their communities and their industry sectors.

The key question is, what are the problems that are aligned with your business in such a way that you have standing to address them? To be seen as sincere, your societal actions must be aligned with your core business operations and value proposition.

Business leaders also need to understand the range of trust needs among their customers. What are you asking them to trust you with? What concerns might they have?

Trust isn't static – it evolves with the relationship. Early on, a customer may be willing to try a product without asking too many questions. Later, when considering a long-term commitment or big investment, their questions change. Businesses need to make answers – about sourcing, practices, values – easily accessible to support that journey from first-time buyer to loyal advocate.

What would you point to as the most significant catalyst in the levels of trust we used to have versus now, and do you have any insights into why that might be?

There's no single cause; our research points to a number of forces putting pressure on trust. But the rise of social media and peer networks has played a massive role. Now, anyone with a smartphone can claim to be a journalist or an expert, which makes people question whether any expert can be trusted at all.

Interestingly, scientists as individuals still score highly in trust, but they are now competing with a greater number of non-credentialed voices. News consumption habits have also fragmented, fuelling confusion over what's real. At a macro level, we're witnessing a redefinition of trust itself. The old signals are fading, and the new ones aren't yet clear.

It's possible Gen Z will lead the way in creating this new framework. In our 2023 research on brands, we asked what makes brand communications trustworthy. Boomers, Gen X and Millennials all said: facts backed by data. But Gen Z prioritized authenticity. They're asking: does this feel real or is the brand just performing? For a generation raised on phones and social platforms, new credibility 'muscles' are forming – based on authenticity, not authority.

The latest report talks about optimism – having led this topic of research for nearly a decade, how optimistic are you that people's trust can be rebuilt?

Trust hasn't vanished – it's shifting. Trust is flowing into new areas: influencers, content creators, unconventional leaders. Traditional institutions aren't receiving as much trust anymore.

While institutions and authorities are struggling to preserve trust and influence, local and peer trust measures remain strong, for now. But the rise of identity politics is putting that under pressure, making people more wary of one another.

That's why we advise companies to make the workplace an island of civility and trust that can then radiate outward. Work should be a space where people feel safe, respected and united by a shared mission. Online, it's harder to create these boundaries – but at work, clarity about who you are, what you stand for and what you won't tolerate is the foundation of trust.

As employers and as brands, businesses have a massive influence in shaping society and culture – and a great interest in ensuring we have the kind of stable marketplace that can only be built through trust. I would say, I am optimistic, and I trust business leaders to make me right over the long term!

What has happened to trust in politics?

Politicians have always battled to be trusted, but their reputations appear particularly poor at present.

The 2024 Ipsos Veracity Index, which tracks British adults' trust in professions, reported that politicians are the country's least trusted group, with just 11 per cent of respondents trusting them 'to tell the truth'.[21] The second least trusted 'profession', with just 15 per cent responding positively, were government ministers.

But there is a renewed focus on the importance of building trust in politics, connected perhaps to an increased desire to demonstrate governments' ability to deliver effective change.

On 5 July 2024, Britain's incoming prime minister made trust the centre point of his victory speech. He talked of a battle for trust which will go on to define the times we live in.[22] He set out a vision of returning politics to effective public service that can be trusted by showing how it can be a positive force in people's lives.

Scrutiny of just how successful Sir Keir Starmer's tenure will be continues, including from within the party he leads, as seen in a commentary on LabourList entitled 'How can Keir Starmer deliver his pledge to rebuild trust in politics?'[23] The author, Billy Huband-Thompson, wrote that it was time for the party to rebuild faith in the functioning of democracy itself.

What has happened to trust in news?

If the public have never trusted politicians, we have historically had faith in the news media to tell us the truth about them. A free press, characterized by careful journalism, diligently sourced and evidenced, has been a vital element in open, democratic societies, and been protected by law. Advertising has helped fund journalism and news media for centuries. So, let's take a look at what's been happening to trust in news in recent years.

The Trust in News Project run by the Reuters Institute is a good place to get a sense of what's going on.[24] It looks at trust in digital news in Brazil, India, the United Kingdom and the United States. This accounts for more than a billion internet users across a huge range of media systems and contexts. Its goal is to understand what drives trust for audiences in different contexts, and to help journalists and publishers build trust in a rapidly changing landscape. Its reports are a highly recommended read for those interested in this area.

In short, falling levels of trust in news media is clearly an area of concern to the profession. The results of the 2024 report were discussed at a Trust Conference in central London in October 2024, in an annual event organized by the Thomson Reuters Foundation.[25] One of the key take-aways was that 'Trust in news is facing many challenges', and the report from the event cited how many speakers highlighted a perception of ever-lower trust in news and journalists. A survey found that only 40 per cent of respondents from around the world trust the news, four points lower overall than it was at the height of the coronavirus pandemic.[26]

There are multiple explanations given for news being less trusted than it was. The speakers at the event talked about attacks on news, the growth of partisan and opinion-based journalism, reporting without factual basis, the negative impact of policies requiring greater transparency and the growing risk from AI which could not be trusted to summarize or label news content correctly.

This was neatly summarized by Nic Newman, Senior Research Associate at the Reuters Institute and a journalist and digital strategist who played a key role in shaping the BBC's internet services over more than a decade.[27] He spoke of the challenges faced from mis- and disinformation, as well as low levels of trust, attacks by politicians and the uncertainties faced by business.

The Reuters Institute's work is rich in findings and recommendations. One with specific reference to advertising in the latest report suggested that some forms of funding (such as advertising or donations) can be viewed more suspiciously by audiences versus other funding models such as subscription.

Note an interesting dynamic at play here over trust, where advertising appears to fund news media and so may be seen to influence the news that they then carry. Historically, advertising has removed the need for newspapers to be funded entirely by governments or owners and organizations with political agendas, but is there a view that advertising spend can be used to further particular views?

Meanwhile in the UK, Ofcom, the regulator for communications services, tracks attitudes to news and trends in news consumption. A 2024 report cites traditional news platforms scoring higher on trust, accuracy and impartiality than online or social media news platforms.[28] Social media was rated lower for accuracy, trust, impartiality and quality, but did perform well for offering a range of views, providing a personal perspective on the world, and one that is of personal importance, the very 'feeling' and 'horizontal' attributes that we have been seeing people valuing earlier in this chapter.

Young people need a country they can trust

In January 2025, UK public service broadcaster Channel 4 published a new research report, 'Gen Z: Trends, Truth and Trust', and called for urgent industry action and regulation to ensure young people grow up and live in a Britain they can trust.[29]

We are going to look at the emerging generational difference in trust of advertising later in Chapter 3 but, for now, let's see what Channel 4 discovered.

This research report looked specifically at Gen Z (13–27 year olds) and highlighted an uncertainty in who and what to trust. Young people, the researchers said, have flatter hierarchies of trust across media, having confidence in posts from friends (58 per cent) and influencers (42 per cent) as much as – and sometimes more than – established journalism. One-third (33 per cent) trust alternative internet-based media personalities vs 12 per cent of 28–65 year olds.

The researchers highlighted emerging trends including growing gender divergence of views around women's equality and a disengagement with democracy. The impact of those trends was described as a lack of reliable information for young people, division and radicalization and a loss of social cohesion. They concluded that a world where trust declines is a more dangerous place; the glue of shared facts that once held us together was leading to greater disconnection from democracy and the weakening of civil society.

Channel 4 put forward solutions which included the introduction of a trustmark, arguing this would help indicate content that is factual and trusted, coming from media that is regulated with professional production standards.

It said that this trustmark would mean tech companies, their algorithms, advertisers and people would understand there and then what is checked and true and what is not.

Channel 4's CEO, Alex Mahon, summarized the aims by saying Gen Z needed a Britain they can trust in return for what they can offer to the future of the nation.

As we think about the role of responsible, trusted advertising, perhaps the public that our industry serves deserves, even needs, a world they can trust in.

Is there a crisis of trust in each other?

But can people be trusted? Before we even get onto the subject of whether advertising can be trusted, isn't trust generally in crisis?

This was a topic that Ipsos, a global market research company, tackled in 2019 in its report Trust: The Truth?[30]

Very few people think trust has been rising over the last 20 years. The perception of large numbers of people around the world is that trust in each other has been falling over the last two decades, as shown in the chart in Figure 1.3.

Perceptions that trust is in decline are particularly high for the institutions we see with some of the lowest levels of absolute trust – the government and the press – but even for our trust in others, slightly more think it has fallen than stayed the same, and very few think mutual trust has actually risen. Ben Page, Chief Executive Officer of Ipsos, concluded:

> This report highlights that trust does not appear to be in terminal decline but is often lower than half a century ago. We find that a much more nuanced conversation has to be had – less about trust per se, and more about what organizations and individuals need to do to be 'trustworthy' in a particular context. There is a lot of painstaking work to be done, but trust can be rebuilt.

FIGURE 1.3 Ipsos, Trust: The Truth?

PEOPLE ARE MUCH MORE LIKELY TO THINK TRUST HAS FALLEN OVER THE LAST TWENTY YEARS THAN INCREASED
Over the last twenty years or so, do you think the proportion of people in [COUNTRY] who say they trust each of the following has increased, decreased, or stayed about the same?

% global average across 24 countries

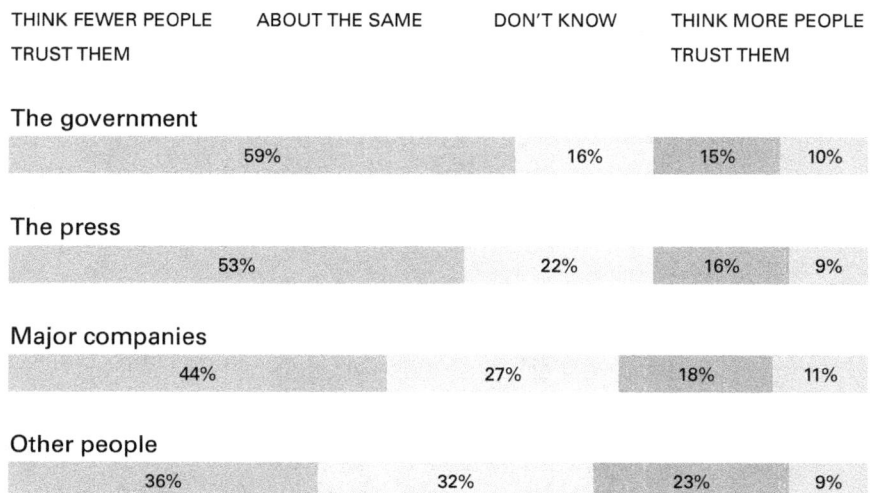

THINK FEWER PEOPLE TRUST THEM	ABOUT THE SAME	DON'T KNOW	THINK MORE PEOPLE TRUST THEM

The government

59%	16%	15%	10%

The press

53%	22%	16%	9%

Major companies

44%	27%	18%	11%

Other people

36%	32%	23%	9%

SOURCE Ipsos Global Advisor

Conclusion

Trust is fundamental to human development, behaviour and social interactions. Society depends on a high level of mutual trust if it is to function smoothly. Leaders, whether in politics or any other sphere, want to be trusted so that they can be effective. They take trust seriously.

It is a much-used word. Trust carries many meanings, both current and historical. It is central to human experience, playing a vital role in childhood development and is ever-present in the games we play, the relationships we form, the media we consume, the products and services we interact with, the leaders we choose and the society we build.

We started this chapter writing about the TV show *The Traitors*. People are fascinated by trust and the concept of whom we can and cannot trust, including how we can successfully betray people's trust in dramatic games. Being trusted (or not!) is box office gold.

But the dynamics of trust within society have been changing. Historically, people trusted those in authority. Secular and religious leaders, whether they deserved it or not, commanded public confidence by merit of their positions. Even if politicians were always treated with some scepticism, the news media – the free press and more recently public sector broadcasters – were relied upon to bring us the truth, and one generally accepted by all.

This change in the way we trust is real; the work of Rachel Botsman and Edelman help explain that clearly, and we're living right in the middle of this change.

Now, instead of a hierarchical or vertical flow of trust, growing elements of society rely more on horizontal or 'distributed' trust – trust across society between equals in communities. Trust that is not necessarily shared across generations or between different interest groups or self-defined communities united by new media technologies. Trust that is matched by higher levels of distrust towards those outside those communities and is often, it seems, based on shaky foundations of truth and objectivity.

The implications for business and for advertising, the mouthpiece of business and of other organizations, are emerging as one aspect of this societal change. To be trusted, which, as the next chapters will detail, is as vital for companies and brands as it is for prime ministers, presidents or popes, requires some new thinking and new approaches.

At LEAD 2019, the Advertising Association's annual industry summit, the journalist Evan Davis told the audience that if they want to be trusted, they should do trustworthy things.[31]

It's a great line to remember. A question, if you will, for a conversation with colleagues about how to build trust in your brand – are you doing trustworthy things?

Advertising, as a constant and highly visible presence in 21st-century society, has a role to play in building – or further eroding – public trust by itself doing trustworthy things. That's a challenge, especially in a frantic and fragmented media environment, so the rest of this book is intended to help you meet it, not just for society's good but your own.

In the next chapter, we're going to look at what's been happening to trust in advertising.

But, for now, we will leave you with a final thought from Anton Chekhov: if we can no longer trust and believe in people, life will become impossible.

Notes

1   The Traitors, Fandom, January 2025, https://thetraitors.fandom.com/wiki/The_Traitors_(franchise) (archived at https://perma.cc/69FG-ZSEQ)

2   E Keslassy and M Ravindran, I'm 100% faithful, you've got to believe me!': 'The Traitors' creator Marc Pos unpacks his reality sensation, Variety, January 2023, https://variety.com/2023/tv/global/the-traitors-creator-marc-pos-interview-rtl-bbc-1235480694/ (archived at https://perma.cc/VY6Y-KV9Z)

3   S McLeod, Erik Erikson's Stages of Psychosocial Development, Simply Psychology, January 2024, www.simplypsychology.org/erik-erikson.html (archived at https://perma.cc/G3YV-JLPD)

4   P Hancock et al, How and why humans trust: A meta-analysis and elaborated model, Frontiers, March 2023, www.frontiersin.org/journals/psychology/articles/10.3389/fpsyg.2023.1081086/full (archived at https://perma.cc/29DQ-A4K5)

5   Trust, N., Oxford English Dictionary, https://doi.org/10.1093/OED/5777528687 (archived at https://perma.cc/D57U-EM6L)

6   The National Trust, Our founders, www.nationaltrust.org.uk/who-we-are/about-us/our-founders (archived at https://perma.cc/AUA5-ZQFS)

7   V Woolf (1915) The Voyage Out

8   Brain trust, Britannica, www.britannica.com/dictionary/brain-trust (archived at https://perma.cc/D257-B6RK)

9   About the NHS, www.stepintothenhs.nhs.uk/about-the-nhs (archived at https://perma.cc/272Y-T7QZ)

10   History of Advertising Trust, www.hatads.org.uk/ (archived at https://perma.cc/5TZQ-CV2Z)

11 W Shakespeare, *The Complete Works of Shakespeare*, 2025, https://
    shakespeare.mit.edu/ (archived at https://perma.cc/JKR4-4CDA)

12 distrust (verb), Oxford English Dictionary, https://doi.org/10.1093/OED/
    3588751189 (archived at https://perma.cc/W3PF-S3LY)

13 2025 Edelman Trust Barometer, Trust and the Crisis of Grievance, January
    2025, www.edelman.com/trust/2025/trust-barometer (archived at https://
    perma.cc/S6CZ-XG5P)

14 R Botsman, www.rachelbotsman.com/ (archived at https://perma.cc/S2N6-
    PQXQ)

15 E Felsenthal, An expert on trust says we're thinking about it all wrong, Time,
    March 2024, https://time.com/6957741/rachel-botsman-trust-interview/
    (archived at https://perma.cc/9WB9-KWML)

16 Ibid.

17 Channel 4 event: Gen Z, Trends, Truth and Trust, YouTube, January 2025,
    www.youtube.com/live/kDDKoPexb2k (archived at https://perma.cc/4Y3M-
    UG7T)

18 London Design Biennale 2025, Rachel Botsman, https://londondesignbiennale.
    com/pavilions/2025/rachel-botsman (archived at https://perma.cc/M5ST-FKAF)

19 Tonia E. Ries, Executive Director, Edelman Trust Barometer, www.edelman.
    com/people/tonia-ries (archived at https://perma.cc/K5Y7-JQAR)

20 Author interview with Tonia E. Ries, March 2025

21 Ipsos Veracity Index 2024, November 2024, www.ipsos.com/en-uk/ipsos-
    veracity-index-2024 (archived at https://perma.cc/LWZ7-FSP8)

22 Reuters, UK's Starmer: fight for trust is the battle of our age, July 2024, www.
    reuters.com/world/uk/uks-starmer-fight-trust-is-battle-our-age-2024-07-05/
    (archived at https://perma.cc/SC2F-RYM4)

23 B Huband-Thomas, How can Keir Starmer deliver his pledge to rebuild trust in
    politics?', Labourlist, October 2024, https://labourlist.org/2024/10/
    government-news-sue-gray-labour-political-trust/ (archived at https://perma.cc/
    7JPF-7V9K)

24 Reuters Institute, Trust in News Project, https://reutersinstitute.politics.ox.ac.
    uk/trust-news-project (archived at https://perma.cc/7U5L-JMAQ)

25 M Adami and G Kahn, Trust Conference 2024: six things we learnt about the
    impact of AI on misinformation and the news business, Reuters Institute,
    October 2024, https://reutersinstitute.politics.ox.ac.uk/news/trust-conference-
    2024-six-things-we-learnt-about-impact-ai-misinformation-and-news-business
    (archived at https://perma.cc/3E8M-XAVQ)

26 Reuters Institute, Digital News Report 2024, https://reutersinstitute.politics.
    ox.ac.uk/digital-news-report/2024 (archived at https://perma.cc/SH9H-SZG8)

27 Nic Newman, Reuters Institute, https://reutersinstitute.politics.ox.ac.uk/people/
    nic-newman (archived at https://perma.cc/FK2P-U899)

28 Ofcom, Attitudes to news, July 2025, www.ofcom.org.uk/media-use-and-attitudes/attitudes-to-news/ (archived at https://perma.cc/99SZ-DBSD)

29 Channel 4 event: Gen Z, Trends, Truth and Trust, YouTube, January 2025, www.youtube.com/live/kDDKoPexb2k (archived at https://perma.cc/KN74-W8H9)

30 Ipsos, The Power of Trust, 2024, www.ipsos.com/en/global-trends-2024/power-trust (archived at https://perma.cc/SV5F-XVQP)

31 Evan Davis, Post-Truth, May 2017, www.evandavis.co.uk/post-truth/ (archived at https://perma.cc/4XL4-MZEQ)

02

Why trust in advertising matters

Introduction

Everyone we talked to for this book and all our background reading agreed on one thing: trust matters to companies, their brands and their success. But why? And why, beyond that, in their advertising? That's the question we will consider next.

This chapter shows that the 'advertising industry', those who work together to bring advertising to the public – advertisers, media owners, tech companies and agencies of all sorts – has long worried about trust.

We will see how those worries have developed alongside advertising's own evolution, along with ideas about how to overcome them. We will see the emergence of evidence that trusted advertising works better, how this has grown in importance in recent years and how some leading brands and businesses have achieved it.

Critically, we will review evidence that trust is linked to advertising effectiveness and, ultimately, business success and profit margins.

This will also lead us in further chapters to consider the anatomy of public attitudes and trustfulness towards advertising, and how understanding those can help us make them stronger.

Why should you care that people trust advertising?

Why should you care whether people trust advertising or not? Why should anyone care? What has advertising ever done for us; what difference does it make?

In short, advertising brings a range of benefits to the economy, society and individuals.

First, the economy. In Advertising Pays 2025, advertising investment is shown to power UK economic activity and jobs in several ways, including:[1]

- Some 3.5 million UK businesses (that's two-thirds of the total) invested an estimated £66.6 billion in their advertising in 2024.
- Advertising supports 5% of all UK employment, representing 1.7 million jobs across the UK.
- The advertising and marketing industries contributed £109 billion of gross value added (GVA) to the UK economy in 2024, 4% of the total UK GVA.
- On average, £1 spent on advertising now generates an ROI of £4.11 for big businesses and £1.89 for small ones.

The report's lead author, Dan Wilks, Director of Credos, said:

> Advertising Pays 2025 reflects on the first quarter of this century and shows the full scale of advertising's value to the UK's changing economy. This report not only demonstrates advertising's economic impact, but its unique position within the creative and professional services, contributing a record amount of GVA towards the UK economy.

Second, society and individuals. The report details how advertising directly funds a broad range of jobs across the UK's media and digital industries, to the tune of £42.6 billion through businesses' advertising investment. Advertising remains the 'currency' that funds and supports valued UK industries and services such as TV and radio programming, journalism, cinema and streaming channels. Online tools such as maps, search and educational content would also be significantly more expensive without advertising income.

Fundamentally, advertising is a force for competition. It enables people to choose between products and services to support how they live. It means the information we all get about product characteristics and capabilities, price points and offers helps us buy better and cheaper. It makes companies work harder to satisfy customers, so that they can communicate and deliver quality and value ahead of their competitors. As such, it's vital in an open economy.

So, there we have it...

Advertising provides jobs, supports businesses to innovate and compete, and does that for companies ranging from a local SME to the world's biggest brands, not just in the UK, but worldwide. People working in advertising provide valuable strategic, creative and technical services to connect all kinds of organizations – businesses, charities, NGOs, public sector organizations and governments, too – to their audiences.

Now take a moment to imagine a world where not one single ad of the many that you see every day can be trusted... how difficult would life be, not knowing what real choices are out there and which ones will be better for you?

Trust in advertising has always mattered

The issue of trust in advertising has been of concern to those in the business for over a hundred years. Ads for 'dodgy' patent medicines and financial schemes just too good to be true troubled the early advertising professionals of the time, just as some still do now in our online economy. But they did not see eye to eye about what to do about those problem ads.

In 1913, leading members of the nascent industry met to consider creating an association to give a national voice to their interests, build wider appreciation of the value of advertising to the economy and the public, and see off the threat of an advertising tax. But one of their goals was also to establish a 'Watch Committee', 'to watch the advertisements... which are appearing and consider carefully the effect on the public of any obviously false or misleading ones, particularly in respect to their likelihood of shaking public confidence in advertising and of weakening the effect of bona fide advertisements'.[2]

There was the connection between trust and success.

The Great War got in the way of progressing this initiative, but soon afterwards the attempt was revived. This time there was disagreement. As *Advertiser's Weekly* reported on 5 February 1926:

> Beneath the placid... surface of the inaugural banquet of the Advertising Association... there was drama.

The draft remit of the proposed association had included a clause 'to make rules and regulations as to the conduct of advertising'. Sir William Berry, then with his brother the owner of the *Sunday Times*, *Financial Times* and a string of other newspapers soon to include *The Daily Telegraph* (talk about a media baron!), would have none of it. This 'unfortunate mistake', as he called it in his speech, was dropped from the Association's objects.

This was to the dismay of, amongst others, Sir Charles Higham, advertising agent, wartime propagandist, ex-MP and later author of *Advertising, Its*

Use and Abuse. In his reply at the banquet, he said he was 'extremely disappointed'. What they needed, he insisted, was the 'laying down of rules and regulations that everyone should obey'.[3]

In fact, he did get some of what he and others like him wanted. The wonderfully named National Vigilance Committee of the Advertising Association (AA) set about developing advertising standards to 'get the advertiser to realize that the only profitable policy was strict honesty'. In 1929 this became the Advertisement Investigation Department to respond to complaints and 'free British advertising from those abuses to which all advertising is subject'. By 1936 those aims had evolved to include the promotion of public confidence in advertising.[4]

Trust, to be won through honesty and built on promoting confidence in the work, was of recognized value. The defence of advertising from government intervention and its promotion as 'an essential part of modern marketing' by the AA's Research & Publicity Department in the 1930s was expressed through campaigns which in 1934 featured posters proclaiming, 'You can place your Trust in Advertised Goods'. The very fact of advertising made manufacturers accountable for the quality of their products and put their reputations on the line.[5]

The ASA's 2024 campaign, of which more later in Chapter 14, is the direct descendant of these early efforts to demonstrate advertising's worth to consumers and business alike, because it can be trusted.

A crisis in the 1970s

Later in the century, it all got more political. The post-war economic boom saw 'ordinary people' acquiring washing machines and cars, wearing clothes and cosmetics of the sort only the privileged had enjoyed before, discovering foods and foreign travel previously restricted to the elite. Britain was becoming a 'materialistic' society whose values were questioned by many, especially on the left.

People, it was felt, were being exploited by commercial interests. A slew of legislation – the 1961 Consumer Protection Act, the Trades Description Act in 1968 and the Fair Trading Act of 1973 – set out to redress the balance.

As the champion of materialism, advertising was attacked. To its critics, it didn't only tempt people to spend too much money – even money they didn't have, but were borrowing – on things they didn't need, but it did so by dishonest means. Exaggeration, ambiguity, mystification and sheer 'puff'

WHY TRUST IN ADVERTISING MATTERS

were just some of the 'countless means of deception in advertising' listed by consumerist Charles Medawar in a speech to the AA's 1974 conference.[6]

The new Labour government of the time tended to agree. As well as fuelling inflation by over-stimulating demand for consumer goods, advertising, said the Minister for Prices and Consumer Protection Shirley Williams, was inadequately regulated. She proposed a National Consumers' Authority, to be financed by a levy on media spend, and set up the Office of Fair Trading to review the ways companies provided their goods and services.

Alarmed by these threats, the industry responded with its own system for maintaining consumer trust. It had already established rules for advertisers through the Code of Advertising Practice (CAP) in 1961, and then an enforcement arm, the Advertising Standards Authority (ASA), the very next year. Its stated objective was 'the promotion and enforcement throughout the UK of the highest standards of advertising in all media'.

We'll come back to the ASA and the crucial part it plays throughout this book, but for now we'll finish with a quote from its first independent Chairman, Lord Drumalbyn, on why, then and now, the industry has cared about trust:

> They (advertisers) are well aware that their most valuable asset is consumer good-will, and they know how easily that can be lost if the goods and services they sell do not live up to what they themselves say about them in their advertisements... Moreover they recognize that the effectiveness of each advertisement will depend to some extent on the general attitude of the public to advertising as a whole. Every advertisement which falls short of the highest standards diminishes public confidence in all advertising.[7]

With that in mind, let's fast forward to what the UK ad industry has been doing about those standards and that public confidence since then.

Trust and advertising in the 21st century

In 2009 there was a new CEO at the Advertising Association (AA).[8] Tim Lefroy took one look at the data on public attitudes to advertising (Figure 2.1) and saw a need, a challenge and an opportunity. The need was evident from the AA's annual survey, which showed a worrying change in opinion. Back in the 1960s and 70s, it had seemed that over 70 per cent of the British public said they approved of advertising; in the 1990s a differently worded question, with the additional option to answer 'neither approve nor disapprove', revealed that only 40–50 per cent felt positive about it, with a big proportion not caring either way. (The addition of 'neither/nor' explains the dramatic drop in approval shown in 1993. Many who had been responding with slight approval were now stating their indifference thanks to the new response.) In 1993, 33 per cent of respondents selected either 'neither/nor' or 'don't know' in response to this question. More worrying still was the decline after the change of question; by 2009, that positive number had dropped even further, to nearer 30 per cent. Something was going wrong.

The challenge was to turn that worrying decline around, which would require time and resources. The opportunity was to rally support from across the advertising industry to create a coalition to restore public positivity and trust, a role only the AA could realistically fulfil, as it uniquely represented all the different groups involved in the business.

Lefroy did just that. With funding from concerned and committed advertisers, agencies and media owners, Credos was established in 2010 as a mini-thinktank under the AA's auspices, with the objective of guiding the industry's efforts in tackling the trust crisis. It started researching the key issues faced by the ad industry and it has consistently done so since then, funded by a group of leading organizations from across UK advertising, known as Front Foot.

First, it was decided a measure of trust was needed to confirm that it related to general attitudes towards advertising. A new question went into

FIGURE 2.1 Levels of public approval and disapproval of advertising since 1961

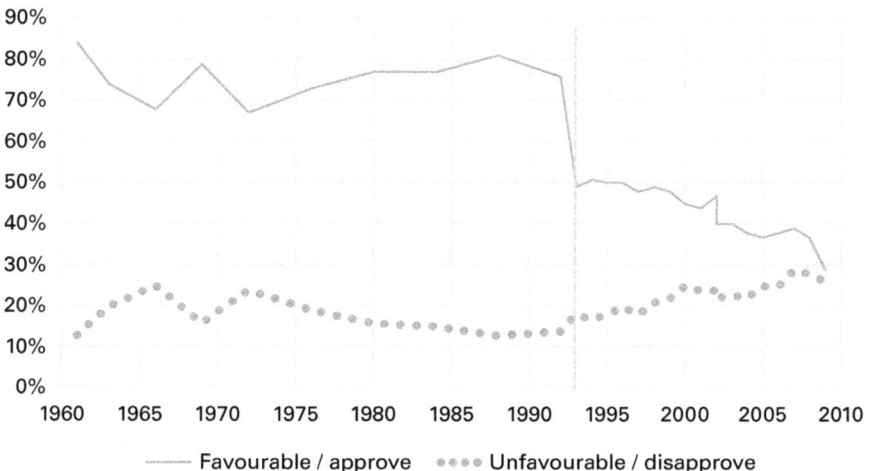

———— Favourable / approve   • • • • Unfavourable / disapprove

SOURCE Advertising Association, 1961–2009

the AA's annual tracking study in 2011 to gauge trust in the industry along-side favourability. Sure enough, the two were and are linked. And both were falling, as they continued to do over the next few years.

All sorts of questions arose from these headline numbers:

- What does 'trust' mean to people?
- Who amongst the population trusts or distrusts advertising?
- Do different sorts of advertising, for different products or in different media, generate different levels of trust?
- Is advertising a special case or just sharing the reported decline in trust in institutions generally?
- Most importantly, perhaps, why is trust eroding and what can we do about it?

We will go on to consider these questions and more in future chapters.

FIGURE 2.2 Public trust v public favourability

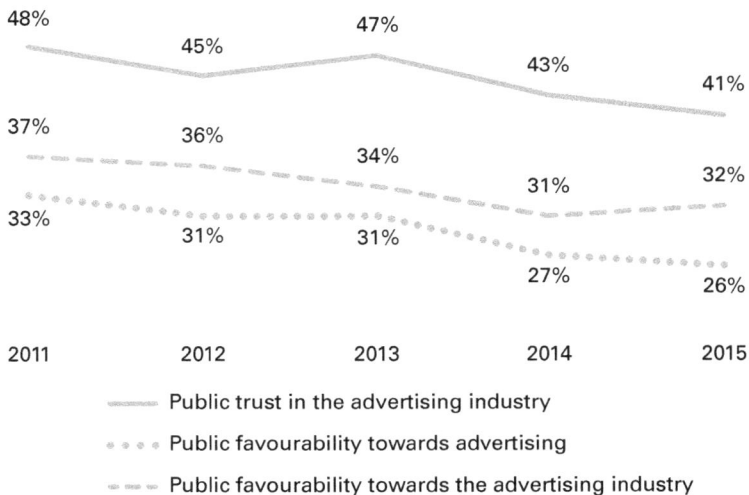

n = c. 2,000 per year

SOURCE ComRes Omnibus survey for Credos trust tracking, 2011–2015

The only way is ethics

The issue came further to the fore in 2014, when Richard Eyre, the Chair of IAB UK, pointed to declining public trust in advertising at the IAB Engage conference. He shared his view that brands have moved from messaging to promises, to market research and finally to trust as the most important way to relate to consumers. He argued that trust would become the biggest success factor.[9]

He went on in the following year to deliver a speech at the AA's LEAD 2015 conference in a mock-presentation to a fictional 'board of the UK advertising industry' entitled, 'The only way is ethics'.[10] He told the imagined board of 'Advertising plc' that it has a problem: the organization has been rapidly acquiring new and exciting technologies that will transform the way it can engage with audiences, but they will only work if Advertising plc is trusted. He warned of an image problem impacting on the potential success of the business right at the moment trust is most needed.

This was from the individual chairing the body that promoted online advertising, whose growth was seen by many as the main source of the 'trust' problem, but by the IAB as an opportunity to get the sprawling internet's house in order, which it has worked to do ever since.

At the same event, Tim Lefroy, the AA's CEO, warned the industry of 'advertising freedoms' coming under attack. The clash between what businesses would like to be able to communicate and public voices rejecting it could threaten the industry's ability to operate without further legal restrictions or ad bans.

The calls to tackle trust because of these risks to the industry and the way it works were loud and clear.

I choose trust

In January 2019, the new AA President, Keith Weed, called for a system change within UK advertising.[11]

The following comes from the seminal speech he gave.[12] It's a call to action that has been central to the work of many in the industry since then. What's interesting to Matt as he reads it back is that, while progress has been made on all fronts, the challenges Weed laid out remain clear and apparent more than seven years on...

> Without trust, advertising has no future. A brand without trust is a product. Advertising without trust is noise.
>
> I'm going to cover what I call the 'Seven Deadly Sins' of advertising. Seeing them all in one place might make some of you feel uncomfortable but we are all advertising adults here!

Annoyance is increasing and quality is declining, with 50 per cent of Brits agreeing that TV ads annoy them.

Over a third of marketers now use influencer marketing and it is set to rise, with 43 per cent expecting to increase their investment this year. But all is not well: fake followers, fake engagement and bad practices are rife.

Just try it yourself… and you will see how easy it is to buy fake followers on Instagram, Twitter, YouTube. There is also evidence of bots, fraud and dishonest business models, damaging the authenticity and trust of influencer marketing.

The good news is that platforms are now taking action and have removed over 1.5 billion fake accounts and content from their platforms since a spotlight was put on these practices at the Cannes Lions Festival of Creativity.

With data hacks becoming more common, people are increasingly concerned about what their data is being used for.

73 per cent of people are concerned about their online privacy with internet companies.

People are seeing news stories that brands are inadvertently funding extremist content producers.

There's $10 billion of estimated fraud in the system, further damaging trust in advertising.

Fake News was the Collins Dictionary Word of the Year in 2017, and search volume continued to be high throughout 2018.

More than half of internet users over 35 find personalized ads annoying, dropping only slightly to 30 per cent amongst Millennials. I really believe personalization is a good thing, but only when it's done well.

And yet, ads will continue to become more personalized with 53 per cent of marketers set to increase personalization.

Personalization will increase but it must be useful rather than low added value and annoying.

Bombardment is leading to more messages than ever and, with mobile, media time has increased by up to 3.5 hours a day resulting in the average consumer now being exposed to up to 10,000 brand messages a day.

Yet advertising is increasing and spreading itself out across more channels – more messages in more places, meaning ads are moving into less trusted environments.

So, what does this mean for us?

We are being blocked – 600 million people are already doing so.

Why?

51 per cent say too many ads are annoying or irrelevant – a similar stat to TV.

47 per cent think ads are too intrusive.

And we are being skipped.

Over 60 per cent of people in the UK say they skip ads wherever they can.

It may look bleak when you see it all in one place. But we have not gone beyond the point of no return. The situation is still very retrievable, if we act.

Our biggest challenge as an industry is trust.

Trust arrives on foot and leaves on horseback.

So, it's trust or bust and we need to act collectively as an industry to thrive.

I choose trust.

Trust is a must

In October 2021, the Advertising Association published a new report, 'Rebuilding public trust in UK advertising', and Weed continued to urge the industry to make progress in this area.[13] In this following excerpt, you will see how he noted, in particular, the need for advertising to be more trusted as the UK, and the rest of the world, recovered from the impact of the Covid-19 pandemic.

Trust is complex and precious. Built up slowly over time, it can disappear much more rapidly; therefore, earning trust and keeping it is an ever-constant and ever-changing challenge. As all the evidence shows, trust pays – with better returns on campaigns and better long-term value for the brands they support.

When this industry is at its best and most responsible, it is trustworthy and makes a valuable contribution to the UK, not just economically but on a societal level too.

It is heartening to hear how the public has responded positively to advertising's output during the pandemic and also the steps we have taken to portray a more inclusive nation. Looking at the challenges coming our way, we should not underestimate the significance of the role advertising needs to play and how important it is that we are trusted.

The advertising we produce will help rebuild confidence as society recovers following the lockdowns of the pandemic. The work we make in the coming years will play a crucial role in helping the UK and international markets respond to climate change. And the way we recruit, retain and develop talent from all backgrounds will shape just how inclusive and successful that work is. All of this contributes to the public's view of our industry and ultimately how trustworthy we really are.

A case of advertising being called upon to step up to the social challenges we face.

Trust is fundamental

It isn't just advertising leaders that believe trust is fundamental to advertising. It's government ministers too.

Sir Chris Bryant, the Creative Industries Minister, gave a keynote speech at the LEAD advertising industry conference in London in January 2025.[14] He shared a piece of advice that was given to him by an experienced ex-minister, Peter Mandelson.

> The one word you can never use in advertising and in politics is the word trust. Because the moment you start talking about trust in politics, people start thinking: 'Oh, can I trust you?' And they nearly always come to the conclusion that they can't.

> But in the end, advertising, I suppose, is fundamentally about trust. It's about trying to persuade the public that you can trust a particular product or that you can trust a particular brand that is promoting a particular product, or that you can trust the person who is promoting the brand that is promoting the product, or that you can trust the space in which you're watching or seeing this particular piece of advertising.

> Of course, to enable trust in all and to create great advertising, that requires all sorts of different things.

The minister neatly captured the significance of trust throughout the advertising process and the challenge advertising practitioners face when thinking about how advertising can build it.

WHY ADVERTISERS NEED TO BE TRUSTED

From 2017 to 2025, Phil Smith was Director General of ISBA, the only body representing brands that advertise in the UK. Smith was a co-chair of the Advertising Association's Trust Working Group (more about that in Chapter 3) and we conducted a Q&A with him to gather his views about the critical importance of trust in advertising.[15]

How important is trust in advertising to your members?

Trust in advertising is a pre-condition for advertising to be effective. But it's part of a larger picture for brands, for whom trust in the brand is also of fundamental importance. Good marketers recognize that trust is also essential for brand profitability and use advertising to create a value exchange with customers to ensure that in return for the customer's attention the advertising gives them something. It could be enjoyment or humour, provide valuable information or be empathetic to the customer's needs, as a 'welcome guest'.

The UK industry's co-regulatory framework for advertising and the Advertising Standards Authority (ASA) are respected worldwide and we know engender public trust. Individual brands are highly sensitized to the risk of ASA rulings against them over, for example, greenwashing or misleading environmental claims. This concern is a boardroom issue, demonstrating how important trust is to brand owners.

What has been your focus to help build trust in advertising as ISBA Director General?

Trust in advertising is achieved at every step in the ad supply chain. Under my tenure, ISBA has focused on the trustworthiness of the media environment, in the areas of transparency, responsibility and accountability. We've focused on the lack of accountable cross-media campaign measurement, which contributes heavily to the negative experience of audience bombardment. Hence, Origin and its purpose – to improve effectiveness and efficiency for advertisers and deliver a better consumer experience. The advertising landscape is changing – it is very dynamic.

How is advertising changing and what does this mean when it comes to your members using advertising to build trust in their brands?

The growth of 'performance' advertising is well documented. Recent advertising market growth has come from businesses that are wholly dependent on advertising to drive their sales and growth. And justifying marketing spend that has instant commercial benefits is much easier than arguing for marketing spend that is defensive or supports long-term goals.

The broad means of connecting with lots of people at the same time, via high-rating mass TV audiences, is no longer achievable due to media fragmentation and declining linear TV viewing reach. Achieving 'social currency' through ads that everyone appears to be talking about is harder to achieve. As a result of fragmentation, the cost of maintaining a brand's media presence simply as a defensive measure has become unsustainable and difficult to defend for an increasing number of companies. In addition, the younger audience may be developing a cynical view towards big corporates and their traditional forms of communication. Instead, they are building their own networks of trusted 'creators', whose values appeal, so we may now need to think about 'distributed trust' and how a brand manages this in the absence of wider social cohesion.

Influencers have a role here, but there is a vulnerability for a brand if it places itself solely in the hands of influencers rather than communicating on its own behalf, creating a dangerous dependence and lack of control. This type of advertising – direct-to-consumer – requires an information exchange, rather than solely entertainment or emotion.

The big question we hear from marketers is 'how do we continually do more with the same or fewer resources?' Creating and sustaining famous brands that are dependent on public trust in the industry and in the brands themselves has never been a more complex challenge.

We will come back to Smith's work at ISBA (particularly on Origin) in Chapter 4, but as we can see here, trust matters greatly to the UK's biggest advertisers.

Trust, business effectiveness and profits

OK, let's get to the meat of why trust is important to advertising in the here and now.

A 2024 Advertising Association report called the 'Value of Trust' included new analysis of the case studies in the IPA's Databank by effectiveness expert Peter Field.[16] This work showed that since 2008, the relationship between building trust in a brand and achieving greater profit has strengthened considerably.

Two decades ago, trust was the least important contributor to profit growth of the seven brand metrics that the IPA monitors, but today, Field observed, it is the second most important, beaten only by the perceived

FIGURE 2.3 The growing relationship between trust and quality with profit and with effectiveness

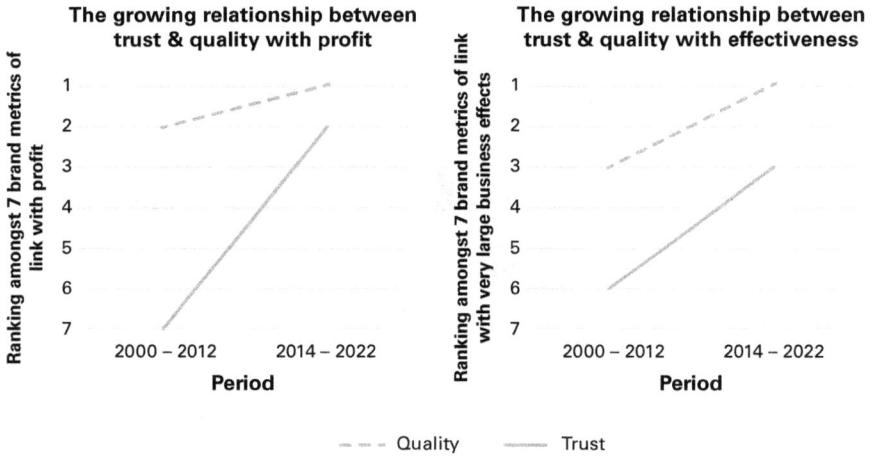

The growing relationship between trust & quality with profit

The growing relationship between trust & quality with effectiveness

– – – Quality   ——— Trust

quality of the brand. He pointed to suggestions that consumers increasingly assess the quality of any brand on whether they trust that brand and its advertising. Given the importance of quality perceptions to pricing power and therefore profitability, it's easy, he said, to see why trust has become so much more important.

The IPA data also suggested that the impact of trust on effectiveness has grown particularly strongly over the last five or six years.

Why is that? Well, for all the reasons we've been exploring already in Chapter 1...

The IPA data suggested there are strong implications for both the nature and placement of advertising if we wish to build trust in our brands. It is therefore vital to consider the implications of both your creative and media choices on how to build trust in your brand through its advertising.

Certainly, the conclusion of the analysis was that advertising that builds brand trust matters to their business performance. Crucially, the winners are the advertisers that commit to trust and make use of the strategies and platforms that grow and sustain it.

Holding advertising to the highest standards

Andria Vidler, Chief Executive of National Lottery operator Allwyn UK, became the new President of the Advertising Association in March 2025.[17]

When we interviewed her for this book, she remarked on just how much things have changed during her career, not just in advertising but in society generally.[18] Who we trust and how we trust has undergone a dramatic and dynamic change, brought about predominantly by technology, with the constant, ongoing challenge for government and society more broadly to adapt, adopt and regulate.

She raised concerns about people from different spheres of life, whether national politicians or social media influencers, presenting their own versions of truth without paying due concern to the facts and the damaging impact that this is having on trust. She expressed surprise at how people seem prepared to trust people they know little about, yet one of the world's most trusted news organizations, the BBC, has had to recently introduce BBC Verify to provide an extra level of credibility to the reporting it presents.

She is clear that trust in a brand comes from much more than its advertising. If you have a can of beans that tastes bad, no amount of advertising is going to get you repeat customers, she says. Likewise, car advertising has particular themes that different brands capitalize on, whether that's safety, design or speed. In that sense, trust is about being true to your message or proposition to the customer.

She is firm in her beliefs that the advertising industry deserves to be trusted. 'We are clear about the rules of engagement,' she says. 'We know the parameters and we know that the accurate marketing of products or services will help to sell them.' You mustn't disappoint people and should have faith in them and their experience of a brand or a product by staying true to that in your advertising.

Vidler's view is that we must always hold ourselves to the highest standards. She acknowledges that there are new players in the advertising industry, making new and disruptive impacts, but she urges the industry not to lower its own standards to accommodate those who can't meet them.

Above all, to remain true to our most important customer, the public. We must have faith in the customer, that the truth about a product or service will prevail, she concludes.

Conclusion

The views of advertising leaders from a century ago through to today remain consistent when it comes to the importance of trust. The way advertising works today may have changed significantly with the impact of technology, but the principles underpinning its success have not. At the same time, the importance of trust to advertising effectiveness has grown, directly linked to business success and the bottom line.

The evergreen truth is that the effectiveness of your advertising relies on audiences trusting what it says. Without trust, it is useless. Making your own advertising as trustworthy as possible is key.

Advertising differentiates your product, service or offering from competitors, and trust in that advertising is fundamental to competing successfully. A lack of trust in the work, in what it says, where it appears and indeed whether it holds to the industry's codes and rules, can have negative effects on your organization and possibly on the wider industry.

We have also seen clear evidence for the growing connection between trust and business results. As the AA's 'Value of Trust' report shows, the relationship between advertising which builds trust in a brand and the achievement of greater profit has strengthened considerably. Bluntly, trust matters more financially now than it has in the past.

We have seen that there are multiple factors involved in how advertising can build (and lose) trust, and that trust is something which needs constant management and nurture over the long term. Yet it can be lost in a moment if you get things wrong.

There is also a sense that if you're working on an advertising campaign, you have a responsibility to think about the bigger picture, and whether the campaign is contributing positively to society or not. This 'moral' obligation is a particularly sensitive one to navigate but we will attempt to do so during this book – it's the balance between achieving short-term advertising results and making a valuable economic and social contribution.

It's not only about trust in individual ads. Trust in advertising generally is good for the economy, and essential for the effectiveness of communications from institutions such as the government and not-for-profit organizations. They, like business, need advertising to function in a trustworthy manner to deliver its fullest economic and social benefits.

In short, advertising needs to be trusted to work, and the best, most trusted advertising work really can make the biggest difference for your organization – to profit margins and to successfully solving problems through great creative work.

So, it's all to play for!

Notes

1   Advertising Association/Credos, Advertising Pays 2025, https://adassoc.org.uk/credos/advertising-pays-2025/ (archived at https://perma.cc/4RC3-8AVY)

2 Minutes, Thirty Club of Great Britain, 20 October 1913

3 *Advertiser's Weekly*, 5 February 1926, History of Advertising Trust archives

4 AA journals, 1925, 1931,1936, History of Advertising Trust archives

5 AA journals, History of Advertising Trust archives

6 *Adweek*, 10 May 1974, the History of Advertising Trust archives

7 *Advertising Quarterly*, 1974, the History of Advertising Trust archives

8 Marketing Week, Advertising Association appoints Tim Lefroy as chief executive, March 2009, www.marketingweek.com/advertising-association-appoints-tim-lefroy-as-chief-executive/ (archived at https://perma.cc/SKX8-Q675)

9 E Owen, Richard Eyre: Trust is the key disruptor, Campaign, October 2014, www.campaignlive.co.uk/article/richard-eyre-trust-key-disruptor/1317353 (archived at https://perma.cc/6RD2-3JJ6)

10 Campaign, Richard Eyre: The only way is ethics?, January 2015, www.campaignlive.co.uk/article/richard-eyre-ethics/1331561 (archived at https://perma.cc/UWW3-HSP9)

11 S Gwynn, Unilever's Keith Weed will be next Advertising Association president, Campaign, July 2018, www.campaignlive.co.uk/article/unilevers-keith-weed-will-next-advertising-association-president/1488820 (archived at https://perma.cc/9RPN-G4WU)

12 Advertising Association, Keith Weed at LEAD '19 It's 'trust or bust', January 2019, https://adassoc.org.uk/our-work/keith-weed-at-lead-19-its-trust-or-bust/ (archived at https://perma.cc/BLL8-4QUC)

13 Advertising Association, Keith Weed 'trust is a must' from 'rebuilding public trust in UK advertising', October 2021, https://adassoc.org.uk/our-work/keith-weed-trust-must/ (archived at https://perma.cc/A98B-6A9T)

14 GOV.UK, Minister Sir Chris Bryant speech at LEAD advertising conference, February 2025, www.gov.uk/government/speeches/minister-sir-chris-bryant-speech-at-lead-advertising-conference (archived at https://perma.cc/9RU7-7MP6)

15 Interview Q&A with Phil Smith, Director General, ISBA, April 2025

16 Advertising Association/Credos, The Value of Trust Report, June 2024, https://adassoc.org.uk/our-work/the-value-of-trust-report/ (archived at https://perma.cc/V5RU-YWG2)

17 L Keitley, Advertising Association appoints Andria Vidler as president, Campaign, February 2025, www.campaignlive.co.uk/article/advertising-association-appoints-andria-vidler-president/1906657 (archived at https://perma.cc/ZU6J-4K9G)

18 Interview with Andria Vidler, CEO, Allwyn UK and President, Advertising Association, April 2025

03

Advertising, trust and the public

Introduction

In this chapter, we're going to review what we know about people's trust in advertising, including their favourability towards it.

To do this, we will take an in-depth look at what the UK advertising industry thinktank Credos (which James chairs) has done over the past 15 years to understand public trust in advertising and what might affect it.

We shall review how the Credos team investigated the subject, the learnings they uncovered and how these were interrogated to build a sense of what the industry can do more of (and less of) to improve levels of trust in the industry and its work.

Our goal is to help you understand as advertising practitioners what makes or breaks the public's trust in advertising.

We should acknowledge here the AA and Credos were of course not the first to explore the issue. Academic studies have long considered different aspects of trust in brands and businesses. A 2023 meta-study of such research by Mansur Khamitov and others in the *Journal of Consumer Research* which the authors describe as 'a big-tent investigation of consumer-trust research' derives from 549 trust-related studies involving almost 325,000 respondents in 71 countries over the five decades since 1970.[1]

Drawing on the findings of this immense body of work to bring out the most important elements of 'consumer trust', the paper divides the constituents of trust into two sets, 'Integrity-based' and 'Reliability-based', to both of which communications can contribute. Weighing up the drivers of both, it suggests that 'Reputation is likely the strongest driver of consumer trust'. Reputation is influenced by several factors, including track record and being seen to have the consumer's best interests at heart.

This meta-study also sees the positive consequences of trust as both attitudinal and behavioural and considers that these benefits for brands have grown in importance in recent years and are most likely to continue to be important in driving people's purchase decisions.

However, very few academic studies appear to have focused on trust in advertising. As far as we know, the regular tracking surveys and in-depth research projects commissioned by Credos are unique.

Trust in advertising: who, where, what and how?

We wrote about the formation of Credos, the UK advertising thinktank, in the previous chapter.[2] Its annual surveys of attitudes to advertising began in 2011 to include questions about trust. As time went by, the team saw some clear patterns emerge, which we can summarize here.

The who

Younger people like and trust advertising more than older ones. Much more.

Age is the only demographic difference of any real significance; socio-economic class, geography, sex, parenthood and political affiliation make little difference to people's attitudes. And it's unique to advertising. Across all the sectors that Credos monitor with the same questions, only advertising shows this degree of age-divide.

FIGURE 3.1 Trust in, and favourability towards, adverts, by age, 2024

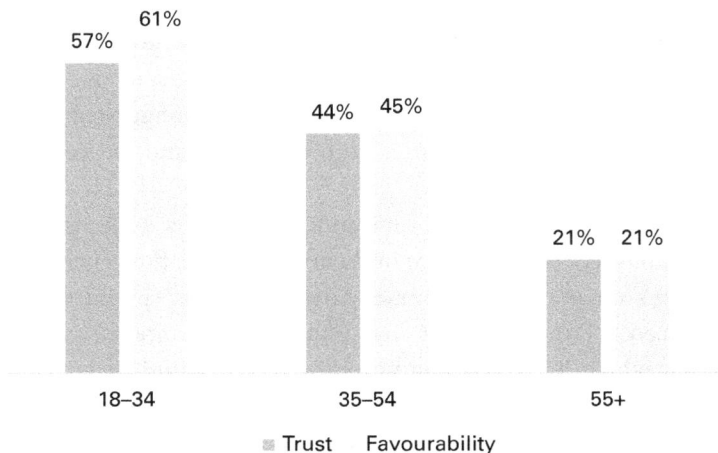

n = 2526
SOURCE Kantar panel for Credos trust tracking, 2024

We can seek to explain this in several ways. First, the older you get (and James speaks from experience here!), the less inherently interested you are in ads. You have, in a phrase, seen it all before; you may well have tried it, experienced it and moved on. You have made your choices, settled on your preferences and are no longer looking for the new. You also have the stuff you need. Of course, ads can appeal, new products and services prove relevant and new choices be made, but simply not to the same degree as when you are young.

A 2024 YouGov survey revealed that degree.[3] It reported that 33 per cent of all respondents said that advertising helped them decide what to buy, but the figure for younger audiences was much higher (at 51 per cent for Gen Z and 44 per cent for Millennials) than for Gen X (31 per cent) and Baby Boomers (17 per cent). The direct influence of ads, or at least our perception of it, clearly declines with age.

Looked at through younger eyes, ads bring a host of fresh and exciting ideas and promises to look out for, maybe to buy or try. As with music, the ads that you see and hear when young are the ones you most enjoy and that stay with you. Few older people buy the music avidly followed by their children or grandchildren; they play what they know and love.

Which is not to say that older people distrust all advertisements. Far from it; they will still trust what familiar brands say to them, depending on other factors we will look at.

The where

The generation gap is partly explained by attitudes to different media – where people encounter ads. Older individuals have not grown up with online media and still treat it with some caution or suspicion compared to the media they have known all their lives. The younger cohorts in our research are 'digital natives', at ease with online life and relaxed about the ads they find there.

This is naturally altering with time and, as the newer advertising formats become established, so confidence in them rises across the generations.

But there's more to it, of course. Advertising has spread to the more individualized platforms built by influencers, content creators and podcasters, which are often communities with a bond of trust between creator and followers or subscribers. For those audiences, these are trusted sources of inspiration and information, and advertisers can benefit from that relationship.

FIGURE 3.2 Trust in selected media channels, by age, 2024

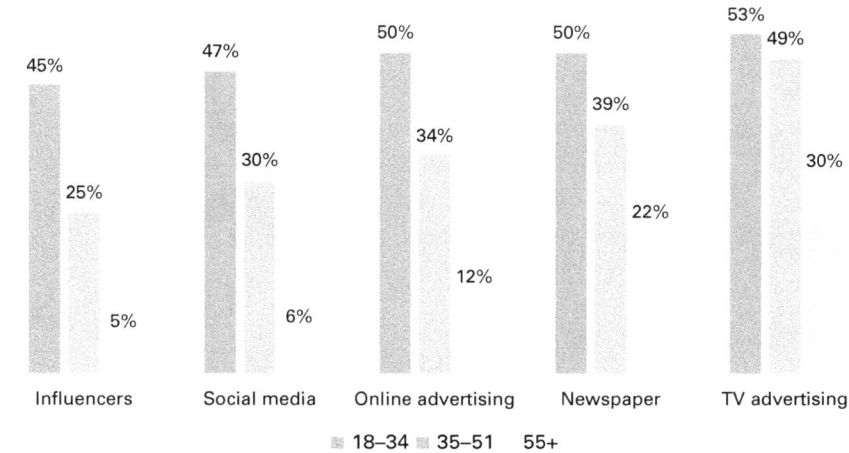

n = 2526
SOURCE Kantar panel for Credos trust tracking, 2024

FIGURE 3.3 Topics of concern in advertising, 2024

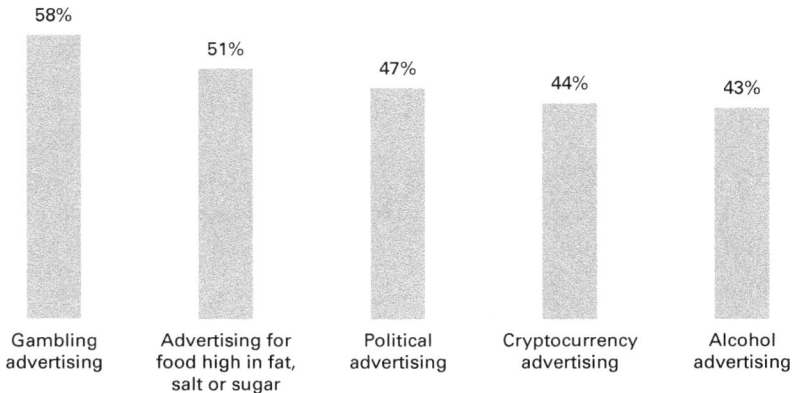

n = 2526
SOURCE Kantar panel for Credos trust tracking, 2024

The what

Just as some advertisers are more trustworthy than others, so are some categories of advertising. Products or services associated with risk and potential detriment attract a level of distrust, so we see gambling, some financial products and political ads, for instance, finding it hard to be trusted. Separating the level of trust in an ad from that in the advertiser, category or brand is tricky.

And the how

Finally, it's the way that you say it. How you tell it. Some ads are better than others at engendering trust, aside from the authority of the facts they convey or the demonstration of evidence to support their claims.

In essence, people trust emotionally engaging and entertaining ads more than overt salesmanship and rational claims. We trust people we like; we will more likely trust ads we enjoy, that strike us as understanding our lives, our sense of humour, what we are about.

So why the decline in trust?

All these aspects of the anatomy of trust in advertising have helped the Credos team understand its nature, shape and trends. But from the beginning, they wanted to find out why trust had suffered overall and how it could be rebuilt or built further. So, in parallel to the regular tracking, they commissioned a series of more focused studies over the years. The fruits of those investigations have led the UK advertising industry along the path of discovery and, in turn, planning and action to help it tackle the issue.

Getting to grips with the issue

The first foray to discover the secrets of trust in advertising came soon after Credos was established. In 2011, it commissioned public research experts Acacia Avenue to talk – and more importantly listen – to a wide range of people over an extended period.[4]

Three waves of qualitative research were conducted over a six-month period amongst a carefully selected variety of people across Britain. These 50 or so people gave the first direct insights into the British public's views on the current role and value of advertising in their lives.

The first findings

In true British tradition, the public proved pragmatic and tolerant in their attitudes to advertising. They felt that they were increasingly 'media savvy' and knew their way round the marketing and advertising jungle. Whether from media studies courses for the young, life experience for their seniors, or articles and documentaries for all, they spoke of their knowledge of advertising techniques, their appreciation of all forms of advertising when informative, entertaining and rewarding, and their resentment towards advertisers who treated them as naïve or gullible.

'Advertisers have spent years trying to pull the wool over people's eyes, but it's not that simple anymore', as one young man said.

James first heard respondents in focus groups saying the same thing back in the 1970s – how much more media-aware and expert they were compared to earlier generations – so perhaps it is a comforting self-delusion that we all indulge. However, he also acknowledges that not only are children and students more likely to have received some media education and even training, but the workplace has fundamentally changed over the years, too, to the same effect.

Whereas in the 1960s, some 55 per cent of the UK workforce were employed in the service sector, that proportion is now over 80 per cent, according to the Office for National Statistics.[5]

Most people work in customer-facing roles, whether face-to-face, online or on the phone. We are nearly all trained in marketing, selling or managing customer experience of one sort or another. We are a nation, if not of shop-keepers, then of customer satisfaction experts. The same is true of much of the world's population, all equipped with phones and the ability to go online. Which means that we really do know the nature of the advertisers' game, perhaps, better than ever.

But back to the 2011 research…

So, who do you trust?

When it came to advertising, Acacia Avenue's findings were clear. For one thing, trust was relative, not absolute. It depended on the viewer, their knowledge of the brand or company and its wider media and social context. Their trust or mistrust was attached not to generic 'advertising' but the particular ad in question. So, a wide range of factors could affect that trust, from the general context to specific triggers, as shown in Figure 3.4.

These factors, to a greater or lesser extent, have remained significant pointers toward how to achieve – or lose – trust in ads throughout our subsequent journey. We will see them resurfacing in later research, along with another significant truth that the 2011 survey revealed.

I believe you, but I don't trust you

Credibility and trust are not the same, reported Acacia Avenue. Believing an ad to be telling the literal truth is one, essentially rational, thing; trusting it

FIGURE 3.4 Acacia Avenue, trust factors

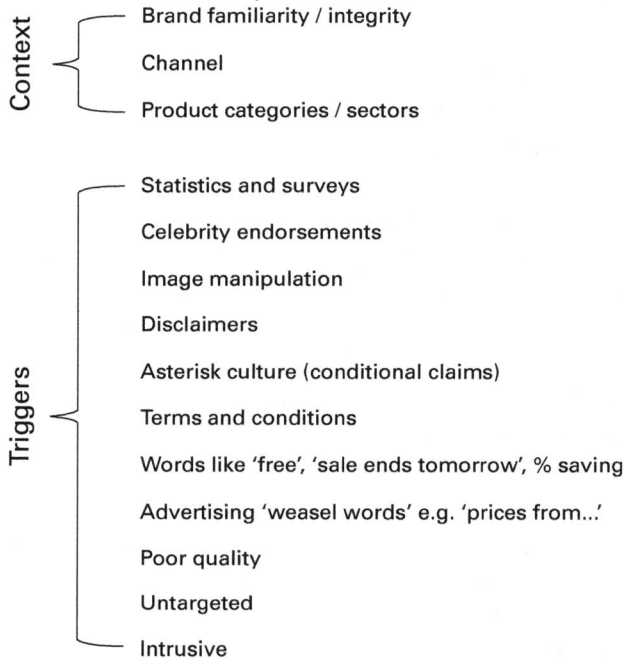

Context
- Brand familiarity / integrity
- Channel
- Product categories / sectors

Triggers
- Statistics and surveys
- Celebrity endorsements
- Image manipulation
- Disclaimers
- Asterisk culture (conditional claims)
- Terms and conditions
- Words like 'free', 'sale ends tomorrow', % saving
- Advertising 'weasel words' e.g. 'prices from...'
- Poor quality
- Untargeted
- Intrusive

comes from a wider and more emotional set of beliefs, knowledge and experience.

Which is why, as Chapter 14 on the Advertising Standards Authority and ad regulation will explore, the ASA's long-cherished slogan, 'Legal, Decent, Honest and Truthful', is expressed the way it is. Honest is different from truthful: the former is a character trait, an approach to life and behaviour; the latter is a statement of fact, or at least of a genuine understanding of something, that can in itself be believed based on evidence. But just because I hear you say a true thing does not mean I trust you more comprehensively. Remember how consumer trust could be 'Integrity-based' and 'Reliability-based' in Khamitov's meta-study? Those terms echo 'honest' and 'truthful' in their difference

So, the question of trust is twofold: do I believe the specific claim or promise in this ad, and do I trust the ad as a whole? Both of these aspects, although distinct, are bound up in how the ad is made, who is in it, where I am seeing it, the brand and company behind it and more. Not always easy to disentangle!

Scepticism and mistrust

Acacia Avenue found the British public to have, overall, a 'healthy scepticism' towards advertising, respondents saying they took ads 'with a grain of salt'. Understanding the commercial intent of most advertising, knowing they promoted the positive and minimized the negative, people's default position was described as one of 'suspended trust'.

That's where factors creating and bolstering trust came in to overcome people's inherent scepticism: reflecting the reputation and heritage of the brand; using a celebrity who fits the brand and has integrity; making a credible, well-evidenced claim; giving recourse if the purchase does not work out.

Mistrust, on the other hand, was felt when an ad was perceived to be intentionally misleading or deceitful. This was aroused most often by 'harder' claims of performance, price or quality that didn't ring true. The 'triggers' in listed in Figure 3.4 show the sort of things that people responded badly to in the study – 'weasel words', small-print caveats, distortions of the truth and poor practice.

'Softer', less assertive ads were more likely to be trusted, a finding which has been repeated since and which we learned more about as we went on, as you will read.

Intruding on people's lives

Credos also learned early lessons from these respondents about 'bombardment', the endless stream of advertising entering their lives. At that time 'digital', online and mobile advertising were building towards the dominance they now exert in the advertising market. Even then, 'intrusive, unsolicited, irrelevant or poor quality advertisements' were resented, with the test groups often feeling besieged but unable to control the flow. As the authors put it:

> The public is not fed up with advertising; it is bored with a huge volume of boring and perceived poor-quality advertisements.

Sometimes this intrusive behaviour crossed the line of what was acceptable and became, in respondents' eyes, an invasion of privacy. Interestingly, the researchers opined that clear lines existed between perceptions of public and private space, with none of the 'blurring' between the two reported elsewhere. They felt that: 'Simply advertising online does not mean that different rules apply'.

The 2011 study set Credos on a path to understand the dynamics of trust in advertising, its complexities and the very human aspects of how and why individuals trust or mistrust the communications they encounter. It gave insights and pointers to how advertising and advertisements could work to earn public trust and led the Credos team to explore further. The research may have been conducted 14 years before the most recent trust studies, but the concerns and challenges it raised have by no means all been resolved, even though many industry players have absorbed and acted upon them.

A fresh look at public trust in advertising

Five years on from Acacia Avenue's first research, the advertising market – and the world – had moved on. Credos wanted to get a fresh picture of the public's views of advertising, particularly from younger people and the parents of small children; groups felt to be particularly affected by the evolution of the advertising landscape.

Acacia Avenue were set three question areas to explore:

1 How was the explosion of social media and mobile, screen-based communications impacting attitudes to advertising and the ways consumers were navigating its new complexities?

2 What was happening to trust? Were controversies over social media, privacy and personal data use, 'fake news' and brands talking up their 'purpose' altering how trust in advertising was being built or breached?

3 What did people know – or care – about regulation? Did they know whose responsibility it was to protect them and their children from irresponsible ads?

So, in July of 2017, Acacia Avenue conducted six focus groups amongst a relatively young mix of people divided into those in their late teens, those in their early 20s without children, and those over 30 with children under 12.[6]

A changing world

The groups soon showed how a changing context was shaping new attitudes to advertising. Think back to 2017 if you can. Unexpected and seismic political change, with Donald Trump's election and the Brexit vote both in the past year, was provoking an unprecedented (at least in the US and UK) polarization of public opinion. This was echoed in – and arguably fuelled by – social media and the propensity of its attention-driving algorithms to draw audiences to extreme views. Nor was it helped by the established news media's phone-hacking exploits, which had culminated in 2012's Leveson Inquiry.

Corporate cynicism had grown, too. Already pessimistic about corporate morality after the 2008 financial crash and its fallout, people had looked to the new tech brands with hope: they seemed to promise higher ethical and more socially benevolent behaviour. But the tax avoidance 'scandal' involving major US 'tech' companies with big UK presence showed that they, too, had feet of clay. Along with a leading supermarket's horsemeat revelations and 'Dieselgate' in the car market, businesses were letting people down too often.

A culture of mistrust had grown, with its own language: 'fake news', 'truthiness', 'alternative facts'. As far as our respondents were concerned, politicians, the media and corporations were all tainted.

A changed advertising environment

Between 2011 and 2017, mobile and online advertising had grown from 33 per cent of UK ad spend to 57 per cent, or to put it another way from £4.8 billion to £11.8 billion.[7] That enormous increase was mostly at the expense of other media but also reflected the ever-increasing number of advertisers as the 'long tail' of smaller companies and even micro-businesses found they could afford their own ad campaigns on targeted digital media. This background inevitably had its impact on respondents' experience of, and feelings toward, advertising.

For one thing, the bombardment registered as a turn-off in 2011 had only got worse. Social media had become a 'never off' companion in people's lives, drawing them on into stories, related links and new posts with no 'off switch'. In that context, advertising seemed to have lost its own 'stopping cues', as the researchers put it, which traditional media had with its timed ad breaks or easily turned pages. Respondents could feel overwhelmed and out of control.

Concerns over privacy surfaced more in this research, perhaps unsurprisingly. Spending more time online and sharing more personal information as they were, media stories of cyber-attacks or the 'danger' of cookies, for instance, prompted some anxiety amongst respondents over how vulnerable they might be. 'Stalking' had entered the vernacular. Overall, the convenience and appeal of the online world outweighed these concerns in people's everyday behaviour, but wariness over advertising's role had increased.

In a climate of strong opinions voiced ever louder in social media, advertisers also faced a wave of instant commentary on, or criticism of, their ads. As the research report described it, 'Social media has become a tool for the public to hold advertisers to account and, indeed, almost a form of public regulation.'

Understanding this new dynamic, some advertisers had put forward more challenging work, with a point of view, a social purpose or ethical values and declarations of authenticity upfront in their communications.

This bolder approach could be very successful – Dove Beauty, This Girl Can and the Axe campaigns were cited, for example, as genuine and positive attempts to 'do more than just sell'.

But what respondents also clocked was that some brands were adopting the mantra of 'purpose', aligning with and championing social causes and presenting themselves as 'doing good', less convincingly. This didn't always wash with the groups: scepticism was evident, authenticity doubted, motivations suspected.

On the other hand, with all the negative news and content washing over them, people showed a natural desire for more optimistic and entertaining distraction in online videos, games and viral content on social media. Advertising was seen to play a part in that, making people laugh or giving a more positive picture of everyday life, which helped respondents feel understood and reassured. As ever, people enjoyed and valued the creativity of advertising, acknowledged its potential to induce positive emotions and appreciated its purpose:

> I don't want my world to become narrower. I don't want to miss out on new things (35–44 yrs)

> I think it would be a bit boring if we didn't have ads… (18–19 yrs)

But the reward for what the researchers called 'the effort equation' had to be fair. As they put it, 'In today's environment, there is too little reward for too much effort'.

Next question: what was that doing to trust?

Changing aspects of trust in ads

Much that was true in 2011 remained so in 2017. That people take advertising 'with a pinch of salt', that trust attaches to individual ads rather than to advertising in general, that a range of factors contribute to trust – the brand, the creative treatment, the media chosen – and that credibility and trust are connected but different, all these stayed valid. But differences had emerged, too, stemming from a changed, more distrustful, political environment and the 'never off' presence of social media.

What about regulation?

The relationship between trust and regulation had evolved, too, over the years. Hardly a big issue to people, most had only vague ideas about it. News of ads being 'banned' and awareness of 'small print' or 'fast-talk' were the most overt signs of regulation that respondents mentioned. Both showed that it existed, which was reassuring, but also that advertisers had to be held in check because of the temptation to overclaim.

Social media had by this time established its own role in holding brands to account, with complaints about advertising more likely to be aired and noticed there than through the more formal channels that people were less familiar with. Mirroring the suspicion that digital advertising lacked rules and regulations compared with traditional media, especially TV, was people's belief that they could and should rely on their own 'healthy scepticism' most of the time. They liked to know that regulations were in place that made advertising more trustworthy, but they understood neither the system nor who was in charge.

It was partly this research that prompted the team at Credos to make an ultimately significant recommendation to the UK ad industry's leaders: to put up the money and resource in skill and thought to launch a campaign advertising the ASA's role and work; to show that an effective 'bobby on the beat' patrolled advertising and kept the public safe from any bad behaviour, wherever it might occur. We shall see how that worked out in Chapter 14.

For now, let's continue our search for the underlying dynamics of trust in advertising and how it gave the industry a path to follow.

A deeper dive

By 2018 there was an appetite amongst the advertising industry's stakeholders to take new action on trust. The Credos tracking survey had shown it reaching an all-time low in 2015, the qualitative research had revealed its dynamics and the AA's newly established Trust Group (more on that in Chapter 4) was looking for real-world policies to rebuild it.[8]

Building on what had been learned so far about the factors likely to impact favourability and trust, the Trust Group, chaired by the heads of the UK's principal advertiser and agency organizations, ISBA and the IPA, wanted Credos to tease out the drivers of trust so that they could be addressed. With this senior, pan-industry working group, the opportunity existed to get authority, resource and energy behind concerted action.

To identify the key drivers of trust in advertising and to quantify their relative importance, a research programme was devised with the agency, Craft.

A sample of 60 respondents completed 10 days of online tasks, capturing and commenting on their day-to-day exposure to advertising in all its guises. Twelve were then selected for visits from the researchers, who accompanied them about their daily lives to see what advertising they encountered and how they felt about it. Film (both self-shot and by the research team), screen-captured tasks and finally in-depth interviews completed the picture. And it was a rich one of people's lived experience with advertising.

Advertising is 'a good thing with downsides'

Surfacing from that immersion, the researchers gave us a nuanced portrait of advertising's place in the public's lives, and the place of trust within that.

Overall, respondents saw advertising as 'a good thing with downsides' rather than 'a bad thing with upsides', with the benefits to individuals, business and society we have already seen in previous studies.

Credos sought to tease apart the tangled issue of favourability and trust, a 'Gordian knot' as the researchers phrased it. It took some doing and we should never expect the two to be quite separate. What and whom people like affects what and whom they trust. Equally, to be trustworthy is a likeable trait. But some conclusions emerged. To quote the report:

Favourability is a more general indicator of satisfaction and, whilst it can be impacted by the same factors that drive or inhibit trust, it often has less serious connotations – whether or not advertising is appreciated on a rational or emotional level and/or the degree to which it is found to be annoying. Such issues are often of personal preference.

Trust tends to have more serious connotations and is undermined when advertising is perceived to be misleading, makes people feel uncertain or uncomfortable... or, in the worst cases, is seen to create (or have the potential to create) harm or offence.

Whereas all sorts of things might affect favourability (and vary a lot by individual), like irrelevance, repetition, volume or annoying content, the 'higher order' factors that provoked distrust were less commonplace.

Factors reducing favourability and trust

Four factors adversely affected both favourability and trust. They varied by individual, according to their media consumption, age, broader attitudes to business and marketing, and personal experience of issues like alcohol or gambling problems.

1 **Intrusiveness:** Rather than just a frustration with the amount of advertising raining down on them – the 'bombardment' issue noted earlier – intrusiveness was defined as unsolicited advertising invading what people considered private places. Here, respondents pointed to examples that are actually outside the scope of legitimate advertising, but which they still regarded as ads – 'junk mail' dropped through the letterbox, PPI-selling phone calls, ads masquerading as emails appearing in the inbox. Perceived intrusion was not only seen in scam or near-scam 'ads', but some online practices that had emerged. Those included display ads on Facebook Messenger, targeted ads that people felt were based on very personal data such as health issues or ads in social media places featuring personal photos taken from people's photo libraries.

2 **Creative content concerns:** Body image was one, and a significant concern for some respondents, perhaps because of their own struggles with weight or because of a family member's problems. Parents, especially of daughters, voiced concern over 'skinny models' and airbrushing creating unrealistic body ideals or showing unachievable outcomes for products. More broadly, discerning *what was* and *what was not* advertising had become increasingly difficult. This research preceded the dramatic rise of influencer marketing, so the words influencer or creator hardly featured, but 'native advertising', sponsored content, and celebrity endorsements that may or may not be authentic were undermining people's confidence in knowing what they were seeing and therefore how to deal with it. They could easily feel manipulated, 'duped' or 'conned'. Not trustworthy behaviour!

3 **Targeting and privacy:** An issue in the news at the time of this research, but most respondents were resigned to companies gaining access to their data and using it to target ads online. For many, it was considered

a cost – *the* cost, perhaps – of using the internet. It was a complicated topic for the majority, and one that worried some more than others. Awareness of how their data was being used had led many, especially the younger participants, to become habitualized to it, even comfortable with it. Others were distinctly uncomfortable. Some resented the harvesting of their personal – as they saw it – information without their knowledge or permission: whether they had kids, their earning power or their personal habits were things they didn't want known and used to target them. Some simply did not know about it until prompted by the researchers and then felt discomforted. The contemporary introduction of GDPR had not impressed respondents, who understood little about it and saw it making no difference.

4 **High profile issues:** The most deeply felt destroyers of trust in advertising arose unprompted during the research – advertising for gambling, alcohol, payday loans, high-interest credit cards and sugary foods. Many respondents had one or more of these as 'hot button' issues because of personal experience of problems with those products, whether their own or a friend's or family member's. The role of personal responsibility was often emphasized, especially when talking of categories where the individual had not experienced a problem close to home, but that some people were vulnerable to forms of addiction or harm associated with such products meant that their advertising was nonetheless criticized. It was often felt to send the wrong message, at odds with people's family or community values, and children in particular warranted special protection. The perceived irresponsibility some saw in advertising seeming to promote anything and everything regardless of consequences extended beyond the high-risk categories listed. It was cited in the emotional or financial detriment that could be generated by NGO ads showing starving children on TV around dinner time, or ads for expensive toys in the run-up to Christmas, even to the promotion of unaffordable (to many) products on tablets or phones used by children. This was not to say that respondents shrugged off personal and parental responsibility in mediating the impact of such advertising, but its ubiquity, volume and appeal could make that difficult. To counter this criticism, the researchers did note people's praise for advertising doing public good by promoting diversity and inclusivity, its public health campaigns (and this, of course, was before the Covid-19 experience of advertising's crucial public service role) and in redressing gender stereotypes. But 'advertising the wrong things' was seen as deleterious to the industry's reputation and trustworthiness.

So, what about trust overall?

When asked whether advertising has become more or less trustworthy in recent years, opinion was divided. Some referred to its regulation as, although understanding of that was low, they felt that it had become stricter. Others, referring to how all-pervasive and diffuse advertising had become, felt that it could not be effectively policed, that the boundaries between what is and is not advertising had become blurred, and that online data use and targeting was a growing worry, so that overall, it had become less trustworthy. Many had no strong view either way.

As in other research considered in this book, feelings towards the brand advertised remained the number one determinant of trust in its ads. As the research partners, Craft, pointed out, brand trust tends to be long term, growing or diminishing over years rather than with a single ad campaign. Moreover, personal experience is more powerful than claims or endorsements, so a brand's reputation rests on a lot more than its advertising.

However, the way a brand communicated creatively and the company it kept in its media context could either reinforce or undermine that reputation. Authenticity – executions without obvious photoshopping, image manipulation, unrealistic models, unfeasible claims or reams of small print T&Cs, but using 'normal people' and credible information, humour and charm – mattered to respondents.

So did the advertising medium. The low cost of entry of online, especially social media, environments was perceived to attract a lower quality of advertisers. A 'lack of quality control' was cited online, too, where perceived lighter regulation – or none – made ads there less trustworthy. Traditional mass media carried more trust in the ads there because of the perceived cost of making and running them, and bigger, richer, more established brands were the more trustworthy.

However, Craft's researchers noted that whereas an unknown brand could make itself feel more trustworthy by using expensive-looking TV ads, an established brand would not sacrifice its reputation simply by advertising online.

Similarly, pop-up ads were pinpointed by some respondents as being an untrustworthy form of advertising, but Craft attributed this as more to do with the types of companies using them than the format itself.

Their researchers also described 'the jury being out' when it came to 'native' advertising and the early iterations of what has now become the booming influencer sector, with respondents sometimes unsure of whether they were seeing 'adverts' or not.

'This speaks to the point about "what is true?", they wrote, 'and is where the goals of the industry appear to conflict with the goals of the consumer. For consumers, good native advertising should not be so native that you can't tell if it's advertising, but from an industry perspective, arguably the opposite is true.'

This is a dilemma we still face today, as we will explore in Chapters 6 and 7.

Last, but described as not least, the media brand in which people encounter an ad was said to have a big impact on trust. This was especially true of smaller brands which reflected the values of the respondent, like a magazine devoted to their special interests or an ethnic TV channel particular to their community.

Quantifying the drivers of trust

That 'deeper dive' into trust, with its in-life, accompanied interviews, participants' videos and their filmed experiences of advertising as encountered day to day, reactions to it and opinions about it, gave Credos a rich seam of understanding about the drivers of trust in advertising and in advertisements.

But it begged questions about the quantitative importance of different drivers and their relative significance to different demographic cohorts, the answers to which could steer industry responses through the AA Trust Group and its work.

The next step, then, was to put some numbers onto the hypotheses generated by the qualitative study, which Credos commissioned Craft to do.[9]

This was a new and defining approach to discover the relative importance of the several 'drivers' of trust and how much they varied within the population. Capturing these insights would enable the AA's Trust Group to focus attention on the factors that mattered and which the industry could address.

With a nationally representative sample of over 2,000 adults, the study used the findings of the qualitative stage to ask people about the factors that influenced their attitudes toward, and trust in, advertising. Using factor analysis to group the answers into clusters and regression analysis to determine their relative significance, the results gave a balanced picture of what drove public feeling.

FIGURE 3.5 Craft, trust factors, 2018

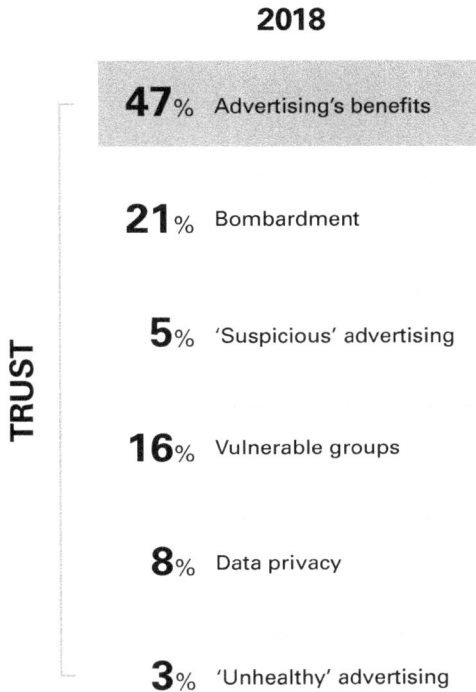

2018

TRUST

47% Advertising's benefits

21% Bombardment

5% 'Suspicious' advertising

16% Vulnerable groups

8% Data privacy

3% 'Unhealthy' advertising

Advertising's benefits, to individuals and society, were well-recognized; in terms of their importance in deciding people's overall favourability and trust scores, they roughly matched the concerns that they felt.

The principal factors driving negative outlooks were volume ('bombardment'), obtrusion (ads barging in unasked-for) and 'vulnerable groups' (the harm that advertising might do to those seen as less able to deal with it all). But volume and obtrusion, annoying as they might be, had a bigger impact on favourability than trust. To undermine trust, the more serious concerns of intrusion, vulnerable groups and suspicious advertising came to the fore.

The report noted that younger people, as seen in the tracking, were less concerned than their elders about these things. It also showed that people who labelled a wide variety of selling and marketing activities, from shop window displays to on-street sampling and sales calls on their phones, as 'advertising' had a poorer opinion of its trustworthiness than those holding to a narrower, more 'correct' view of ads as restricted to (usually) paid-for media.

These findings echoed the qualitative research insights but also gave the AA's Trust Group some headlines to focus on for industry action.

Tracking the 'good' and 'bad' – three years on and two years later

In mid-2021, as the country was reaching the tail-end of the extraordinary Covid-19 experience, with its lockdowns, its economic dislocation and advertising's response to both, Credos repeated the survey and analysis,[10] as it did two years later,[11,12] with Covid-19 behind us but its consequences echoing through society, business and advertising. Each wave saw the same big factors prompting respondents' likelihood to trust or distrust advertising, but their relative significance waxed and waned, in particular amongst different age groups.

In 2023, the research not only repeated the quantitative interrogation of the drivers of trust but took a fresh qualitative look at the context in which people formed their views. The quant analysis delivered the same 'top drivers' as before, the most significant being the positive impact of engaging and enjoyable creativity in advertising, with bombardment in all its forms staying the top negative driver.

But, as in 2021, some intriguing changes lay below those headlines. Whilst bombardment had become significantly more of an issue for younger audiences, their concerns over suspicious advertising had reduced, although remaining higher than back in 2018. That advertising could negatively affect vulnerable groups had risen in significance instead, as had advertising's positive social contribution.

These swirling undercurrents can and did generate all sorts of theories as to their causes. Had the recovery and surprisingly dynamic growth of advertising spend, especially online, post-Covid triggered a spasm of dismay over its sheer volume, leading to the spike for 'bombardment' amongst younger people? Had the platforms' efforts to improve the advertising experience of their users led to the reduction in perceived 'intrusion'? Had the ASA's own new and better funded advertising campaign had an impact on perceptions of how many ads were misleading?

Maybe. But the big truths about how to secure trust in advertising held:

1 Do truthful advertising that people like, respond to emotionally and find value in.
2 Don't intrude on people's private spaces.
3 Try to make sure the public knows that advertising is well-regulated.

FIGURE 3.6 Craft, trust factors, 2018, 2021 and 2023

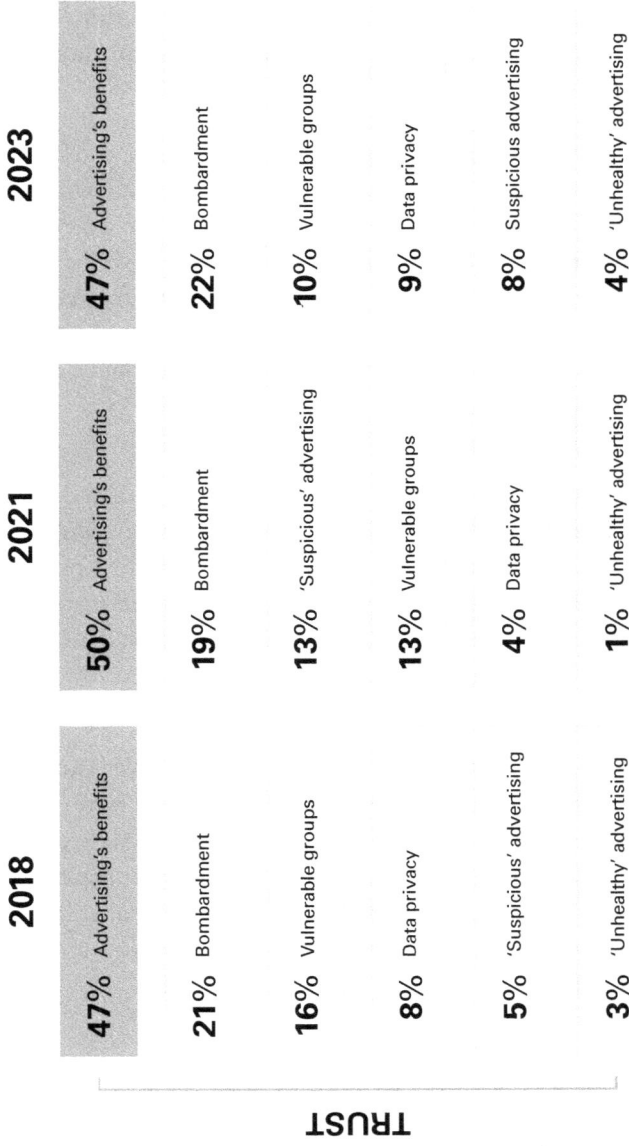

	2018	**2021**	**2023**
TRUST	**47%** Advertising's benefits	**50%** Advertising's benefits	**47%** Advertising's benefits
	21% Bombardment	**19%** Bombardment	**22%** Bombardment
	16% Vulnerable groups	**13%** 'Suspicious' advertising	**10%** Vulnerable groups
	8% Data privacy	**13%** Vulnerable groups	**9%** Data privacy
	5% 'Suspicious' advertising	**4%** Data privacy	**8%** Suspicious advertising
	3% 'Unhealthy' advertising	**1%** 'Unhealthy' advertising	**4%** 'Unhealthy' advertising

Some things about trust are beyond advertising's control

Those aspects of being trustworthy are largely under the advertisers' control. Other important factors in the trust equation are not, as the qualitative research showed. Craft's interviews in this wave confirmed three overarching themes that could predetermine individuals' attitudes to advertising when quizzed.

1 'World view'

Attitudes to advertising nest, Craft's researchers found, within a broader set of values and opinions about society and business in general. Those feeling that a consumer-led market economy was at odds with their personal values were naturally critical of advertising and unwilling to credit ads with their trust. Others, more comfortable with the status quo, accepted advertising as a necessary, even welcome, element in a healthy economy; a greater propensity to trust it followed.

2 'Media socialization'

This also underpinned people's expectations of and attitudes towards advertising. The media world in which someone has grown up affects their outlook on what to trust and what not to, so that older people were sceptical of relatively unfamiliar 'new media', whereas younger respondents felt at ease with a wider range of channels and platforms. Their confidence and trust in those media were consequently greater.

3 'Definition of advertising'

Participants' answers to the question of 'what is advertising' made a difference. The public, as seen in the earlier research, have a much broader definition of advertising than the industry. It can include every sort of 'selling communication' from sponsorship to window displays to packaging and, as we have noted, scams and fraudulent phone calls. To trust that entire gamut of marketing and selling techniques everywhere they encountered them was unlikely. Context, as we have seen, is key.

PUBLIC TRUST IN ADVERTISING: WHAT NEXT?

By Dan Wilks, Director, Credos

Measuring trust often feels like trying to nail down jelly, or rather how I imagine that would feel. Trust is difficult to define, it's instinctive and it's highly personalized.

Now try to measure trust in advertising. Most people have trouble even conceptualizing advertising in a general sense – it is ever-evolving and takes too many disparate forms. On top of that, the public's definition of advertising tends to be much broader than the industry's own. It can become so broad that it encompasses capitalism, corporate behaviour and consumer culture as a whole.

But just because something is difficult, doesn't mean you shouldn't try. And as illustrated in this chapter, at Credos we've been trying for over a decade. We've learnt much in that time, including some eternal truths of what drives trust in advertising and what doesn't.

These learnings have enabled the industry to take action in many areas to increase public trust. But there is still much work to do, and more questions that deserve answers. This is to be expected in an industry changing as rapidly as advertising. Some things we know to be true today may not be so in a year or two.

That's why we've commissioned the leading research agency, Opinium, to identify what drives a person to trust or distrust advertising in 2025. This project looks to update our existing bank of knowledge and specifically investigate emerging themes related to age, influencers and AI.

The new research employs various qualitative techniques across three phases, with daily in-the-moment diaries to capture reactions to advertising as they happen; family debates, providing an unfiltered generational view on trust in advertising; and in-depth ethnographic interviews deep-diving into what really drives both trust and distrust.

At the time of writing, the research is in the fieldwork stage. However, I can share a preview of the emergent findings so far.

New areas of interest

Though still in its early phases, the research has already revealed several nascent themes and perspectives:

- AI is quickly adding more complexity to trust in advertising. People see the potential of AI to be creative and efficient, but many feel uneasy. AI is moving fast, can feel inauthentic and it's not always clear what's real. Greater transparency, clarity on use and regulation were seen as key to building trust.

- A stark generational divide in what drives trust is very apparent. That's nothing new, but some interesting nuances have emerged:

  o Older generations are more likely to trust ads that are clear in intent and execution, whereas younger generations appear more responsive to how the ad made them feel.

- o   Micro-generational differences are emerging amongst younger people, where two/three-year differences are significantly impacting how advertising is both consumed and perceived.

- Gen Z are often highly attuned to influencer tactics, feeling naturally able to spot when promotions seem insincere, 'off brand' or purely financially motivated – all driving distrust.

- Though people tend not to have defined categories of influencers, there are natural distinctions developing between influencers, celebrities and content creators. The latter are received more openly and their commercial content often described as "integrated" or "personal".

The eternal truths

As you would expect, the initial findings echo many of the themes that have consistently been found to influence trust in advertising over the past decade:

- Bombardment remains a key annoyance, particularly on social media, where people feel that the volume and repetition across platforms is relentless and getting worse.

- Trust remains highest in traditional advertising channels, particularly TV. The view remains that online advertising is largely unregulated.

- Advertising of controversial categories remains a frequent driver of distrust across generations. Gambling remains the most commonly cited, although concerns around unrealistic beauty/health standards and crypto get-rich-quick schemes were common amongst the young.

- Scams remain top of mind for all ages, with misleading buys cited frequently, resulting in increased in distrust and suspicion.

I re-iterate that these represent just initial themes identified in the research so far. They may develop, morph or diminish as it continues. As in previous years, we plan to test the qualitative findings through follow-up quantitative research to ascertain their relative importance and scale.

It will then be up to industry, spearheaded by the Advertising Association's Trust Group, to identify what action can and should be taken to further build the public's trust in what we do.

We stand at a pivotal point for trust. As advertising continues to change through the application of technology, so do the various ways in which trust can be secured – but also destroyed. Ensuring ads can be trusted by the people that receive them must remain a core principle of our industry.

Conclusion

We have worried away at the issue of trust in advertising for over a decade. It is too central to the reputation and success of our industry to neglect.

We have learned that it is affected by many things. Some, like the very different world views individuals may hold much more deeply than any views on advertising, or the life experiences of succeeding generations that determine their media choices, lie quite outside our control. We can try to understand them, deal with them and perhaps ameliorate their impact on people's trust in the ads they encounter, but we cannot fundamentally alter them to our benefit.

Others, such as the consequences of the ebb and flow of advertising investment into different advertising media as technologies spur new forms of communication and marketing, have proved hard to address collectively in a competitive environment. Efforts to do so continue and, in an industry that in the UK at least is characterized by a surprisingly co-operative mindset, there has been some success through voluntary self-regulation and standard-setting. The commercial benefits of limiting the sorts of repetition, intrusion or 'bombardment' that frustrate audiences also help in winning adherence to better practice. Later chapters will show how the industry and its regulators are tackling problems of misleading or 'suspicious' advertising, too.

And some factors we have identified and communicated for advertisers to use to their advantage. For those for whom 'content is king', there is guidance to improve the quality of their work. For those believing that 'the medium is the message', there is advice on media choice, too. Both are key to trust.

Nor is our journey of discovery over. In 2025, as we write, the new research programme is in hand at Credos. The thinktank wants to sharpen the appreciation of where and how we can push for further industry action based on new and deeper understanding of the public mind and advertising's place within it.

Notes

1   M Khamitov and R Koushyar, Consumer trust: Meta-analysis of 50 years of empirical research, *Journal of Consumer Research*, August 2023, www.researchgate. net/publication/373448534_Consumer_Trust_Meta-analysis_of_50_Years_of_ Empirical_Research (archived at https://perma.cc/8PHU-MS3Z)

2   Credos, the UK advertising thinktank, https://adassoc.org.uk/credos/ (archived at https://perma.cc/J7SV-GQPJ)

3   J Fernandes, Advertising by age: Platforms and content that influence consumer behaviour, YouGov, October 2024, https://business.yougov.com/content/50751-advertising-by-age-platforms-and-content-that-influence-consumer-behaviour (archived at https://perma.cc/244M-HY6P)

4   Credos forum: Monitoring the public's opinion of advertising, by Acacia Avenue, July 2011, available from Credos archives

5   Long-term trends in UK employment: 1861 to 2018, Office for National Statistics, April 2019, www.ons.gov.uk/economy/nationalaccounts/uksectoraccounts/compendium/economicreview/april2019/longtermtrendsinukemployment1861to2018 (archived at https://perma.cc/T4WJ-SJKA)

6   Public perceptions of advertising in 2017, Credos, by Acacia Avenue, September 2017, available from Credos archives

7   Advertising Association/WARC Expenditure Report 2025, www.warc.com/about-media/expenditure-report (archived at https://perma.cc/8PGT-GT4A)

8   Public trust, Advertising Association, https://adassoc.org.uk/our-work-category/trust-in-advertising/ (archived at https://perma.cc/T4AY-J3M5)

9   Advertising favourability and trust research, Credos & Craft, 2018, https://adassoc.org.uk/our-work/new-credos-report-highlights-how-consumers-want-advertising-to-change/ (archived at https://perma.cc/B36E-NXK9)

10   Putting numbers onto the insights: The quantitative 'Drivers' study, Credos & Craft, 2018, available from Credos archives

11   Drivers of Trust in Advertising 2021 – focus on suspicious advertising, Credos & True Stories, available from Credos archives

12   What drives the public's trust in advertising', Credos & Craft, 2023, available from Credos archives

04

How advertising
builds trust (or fails to)

Introduction

Now we're going to review more work by Credos to identify the 'drivers' of people's trust in advertising – both the positive and negative things we can do that affect trust – and consider how action around each can create a positive boost to public trust. These drivers are key to shaping people's trust or distrust in advertising and the chapter draws out ways in which advertisers and their industry bodies either do or can influence them.

We will also consider a range of examples from across the industry through real-world examples of industry codes, research reports, campaigning initiatives and awards, which may provide further stimulus for action to maintain and build trust in advertising.

The key drivers of public trust in advertising

As we saw in the previous chapter, Credos developed a model in 2018 to identify what drives people's trust in advertising, which was replicated in 2021 and 2023. It used the same nine clusters of drivers every time. These nine drivers were then ranked in terms of their overall impact on the public, with percentage scores indicating the relative importance of each in determining someone's level of trust.

As shown in Figure 4.1, the enjoyment of the ads that people see and hear is the most important driver of trust, followed by the most prominent negative driver, bombardment.

FIGURE 4.1 Key drivers of public trust in advertising

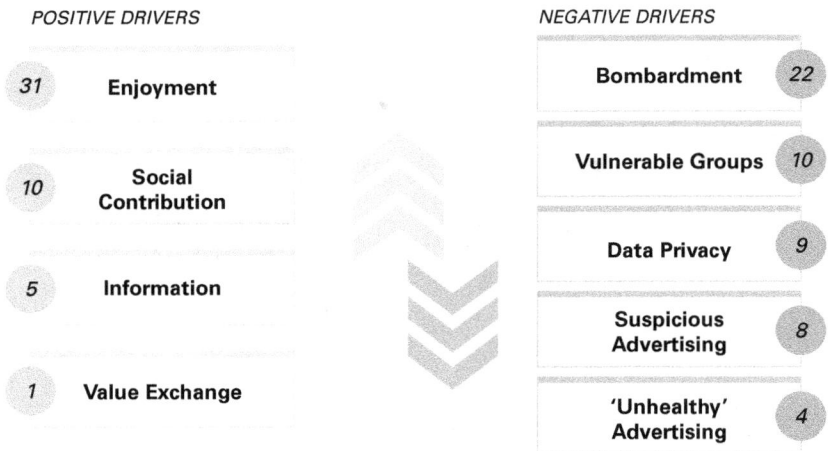

POSITIVE DRIVERS

31	Enjoyment
10	Social Contribution
5	Information
1	Value Exchange

NEGATIVE DRIVERS

Bombardment	22
Vulnerable Groups	10
Data Privacy	9
Suspicious Advertising	8
'Unhealthy' Advertising	4

The social contribution that advertising can provide, advertising to vulnerable groups, concerns around data privacy and 'suspicious' advertising were also important drivers, for better or worse. The information advertising provides, as well as 'unhealthy' advertising (e.g. for alcohol or food high in fat, salt or sugar), and advertising's 'value exchange' with its audiences also impacted trust but to a lesser extent. These findings have remained fairly consistent between 2018 and 2023.

Let's look at each of the drivers in turn, starting with the four that each have a role in positively boosting people's trust in advertising.

The positive drivers

ENJOYMENT

Most important to the public's experience of advertising is enjoyment.

By this we mean advertising's entertainment value, and its ability to engage our emotions. As with people or brands, the more you like an ad and feel an affinity with it, the more likely you are to trust it. You will have noticed that in the last chapter – liking and trusting ads are pretty well aligned.

Within that broad description of enjoyment, Credos uncovered five pillars, one or more of which are seemingly required for an ad to engage us successfully.

FIGURE 4.2 The percentage of people regularly encountering the following elements of enjoyable ads

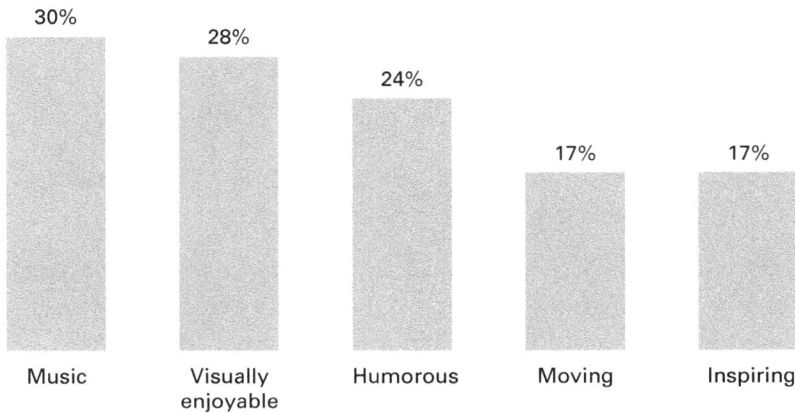

| 30% | 28% | 24% | 17% | 17% |
| Music | Visually enjoyable | Humorous | Moving | Inspiring |

As you see, the top three are very much the entertaining elements – music, good visuals and humour; the other two are the more emotional – that the ad is moving or inspiring. The lesson is clear: make enjoyable ads if you want people to warm to you and your message. It is not only Credos research that has emphasized the same point – we will explore this in more detail in Chapter 13.

However, a long-term drift toward 'performance advertising', often short term in its goals, has been very apparent in how most advertisers are spending their budget, especially as online spend has become dominant. You may well ask if this is wise for the longer-term health and success of their brands.

REAL-WORLD EXAMPLE
Festive ads

The following is work by Kantar to understand the positive effect of the UK's Christmas advertising season.

This is a moment each year when companies unveil their big brand campaigns to win attention and custom in the 'golden quarter' for sales. The season often includes some of the most enjoyable ads of the year – the biggest single driver of public trust in advertising. Kantar's analysis of 2024's biggest campaigns show this in full effect, including the use of music, humour and emotion, all cited as important in the Credos work.[1]

These were the best performing, most enjoyable work, according to Kantar.

The funniest ad was TK Maxx's Festive Farm, an ad which ran first in 2023 and was run again in 2024, featuring a couple on a farm, gifting designer knitwear and festive clothing to a cast of creatures including Lil' Goat, Big Al the Alpaca, Hattie the Hedgehog and a pair of geese called Drake & Demi. Kantar's research showed that one in four people said they laughed out loud at Christmas ads in 2024, marking a return of the use of humour in advertising.

The award for most enjoyable music went to Coca Cola with its 'Holidays Are Coming' and this is what Kantar had to say about its performance:

> Music has the unique ability to evoke emotion and create enduring memories. 'Holidays Are Coming' once again reigns as this year's most enjoyable track. Though the visuals may have been altered using AI, the ad retains all the ingredients that make it so powerful—it remains as effective as it was in previous years.

The most enjoyable ad was from Marks & Spencer, for M&S Food and the campaign 'Party Like Dawn', which featured the comedian Dawn French as herself and as the voice of the M&S Fairy, navigating the challenges of hosting a festive party for friends.

The overall winner was Cadbury's Secret Santa, which Kantar describes as 'a simple story of generosity', told and retold effectively since its debut in 2022.

Lynne Deason, Head of Creative Excellence, Kantar, noted:

> The enjoyment of ads is the strongest driver of public trust – how can the industry ensure more people enjoy more ads? Develop a creative effectiveness culture with your target audience at the heart of it. Ask yourself: Are your ads entertaining? Or are they crammed full of product features conveyed in a boring ad that nobody will even notice? Creativity and originality are essential. Why should people want to spend time with your ads instead of all the other things that are competing for their attention? Humour is a fantastic way to create enjoyable ads, but there are so many creative ways to achieve this. Ensure your ads are a welcome part of people's lives, not an unwelcome interruption.

SOCIAL CONTRIBUTION

The social contribution advertising can make comes next in importance. Although the level is way behind enjoyment for most people, Credos' research does show this factor has been rising in importance in recent years.[2]

Firstly, the findings indicate the public are pretty positive about the role that advertising plays in society, with 44 per cent feeling it has a positive effect on society – 7 per cent being very positive and 37 per cent fairly positive.

More specifically, 44 per cent of respondents feel that advertising drives social change, and this figure has risen significantly since 2016.

Figure 4.3 shows the percentage of the public who feel that way by age group: the overall figure has risen every year since 2021, climbing from 34 per cent in 2021 to 44 per cent in the first half of 2024.

As we can see, the young are much more positive about advertising's ability to create social change, consistent with much of Credos' research into trust in advertising: 57 per cent of 18–34 year olds believe it does so, compared to just 30 per cent of those over 55.

In 2020, the Advertising Association and Credos published Ad Pays 8: UK Advertising's Social Contribution.[3] For the first time, that report identified five key areas where advertising can be seen to make a social contribution:

1 Raises awareness and/or money for good causes.

2 Encourages individuals to seek help or make changes in order to lead happier, healthier lives.

3 Brings people together around important cultural events/messages.

4 Promotes products and services that are good for society/for the planet.

5 Promotes a more harmonious society.

FIGURE 4.3 Percentage of respondents who feel that advertising drives social change, 2021–2024

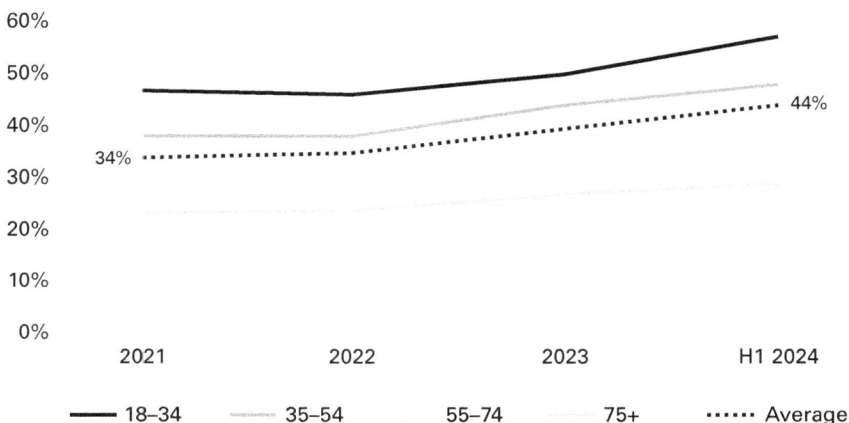

FIGURE 4.4 Percentage of respondents who often come across advertising with different types of social contribution

How often do you come across advertising that...?

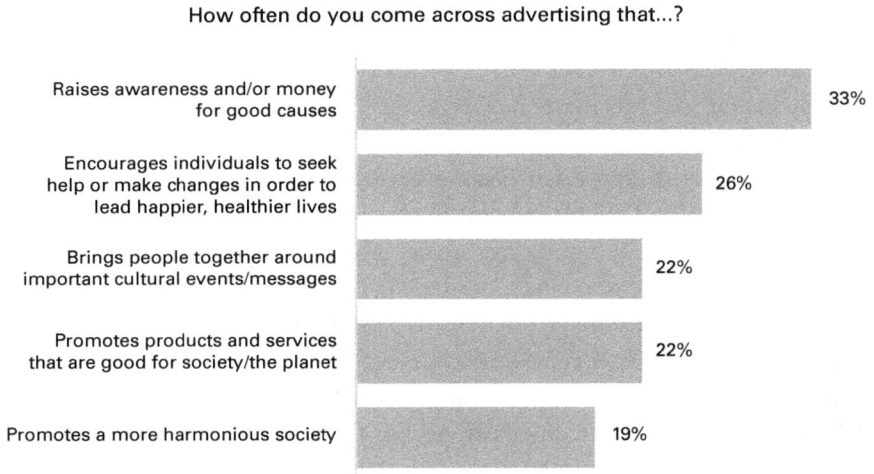

These areas arose organically through qualitative research with people before being validated in a quantitative study.

Credos has continued to track how often people come across these types of advertising and Figure 4.4 shows the prevalence of the different types of social contribution people recognize in advertising.

It is important to continue to monitor and understand this link between people's trust in advertising and the social contribution that advertising can make, particularly when we reflect on learnings in the first two chapters. Remember how people are looking to business to help solve problems and to be trustworthy in their advertising and communications while doing so.

Taking a step back, we can broadly view how people see advertising's social contribution in two ways. Let's consider a couple of examples to help demonstrate trusted advertising (and its social contribution) in action.

REAL-WORLD EXAMPLE

HM government coronavirus advertising campaign 2020–21

Advertising can provide information considered useful for society, like public health messaging from government or from charities.

Harnessed correctly, advertising is a powerful tool for encouraging and enabling positive behaviour change. Credos research found that over a third (34 per cent) of the public agree that some advertising has had a major impact on how they think about things.

Possibly the best example of advertising's role in effecting behaviour change at scale was during the Covid-19 pandemic.[4] The pandemic 'necessitated the biggest communication and information campaign in the 100-year history of Government Communications', needing to reach every person in the UK to engage them with critical information that they could trust. Advertising was the most effective way to communicate this message to the public.

There were several campaigns that ran throughout the height of the Covid-19 pandemic, including a TV campaign featuring ethnic minority stars urging those from the BAME community to get vaccinated and addressing cultural concerns around vaccination. While it is difficult to isolate the impact of advertising alone, the campaigns were a crucial tool for the government in spreading awareness and information at speed, resulting in high vaccination rates.

REAL-WORLD EXAMPLE
Campaign Ad Net Zero Awards 2022 (to present day)

Advertising can play a role in portraying society in a positive way, helping people to make decisions about more sustainable choices and featuring a broader range of people and lifestyles.

Credos data shows over a third (34 per cent) of people agree that advertising helps them make more sustainable purchases. That number rises to 50 per cent of 18–34 year olds who are particularly positive about this value of advertising to make a trusted and valuable social contribution to them.

It is partly in recognition of this reason that the Advertising Association partnered with Campaign Magazine back in 2022 to run the Campaign Ad Net Zero Awards,[5] a special set of awards that requires all entrants to demonstrate proof of both commercial and sustainable success. The awards take place each year with a growing bank of inspirational examples for the industry to draw learnings from and build into future campaigns.

Previous Grand Prix winners include Sky for its long-term work around climate action; the Sky Zero Footprint Fund which helps sustainable businesses, whether established or start-ups, present their products and services on TV; Hellmann's 'Make Taste Not Waste' campaign that tackles food waste (and helps people save money); and ITV's partnership with eBay for Love Island that helped popularize pre-loved (second-hand) clothing with millions of young people.

PROVIDING INFORMATION

Providing information is what advertising is classically meant to do, at least as far as economists are concerned. And it is vitally important, of course, in telling us about prices, product features, innovative services, special deals or a host of other things. Without advertising boosting – or even forcing – competition, we would have neither the choice, quality or keen pricing that an open and healthy economy requires. But information doesn't seem to build trust as much as the 'softer' aspects of advertising's role that are ranked a lot higher, at least amongst the positive drivers that Credos has identified.

However, that ads can be expected to tell the truth does count, and any information contained in advertising should of course be factually correct.

REAL-WORLD EXAMPLE
Can you add an extra layer of trust in your advertising?

It may be possible to take extra action to ensure that information is trusted, as the following demonstrates.

Kantar worked with Trustpilot to measure how the inclusion of a Trustpilot message within TV advertising might add an extra level of trust.[6] People were shown one of eight brand adverts and these 30-second videos covered four separate industry categories – consumer electronics, financial management, furniture and car retail and each had two versions – the only difference being the inclusion of Trustpilot ratings.

The research showed how including Trustpilot within TV advertising had a positive brand equity impact on all of the brands in question. All measures directionally benefited on average, with some of the strongest overall lifts seen for perceived brand worth, brand confidence, and positive feelings around customer service.

Kantar argues here that if you are making an explicit trust-based claim in your advertising, whatever the size of your business, it is more effective if you back that with third-party verification.

VALUE EXCHANGE

Finally, the 'value exchange' that advertising represents, giving us access to media and services either free or for a lower price. Again, this is a critical aspect of advertising's value to society, whether in sustaining a plurality of news sources or enabling online platforms to 'give' us free social connections, maps, weather forecasts or entertainment. But it seems one taken for granted or not well understood by the public, and only a small factor in driving trust.

It's worth asking at this point whether the advertising industry has done enough to explain the value it provides to people in terms of free or discounted content, of news and investigative journalism? Or, perhaps most significantly, the value exchange for the range of free digital services that we now take for granted?

Imagine, for example, how much you might have spent by now if Google had charged you a few pence every time you conducted a search or even more for when you used its Google Maps service? If TikTok billed a fee for every video you viewed? Or if Facebook ran on a subscription model to stay in touch with family and friends?

This isn't a naïve propaganda point on behalf of the global tech companies that have come to take up such a large presence in the advertising industry. But it is a genuine question about how much value we would place on these things if there was a micro-payment involved every time we did it, rather than free, unlimited access which has been funded through advertising revenue.

The following example shows how we might put a monetary value for people on that value exchange.

REAL-WORLD EXAMPLE
The digital dividend

This ground-breaking work helped to explain new types of 'value' that people get back from digital advertising.

In September 2023, IAB UK published a study entitled 'The digital dividend' which, as its CEO, Jon Mew, said at the time, had a clear aim to quantify the value of digital advertising 'to the vast majority of people who depend on free digital services every single day'.[7] This is what they found:

- Digital advertising saves UK consumers a total of £18 billion per year by providing free access to online services, which is over £600 per household:

  o £580 per year, per household from not having to pay to use free ad-supported online services.

  o £58 per year, per household by enabling consumers to find cheaper retail products online.

- The cost-of-living crisis had heightened the value of free online services:

  o 70% of adults say it is important to them that these services are available for free.

o 28% of adults have used free, often ad-supported online entertainment more in the last year.

- Digital advertising was saving UK consumers time, as well as money. IAB UK's consumer survey with Public First showed:

  o 72% of UK consumers save time by shopping online rather than in physical shops, and 61% say they save money by doing so.

  o UK consumers really value the ad-supported digital services that they access for free. When asked how much they would have to be paid to give up access to these services, it works out at £14,600 per household per year.

Those, then, are the positives, the elements of people's advertising experience that drive their trust in it.

They are evenly matched by negatives, though: aspects of advertising that push people away from feeling they trust it and, by extension, its messages...

The negative drivers

BOMBARDMENT

Those people that identify ad bombardment as an issue are the most likely to distrust advertising. It has consistently been the number one cluster of factors driving distrust by some distance in each of the 2018, 2021 and 2023 studies. However, in 2023 it also became the most important driver for 18–34 year olds, marking a significant change from 2021.

When asked to rank the four components of bombardment in order of annoyance, respondents clearly identified obtrusion – the delay or interruption of the content experience – as the biggest source of annoyance. This was followed by repetition, volume and irrelevance.

The rank order of the four components remains the same regardless of age, but the nature and level of annoyance changes. Obtrusion is most annoying for 18–34 year olds and largely explains why bombardment has become such an issue for this age group. For older people, interruption by advertising has always been accepted as part of the deal; not so for younger people. They are less used to being interrupted and feel that is happening more now than previously on the platforms they use most.

Repetition, on the other hand, is most annoying to older people, who are subject to a smaller pool of advertising and so more affected by repeat viewings. Likewise, volume is more of an issue for older people, having witnessed

FIGURE 4.5 The four components of bombardment

Bombardment   *What drives it?*

1   **Obtrusion** - *advertising that delays or interrupts what you are trying to do*

2   **Repetition** - *advertising that you've seen/heard too many times and feels repetitive*

3   **Volume** - *the amount of advertising you come across generally*

4   **Irrelevance** - *advertising that isn't relevant to you personally*

what they perceive to be an explosion of advertising in their lifetime. Irrelevant advertising is the least annoying factor across all ages. Most consumers simply accept that not all advertising will be relevant to them, but many also understand the 'deal' whereby more relevant advertising means more personalized targeting, driven by what some perceive as intrusion into their privacy.

The next example explains how advertisers might just seize this nettle and resolve the issue, bringing multiple positives as a result.

REAL-WORLD EXAMPLE
Origin

This initiative, led by a UK trade body, seeks to resolve the issue of excessive advertising frequency.

ISBA, the UK trade body for brand owners and part of the World Federation of Advertisers (WFA), has launched a platform called Origin, which is being tracked with interest by advertisers around the world.[8]

The trade body describes Origin as 'a cross-media audience measurement platform that allows marketers to accurately measure deduplicated reach and frequency of ad campaigns, across different media channels and across the ever-increasing number of different ad formats'.

The goal is to drive greater effectiveness and create less waste across advertiser's media planning. This will result in a better audience experience by reducing annoying frequency.

Over 50 funding stakeholders are involved in the service design including 32 major advertisers who from September 2024 took part in the Origin Beta trial. Triallists include Vodafone, HSBC, NatWest, PepsiCo, P&G, Red Bull, Tesco, Unilever and Virgin Media O2. The trials successfully concluded in June 2025 providing clear use cases and important feedback on the future roadmap of additional features. In July 2025 the platform extended its availability to a further tranche of advertisers.

Phil Smith, Director General, ISBA described Origin as 'our members' most important strategic priority and is likely to remain so for some time. It has been driven by brand-owners' desire to deliver more effective advertising in an ever-changing and increasingly complex media environment.'

Origin is the UK programme to bring to life the WFA's global cross-media measurement principles and while first to market, it is being closely followed in the US by the Association of National Advertisers (ANA) Aquila initiative. There is keen interest from many more markets and demand from global advertisers to have a consistent measurement platform available in as many markets as possible.

Might it be a silver bullet to tackle the public's biggest single negative issue with advertising – bombardment? Only time will tell.

VULNERABLE GROUPS

Advertising to 'vulnerable groups', which leads to wider distrust, is largely cited by older age groups, recording relatively little impact for 18–34 year olds, according to Credos.

Concerns in this area, where they exist, fall into two categories. The first is advertising, which is felt to 'unfairly' target vulnerable groups such as children, the financially insecure or addicts. However, concern varies significantly by category and from person to person, often being closely linked to individual experience of personal or family and friends' problems.

The second is a much more widespread set of views relating to web-based advertising that divide along generational lines. Younger people worry that the old are not digitally savvy enough to spot online scams and what is and isn't advertising. Conversely, older people worry about impressionable youngsters exposed to misleading advertising on social media.

Let's take a look at an initiative working to address concerns that may be damaging trust in advertising.

REAL-WORLD EXAMPLE
Supporting conversations about young people's online experiences

This example is about helping young people (and their parents and guardians) to understand and have a better, safer time online.

Media Smart, the UK advertising and media industry's education programme, helps young people understand advertising wherever it appears and inspires them to consider the sector as a career choice.[9] It is a not-for-profit funded by advertisers, agencies, media owners, trade organizations and tech companies which provides guides for 7–25 year olds, engaging teaching resources and expert advice for parents and guardians.

In March 2025, it partnered with TikTok for a campaign called 'Teens, Social Media & You' to support parents and young people aged over 13 to have conversations about their online world.[10] The campaign, which was rolled out first in the UK before launching in EU territories, saw TikTok content creators invite their audience to a crash course in digital creation, advertising content and online safety. At the time of writing, it has had 50 million views.

Media Smart worked with youth creative agency, Livity, to identify three key areas that Teens, Social Media & You will address: staying safe online, specific tools and features such as Family Pairing, and healthier habits. Alongside the videos, a downloadable guide was published on Media Smart's website, which answers commonly asked questions around screen time and mental wellbeing, helping teens deal with harmful content online and identifying what's okay to share.

Rachel Barber-Mack, Director of Media Smart UK, commented that 'it has never been more critical to support parents' understanding of their young people's online environment, particularly following the pandemic which led to a significant increase in daily screen-time'.

The campaign built on Media Smart's expertise in helping young people understand advertising and the online world. It was a follow-up to 'Adverts, Creators and You', a partnership with TikTok which launched in 2021 to help teens differentiate advertising and organic content on platforms.

DATA PRIVACY
Though understanding of the technical aspects of data consent and control are minimal, there is a widespread, if vague, sense of unease. According to Credos, people feel that they are not in control of their own data and what happens to it. Neither are they sure that they have truly given their consent for their data to be used in quite the ways that they suspect it might be.

REAL-WORLD EXAMPLE
The Data & Marketing Association: its code and the importance of trust

This code by a UK trade body helps set the standard for its members around the use of data to help protect and build trust.

The UK's leading data-driven marketing trade body is the Data & Marketing Association (DMA), with over 700 member organizations and a 27,000 marketer community. It has an established code with which all members must comply.[11]

Within what has become a complex web of legislation and regulation, the Code is an ethical framework that sets the standard for the data and marketing industry.

As described by DMA CEO Rachel Aldighieri, 'it is about putting customers first. It's about being transparent, authentic and responsible. These are the qualities that build trust and loyalty – things every business needs to thrive.' Recently a 'people principle' has been added to the Code. It, too, is focused on fuelling trust by ensuring that marketing teams are trained to do the right thing with data and that they are diverse, to mitigate bias in data – a factor Aldighieri notes as particularly important as the use of AI grows.

The DMA, in collaboration with the Global Data & Marketing Alliance and Acxiom, produces research on data privacy and consumers, which consistently shows trust to be the single biggest factor influencing whether consumers are willing to share their personal data. In the latest survey, 85 per cent of consumers said it was the most important, although only 39 per cent globally felt that they could trust businesses with their data.[12] Transparency, control and the perception of benefit were noted as the key drivers of that all-important trust.

These drivers are reflected in the DMA Code, which requires policies and practices that will deliver positive consumer-driven outcomes – that 'Organizations have a clear understanding of the value exchange when sharing personal information. Organizations are open, honest and upfront about why they are collecting data and how they intend to use it. Organizations are sensitive to their customers' needs and avoid marketing that is intrusive or excessive. Organizations recognize vulnerable customers and market to them responsibly… Customers have control of their personal data.'

In line with the importance of justifying consumer trust in how their data is used, the DMA's manifesto declares that 'We want all marketers to be able to 'do data right'. In turn, helping marketers 'be more customer'. Marketing growth is fuelled by integrity. We want customers to trust who sells to them. Being honest, smart and powerful means everyone wins – business, consumers and the whole economy.'

SUSPICIOUS ADVERTISING

'Suspicious advertising' tends to refer to advertising malpractice. The term includes a variety of issues ranging from hidden ads and misrepresentation right through to fake ads and scams.

As detailed in the AA's Value of Trust Report, in 2021, the failure of many influencers to be open and transparent when promoting products appeared a significant driver of distrust amongst the young.[13] However, by 2023, increased consumer savviness, alongside action taken by the ASA, tech platforms and the influencer industry itself to increase transparency, had greatly reduced concerns in this area. The authors of the report state this clearly illustrates how quickly public perceptions can and do change, and the impact that decisive industry-led action can make.

However, the report confirmed that the advertising of bogus, counterfeit or low-quality products on social media remained a universal concern. Most often associated with the health, fitness and wellbeing categories, or with digital 'get rich quick' schemes, this tended to impact younger people simply because they encountered it more.

Scam communications are perceived to have increased considerably during the pandemic and significantly impacted trust in advertising across all age groups. Almost one in five (19 per cent) people saw advertising and scams as one and the same, making no distinction between legitimate brand advertising and those from nefarious sources. Even those who make the distinction between genuine ads and scams can still have their views of advertising subtly coloured by the similarities between them.

Several different initiatives are in play to tackle scams. In the UK, these include the UK government, the UK Safer Internet Centre, the ASA's 'scam alert' system and prominent individuals such as Martin Lewis from Money Saving Expert. But people look to the advertising industry to act on this problem, which goes right to the heart of their trust (or distrust) in advertising, and with industry funding and leadership, Media Smart has worked to do so.

REAL-WORLD EXAMPLE
Tackling scam advertising

This campaign tackles the issues of scams head-on, by equipping young people with the knowledge of what to look out for and avoid.

Media Smart's work specifically targets topics that 13–25 year olds have said they are most worried about, with scams featuring high on the list. It worked closely with youth-focused communications agency, Livity, to develop animated films and resources that deliver a clear message about 'scam flags'.[14] This might be about cryptocurrency scams or fake online shopping deals, unauthorized access to webcams or false scholarship offers. A build-up of 'red flags' highlights when an offer seems too good to be true, it probably is.

Safer Internet Day, run by the UK Safer Internet Centre, takes place every February.[15] In 2025 it shone a spotlight on scams, responding to fraudulent online activity growing in frequency and sophistication with the theme 'Too good to be true? Protecting yourself and others from scams online'.[16]

Media Smart ran its 'Scam Flags add up to a Scam' for Safer Internet Day 2025, co-branded with the UK Government's National Campaign Against Fraud – STOP! THINK FRAUD (which first launched in 2024).

Media Smart's online toolkit provides practical advice on identifying scams, reporting them to the appropriate authorities – including social media platforms, Action Fraud and the Advertising Standards Authority – and where those affected can go for support.

At the time of writing, the 'Scam Flags add up to a Scam' campaign had achieved significant reach, with 182 million media impressions. The campaign provided support for both students, teachers and parents, offering a downloadable guide and video content for use in the classroom and at home, all accessible through a dedicated hub on the Media Smart website.

Thousands of organizations get involved in Safer Internet Day each year to promote the safe, responsible and positive use of digital technology for children and young people. In 2025, questions being considered included:

- How is changing technology like generative AI going to impact the approach of scammers?
- What role can the government and internet industry take to tackle this threat?
- And what changes would young people like to see to help protect themselves moving forward?

There is an opportunity to do more to address this challenge to trust through even greater support by the advertising industry for Media Smart and Safer Internet Day.

UNHEALTHY ADVERTISING

Finally, 'unhealthy advertising' for HFSS food and drink products and alcohol formed its own factor driving distrust in advertising. However, despite the scale of the debate about these products in the media and even parliament, the importance placed on this issue by the public was relatively low.

This low level of apparent concern may be surprising to advertising's critics and reassuring to the industry. However, as we have already outlined in earlier chapters, there is clearly increasing scrutiny on advertising and its perceived links to societal problems such as obesity, with the possibility of intervention as and when the industry is not judged trustworthy enough to address the issue itself.

REAL-WORLD EXAMPLE
Marketing and advertising alcohol products

On occasions, an industry can take further responsibility for setting standards for its own advertising and marketing, as shown here by the drinks industry.

The advertising of alcohol has long been a target for health lobbyists seeking to restrict how, when and where advertising for all kinds of alcohol brands can appear. The drinks industry has long known this challenge and introduced the Portman Group's Code of Practice back in April 1996.

For nearly 30 years this has set the minimum standards for alcohol producers to market their products responsibly.[17] It covers the naming, packaging and promotion of any alcoholic products which are marketed in the UK and now has 12 code rules which all producers must abide by if they are selling or marketing a product in the UK. It ensures that alcohol is marketed in a socially responsible way, only to those aged 18 and over, and in a way that does not appeal particularly to those who are vulnerable. The Code is supported by the industry, including producers, importers, wholesalers, retailers and trade associations.

Action taken since 1996 has resulted in nearly 200 inappropriate and irresponsible products being removed from shelves. It has acted against products including TNT Liquid Dynamite (1996) for association with dangerous behaviour, Bullshit Lager (1997) for likelihood of appealing to under-18s, Cannabis Vodka (2002) for association with illegal or illicit drugs, Quickie Wine (2021) for a direct link to sexual activity and causing serious or widespread offence.

The drinks industry also faces a challenge in advertising the new low or no-alcohol versions of popular, well-known brands. One example of a recent ruling was for Heineken's 0.0 product featuring Formula 1 driver Max Verstappen, with concern raised around the issue of 'drinking and driving'.[18] The ad was judged to have not made the 0 per cent ABV clearly enough in its execution.

Taking action to rebuild public trust in advertising

Supporting the Credos thinktank every step of the way in its work to understand the public's trust in advertising has been a Trust Group, formed by the Advertising Association in 2018 and chaired by the Director Generals of the IPA and ISBA.[19] Members of the group have always been drawn from across the industry, representing the interests of advertisers, media owners, agencies and tech companies in a drive to find ways to rebuild trust.

This is how the Trust Group was described back at its launch in February 2018:

'To seek the truth and live by it' was one of the Advertising Association's founding pledges in 1926. Unsurprisingly, truth remains high on the Advertising Association agenda in 2018.

As an organization we are now informing a working group which engages our Council members in the biggest challenge the industry faces – trust in advertising.

We believe that the end-user of the UK's advertising industry deserves the very best advertising has to offer – client, agency, media and public.

What does the very best look like for each of these end-users and how do we get there? And how do we get there faster than other territories dealing with similar issues?

The first output was the Trust Action Plan, published in 2019, which set out five bold industry-wide actions as follows:[20]

- To reduce advertising 'bombardment'.
- To reduce excessive advertising frequency and re-targeting.
- To ensure that the ASA is 'best in class'.
- To ensure that data privacy matters.
- To show that advertising can drive social change.

In February 2020, the group published *Improving the Public's Advertising Experience*, after work by industry consultants Derek Morris and Nick Manning with Credos, including a full review of available data, alongside qualitative interviews with a select group of the UK's biggest advertisers, their agencies and leading media owners.[21]

Advertising's top driver of public negativity – bombardment – and excessive frequency and retargeting was prioritized with this guidance for all advertisers:

1 Make your advertising welcome in people's lives.
2 Place business effectiveness above efficiency.
3 Achieve full visibility of where your advertising goes.
4 Ensure every impact and exposure matters.
5 Deploy the necessary resources to track, measure and manage this programme.

In October 2021, the group published *Rebuilding Public Trust in Advertising*, which built on many of the findings we have discussed in this chapter, particularly around the positive and negative drivers.[22]

The Advertising Association's Chief Executive, Stephen Woodford, said: 'The public's trust in our work isn't a nice-to-have, it's a must-have. As all the evidence shows, trust pays – with better returns on campaigns and better long-term value for the brands they support.'

That payback on trust was then further evidenced in the Value of Trust report which the group published in June 2024.[23]

As we write this book, the group continues to push forward with its understanding of how the public's trust in advertising is shaped by the dynamic changes in the advertising landscape, and what can best be done to manage, protect and enhance the public's trust in its work.

Conclusion

We have a good understanding of how people's trust in advertising is constructed.

We have seen a clear map of the positive things that we can do as advertising professionals: deliver advertising that is enjoyable, makes some sort of positive social contribution, provides useful information and makes good on a value exchange. In short, advertising that provides people with something they appreciate in return for their time and attention. Such advertising can be done and often is.

We have also seen the things that have a detrimental impact on people's trust in advertising and drain away their goodwill. Firstly, simply bombarding them with too much advertising. Just because there is seemingly unlimited advertising inventory, thanks to the growth in digital advertising opportunities, doesn't mean we should produce unlimited numbers of ads. Nor does it mean that there is a positive value to you and your brand in excessive frequency or repetition of your campaign to the target audience.

Secondly, there is a big message in here about 'responsibility'. People look to the advertising industry to take responsibility for what is seen by those deemed vulnerable groups and to take positive action to address concerns. They want to be reassured that their data is used responsibly. They expect the industry to help educate people about scam or fraudulent advertising, often committed by criminal organizations, and do everything in its power to stop it. They also want to see reasonable steps to tackle unhealthy advertising, or risk action being taken by regulators on their behalf.

In the UK, the industry as represented by members of trade bodies has consistently asked and funded its thinktank and trade body (AA) to pursue the issue of trust in advertising. The people responsible for UK advertising want to understand its dimensions, dynamics and details better, because they believe that if they do, then they can improve the effectiveness and approval of the work they invest their time and money in.

We know trust is a fundamental human value, so it has to be taken seriously in the context of advertising as in any other. The work to date has revealed complexities and currents that underlie the seemingly simple question of whether people trust ads. The more it is explored, the more is discovered of what can be done to affect it, but the more intricate and many-factored it has proved to be. A simple question, maybe, but with no simple answers.

What's clear is a concerted effort is required to improve the public's experience of advertising. Understanding that as we do, it seems a folly not to address the issues, and many in the business are intent on doing so.

Notes

1   The best Christmas ads 2024, Kantar, www.kantar.com/uki/campaigns/the-best-christmas-ads (archived at https://perma.cc/4GZA-TEBQ)
2   The Social Contribution of UK Advertising 2024, Advertising Association & Credos, July 2024, https://adassoc.org.uk/our-work/the-social-contribution-of-uk-advertising-2024/ (archived at https://perma.cc/2JGH-3X9V)
3   Advertising Pays 8: UK advertising's social contribution, Advertising Association & Credos, https://adassoc.org.uk/ad-pays-8/ (archived at https://perma.cc/G22E-RERP)

4   The Social Contribution of UK Advertising 2024, Advertising Association & Credos, July 2024, https://adassoc.org.uk/our-work/the-social-contribution-of-uk-advertising-2024/ (archived at https://perma.cc/W7E9-65RQ)

5   Campaign Ad Net Zero Awards, www.campaignadnetzeroawards.com/ (archived at https://perma.cc/VEM9-B92A)

6   Trust Matters: How trust validation builds brand value, Kantar, February 2024, www.kantar.com/uki/inspiration/brands/trust-matters-how-trust-validation-builds-brand-worth (archived at https://perma.cc/9GUX-X2MK)

7   The Digital Dividend, IAB UK, September 2023, www.iabuk.com/digitaldividend (archived at https://perma.cc/MAB3-VZZR)

8   About Origin, ISBA,www.isba.org.uk/knowledge/origin (archived at https://perma.cc/PTX2-UT9K)

9   Media Smart, About us, https://mediasmart.uk.com/about-us/ (archived at https://perma.cc/PJ5S-D245)

10 Media Smart, TikTok: Teens, Social Media & You, https://mediasmart.uk.com/tiktok-teens-social-media-and-you/ (archived at https://perma.cc/SH39-WG6D)

11 DMA, The DMA Code, July 2025, https://dma.org.uk/the-dma-code (archived at https://perma.cc/84WH-Y2WL)

12 DMA, UK Data Privacy: What the Consumer Really Thinks 2022, December 2022, https://dma.org.uk/guide/uk-data-privacy-what-the-consumer-really-thinks-2022 (archived at https://perma.cc/D9CB-P5ZT)

13 The Value of Trust Report, Advertising Association & Credos, June 2024, https://adassoc.org.uk/our-work/the-value-of-trust-report/ (archived at https://perma.cc/5FED-8QKH)

14 Scam Flags add up to a Scam, Media Smart, https://mediasmart.uk.com/scams/ (archived at https://perma.cc/S3QA-LM3D)

15 Safer Internet Day, 11 February 2025, https://saferinternet.org.uk/safer-internet-day/safer-internet-day-2025 (archived at https://perma.cc/MJW5-ABWN)

16 Safer Internet Day: Helping young people avoid scam ads, Politics Home, February 2025, www.politicshome.com/members/article/safer-internet-day-helping-young-people-avoid-scam-ads (archived at https://perma.cc/97BX-XM2X)

17 28 years of the Portman Group Code of Practice: A look back over the years, Portman Group, September 2024, www.portmangroup.org.uk/28-years-of-the-portman-group-code-of-practice-a-look-back-over-the-years/ (archived at https://perma.cc/GXM2-2EWR)

18 ASA Ruling on Heineken UK Ltd t/a Heineken, Advertising Standards Authority, December 2024, www.asa.org.uk/rulings/heineken-uk-ltd-a24-1251637-heineken-uk-ltd.html (archived at https://perma.cc/F2V2-JBSC)

19 Addressing the issues of trust, Advertising Association, February 2018, https://adassoc.org.uk/our-work/addressing-the-issues-of-trust/ (archived at https://perma.cc/A74Y-6XVD)

20 Arresting the decline of Public Trust in UK Advertising, Advertising
Association, March 2019, https://adassoc.org.uk/our-work/report-arresting-
the-decline-of-public-trust-in-uk-advertising/ (archived at https://perma.cc/
S9EY-QSEK)

21 Improving the advertising experience, Advertising Association, February 2020,
https://adassoc.org.uk/our-work/improving-the-advertising-experience/
(archived at https://perma.cc/75GT-GBZ2)

22 Report: Rebuilding public trust in UK advertising, Advertising Association,
October 2021, https://adassoc.org.uk/our-work/report-rebuilding-public-trust-
in-uk-advertising/ (archived at https://perma.cc/VS8F-K7R6)

23 The Value of Trust Report, Advertising Association, June 2024, https://adassoc.
org.uk/our-work/the-value-of-trust-report/ (archived at https://perma.cc/
B2CW-79A5)

05

Trust: The secret sauce

Introduction

As we set out to write this book, one of the most important things we wanted to do was to gather the views of leaders from across the advertising ecosystem about trust: how it features in their thinking and the conversations they have about their work with colleagues.

In this chapter, we're going to share a range of interviews we conducted with leaders from brands, agencies and media owners. We generally began an interview with a simple question about whether trust mattered to them and, if so, why? How important was it? And what sort of things did 'trust' then impact on as they developed advertising campaigns in their day-to-day work, either for the brands they worked at or for the clients they represented?

Plot spoiler.

Trust always mattered. In the immediate sense, it was obvious, of course trust matters. But as each conversation developed, the nuances around trust and advertising emerged, as did the way marketers and their advertising partners think about it and weave it into effective advertising campaigns.

We've called this chapter Trust: The secret sauce because we're aiming to unlock useful insights from some of the best people in the industry today that you may find useful to your own work. Insights that informed the direction of subsequent chapters where we will dig deeper into some of the big themes that we surface.

So, here's what people shared with us about trust and why it matters when you're thinking about your advertising.

There's a science to trust

Dan Bennett, Behavioural Science Lead, Ogilvy

The truth about behaviour change science is it brings a number of inconvenient insights, says Bennett.[1] He commented that requests to him for insights about trust have been rising over the past few years, with particular recent interest from FMCG (fast-moving consumer goods) clients to address concerns around ultra-processed foods, and restaurant chains looking to rebuild customer bases after the Covid lockdowns.

Firstly, there is a real difference, he says, between being liked, which offers a short-term benefit, and being trusted for the long term. However, there is no direct route to building that trust.

He encouraged us to take a step back to consider human evolution and how we have been programmed over hundreds of thousands of years. This understanding of how we have evolved is important because it means we can then bring about effective behaviour change, he argues, rather than hope that falsehoods might work.

He talked about physiognomy, the act of reading things about people from their faces, much as our ancestors did before the use of language and which we continue to do. The social programming to align with 'people that look like us' is one way we read the world around us, an innate process that was (and remains) critical for survival.

This judgement to 'trust' or not, says Bennett, is something predominantly delivered by our System 1 thinking. That's the 'automatic' part, where decisions are made almost instantly, effortlessly and unconsciously. In that sense, trust is instinctive. We might try to rationalize why we 'trust' someone or something using System 2 thinking, through reflection, but the fundamental decision has already been made.

There is a science to trust, believes Bennett and he cited The Trust Equation, a formula that identifies and relates the elements of trust.[2]

> In The Trust Equation, for someone to 'trust' you, three factors are first added together – C+R+I.
>
> The first is Credibility (you know your stuff).
>
> The second is Reliability (you always deliver).
>
> The third is Intimacy (I feel safe with you).
>
> The total effect of these three factors is then divided by a fourth factor – S.
>
> This factor is Self-Orientation (are you focused on my interests or yours?).

We can see how this equation can help understand what constitutes trust, whether in a person or a brand – the factors have often cropped up elsewhere in other interviews, albeit described in slightly different ways.

He reminds us that trust is not about dominance but is akin to 'soft power'. Bennett describes trust as a gas, not a solid.

He believes it is the job of everyone working in advertising and marketing to change behaviours, that marketers and their partners are mind-changing machines.

So, when it comes to changing behaviour, one approach is to think how people can be nudged by people like them. Bennett cited two effective examples of this in practice.

First, the BrAIDS With AIDS campaign across African Caribbean and Black communities internationally.[3] Hairdressers rather than health practitioners are deployed to assist HIV/AIDS prevention by offering sexual health advice within the trusting and sympathetic relationships they have with their clients; a nudge, not a lecture.

Second, the Mayor of London and Ogilvy UK's 'Say Maaate to a Mate' campaign to nudge men and boys to say 'Maaate' to their mates to challenge misogynistic behaviour toward women and girls.[4] The resulting integrated campaign, combining creativity and behavioural science, presented 270 possible different scenarios for when you might say 'Maaate' to one of your mates as a trusted friend, not a distant authority figure, to make them think again.

However, this instinct to trust 'people like us' is also a challenge for trust in work around DEI and representation, where 'people not like us' are introduced. This reinforces the need for authenticity in representation, if you are aiming to elicit a trusted response.

He noted that the marketing world seems to be heading fast towards influencers and, aside from their relatively low cost, he expressed surprise at marketers' willingness to surrender control of their brands to others. However, he did recognize the growing importance of people, not institutions, to Gen Z. If institutions aren't delivering, why would you trust them, he asks, and reminds us that evolution means people trust people. With that, there's little surprise that CEOs and directors are becoming the faces of businesses, large and small.

The challenge ahead within behaviour change and trust, he says, is to truly understand who is most likely to trust whom. Who will be most trustworthy in the eyes of a 17-year-old boy, or a 35-year-old woman? Will it be possible to matchmake influencer and audience, based on the likelihood of trust? Psychographic profiling, as used to overcome vaccine hesitancy amongst different audiences trusting different people, can help.

However this thinking develops, Bennett expects the interest in trust to continue to grow, and he finished with another useful analogy for us to reflect on: trust grows like the coconut tree but falls like the coconut; nurture it.

THREE KEY TAKEAWAYS

1 Trust is instinctive, based on thousands of years of programming through social evolution.

2 The Trust Equation may be a helpful way to think about trust in you and your brand.

3 People trust people, which is why we are seeing the rise of people (influencers) we can trust.

Building trust across the generations

Pete Markey, Chief Marketing Officer, Boots

Boot is the UK's leading health and beauty retailer with over 1,800 stores, ranging from local community pharmacies to large health and beauty destinations. Markey, its CMO, is also ISBA President and Chair of the AA's Front Foot community, which brings together UK advertising practitioners to rebuild trust in advertising, backing the work of Credos and the Trust Working Group.[5] He provides us with a big brand advertiser point of view on the value of trust in advertising.

'Trust is really important to us at Boots, it's what makes the brand,' says Markey. 'So much so, that it's right there in our purpose: "With you for life". It effectively says, "trust us" because when people come to Boots, we want them to trust that we can help them feel better and never let them down, no matter what sort of day they are having.'

Markey shares how Boots offer solutions in health and wellbeing, beauty and a wide range of things that can make everyone's day a little better. Our customer might be having an amazing day, he says, and be looking for a new aftershave for a date that night, or they could be having a bad day, they're full of cold or their baby's got colic, and they're looking for help. In every scenario, Markey needs Boots to be a trusted source, whether for delivery of prescriptions, advice on ailments or recommendations on beauty products. There's a grittiness in trust, Markey believes, and it's driven through the brand and its marketing activities to make sure customers know Boots cares about them whatever their day is like.

In Boots' approach to advertising, Markey always begins by identifying an insight into people's lives and asks, 'how does Boots meet that?' Alongside trust, he believes there is a vital need to always be relevant. A recent campaign, 'Make More Room For Beauty', was in response to the often quite sudden growth of beauty brands on TikTok to let people know these will be in stock in store. Another, 'The Health MOT', is a free service for 40+ year olds in England that has helped save lives by identifying people with serious health conditions and sending them for further treatment.

Like other marketers we have spoken to for this book, Markey is increasing the use of 'trusted influencers' in the advertising mix. Boots carefully vet the influencers the company works with to ensure there are no skeletons in their closets which could cause unwanted blowback on the brand. But 'beauty is influencers', Markey asserts, with brilliant content creators emerging, and marketing spend with them having doubled over a couple of years.

While he acknowledges that spend on influencers will continue to grow, Markey is very clear that they will not replace TV for the company. Boots has a 'one AV' strategy for TV, live and on-demand, and he believes that TV is 'amazing' in the marketing mix.

He expressed concern about low quality or 'lo-fi' content on social platforms and is convinced people can tell the difference between a good and a bad ad, responding to the first more than the second. The challenge of attracting attention in just a matter of two to three seconds begs the question: how much time do you have for someone to trust the message you are sending? So, Boots invests in higher quality production for social too, first to secure and then to keep that attention for longer.

Boots has to talk to everyone across the generations, says Markey, and as an example, points to the particular importance of TV and a big advertising campaign during the Christmas season, in order to be in the company of the country's other top brands.

Its 2024 Christmas campaign focused on the Boots beauty category in a bid to become the number one beauty gifting destination at Christmas. The campaign 'Make Magic' celebrated brands such as Bubble, Byoma, Sol de Janeiro, Made by Mitchell and No7, with a plan to attract younger beauty enthusiasts, retain its core customer base and for the first time target men with partners who needed help with gifting.[6] The cast for the ad saw two beauty influencers join Bridgerton star Adjoa Andoh as Mrs Claus. @soph, a Londoner behind the YouTube channel Soph does life, and @snatchedby-will, a make-up artist called Wiliam Grande, both help Mrs Claus by testing the Boots beauty products as her trusty 'elf-fluencers'. This ad was extended, through the two 'elf-fluencers' into a TikTok live shopping event, a powerful cross-promotion which increased Boots' profile, reach and 'trust' across all audiences.

Markey and his team measure trust in a variety of ways, including consumer polling, alongside scores in the tracking they run for brand saliency, buzz and relevance. Buzz, in particular, can be a good measure of trust, he says, and highlights how an error with wrongly packed medication was an example of where 'buzz' negatively impacted on customer trust but was quickly rebuilt once the error was addressed. In a world where brand choices seem increasingly fickle, trends can be very short lived and generational differences are very evident, Markey acknowledges it's a challenge for marketers to manage the balance between long-term trust and immediate relevance. Boots needs both.

THREE KEY TAKEAWAYS

1 Boots aims to be a trusted source for whatever the customer needs to make their day a bit better.

2 Insights help Boots to make sure the company is always relevant to what customers are looking for.

3 Influencers are growing in importance to build trust as part of the advertising mix, but maintaining quality of content production for the brand is vital.

Sometimes you've just got to trust your gut

Katie Jackson, Chief Marketing Officer, Channel 4

We started by asking Jackson whether trust mattered when it came to Channel 4's advertising. She said that the answer should be obvious: yes, of course, trust matters for a very simple reason.[7] If you don't trust how a business is showing up, then you are not going to engage with them. The brand needs to build trust to open up a conversation and connect.

Jackson's background prior to Channel 4 was agency-side where the goal is for the client to trust the agency, for two reasons. The first is transactional trust – when the client interacts with you, the delivery is seamless. The second is relational, what she described as the soft power element, where you go beyond the price, product or service to a rapport where you talk a language that connects with them. Without this, it is difficult to truly build trust, and she questioned whether brands pay enough attention to the relationship aspect of advertising.

The Channel 4 team pay constant attention to brand health and measure affinity (how much the audience feels the brand is 'for someone like me') which Jackson acknowledged was a proxy for the relational trust people have in it. For Channel 4, there are generational and demographic differences in trust levels, as well as in the idea of what advertising actually is now, moving from a classic TV ad like the Guinness 'Surfer' to an individual post on Instagram.

Jackson argues, though, that the fundamentals remain the same – a good marketer mines the insights, finds the relevance and talks to the target audience in the right way.

It's worth remembering here that Channel 4 is a unique media brand, a public service broadcaster with a license to provoke and challenge with its programming, including its news content.[8] Its remit is to champion unheard voices, innovate and take bold risks, inspire change in the way we lead our lives and stand up for diversity across the UK.

This brief means it has a range of competitors, from global streaming platforms and entertainment platforms to fellow UK broadcasters and news operations. It must build affinity (or trust) in its different propositions but always find a way for that to support the masterbrand, too.

Channel 4 is advertising-funded, so, as well as the provocation it is expected to deliver, it has to win commercially attractive audiences. That makes its advertising a key business tool which it must get right. It is not just allowed to play in a special, protected space.

The past decade or so has seen, according to some critics, a homogenization of advertising, a coalescence around average work driven too much by data and research. This is a view that Jackson agreed with, arguing the advertising industry needs to trust its gut more, which is why Channel 4 relies on its in-house marketing team to deliver its advertising; evangelists for the brand who really understand it. She encourages her team to try and avoid just adopting best practice principles and instead look to break them with all the risks that carries but with the reward of increased trust as a result from campaigns that really matter.

She cited the Paralympics work by Channel 4, which began in 2012 and has now run for four consecutive games, as an example of strong brand advertising that has consistently built affinity with Channel 4's audience by challenging perceptions.[9] Other bold campaigns featured the business and political elite in carbon skid-marked underpants for its 'Change Climate' season,[10] or Black presenters, actors, writers and experts, contributors and programme-makers in its 'Black To Front' which began in 2021 to challenge and leave a legacy for increased Black representation on and off screen.[11]

Every step of the way, Channel 4 embraces risk in its advertising, using its gut feel understanding of the brand to develop and deliver campaigns, and by doing so successfully build its affinity with the audience.

THREE KEY TAKEAWAYS

1   Channel 4 tracks how much people feel the brand is for 'someone like me', its affinity, as a proxy for how trusted it is by key audiences.

2   Taking risks with campaigns that really matter to your audience can lead to greater relational trust as a result.

3   To successfully build trust, your advertising has to be something you and your team really *feel* and believe fits the brand.

Trust works sideways

Charles Vallance, Chairman, VCCP

We trust sideways, said Vallance.[12] We trust people like us; any brand that isn't connecting with people rightfully loses their trust.

He went on to share the view that unlike politicians, advertisers are fighting a permanent election campaign where people have the right every day to vote for or against the brands they choose. He mentioned high-profile examples – Gillette, Bud Light, Jaguar and, most recently, the Oasis ticket pricing furore – where the campaigning goes wrong and the impact on trust (and business performance/reputation) is, in his view, tangible.

Vallance was also of the view that central to building trust is optimism, pointing back to the early 1990s with the launch campaign for new mobile company Orange, with its 'The Future's Bright, the Future's Orange' strapline, heralding a time he saw as a flowering of a number of new big British brands. Gillette, too, had a history of aspirational men's ads that promised to help users be 'the best a man can get'. He connects this need for optimism with people's need to believe that things can improve in their own lives, for them and for their children, and an innate drive humans have for progress. Brands can, he argues, build trust by connecting with that and supporting it in some way.

On the other hand, he criticized brands or companies that 'patronize' their audiences with advertising that presents well-intentioned but contrived portraits of modern life far from the experience of their customers. In an increasingly complex society with heightened cultural sensitivities and risk of offence, brands have to walk a fine line between promoting inclusivity and going too far in presenting role models seen by many as inauthentic. Careful considerations over casting, for instance, are built into VCCP's way of working. The 'body language' of a brand, Vallance suggested, is picked up by viewers from its ads: inauthenticity is unconvincing; credibility, authority and believability go hand in hand, and it is vital to avoid double standards either in your communications or your real-life brand behaviour.

He also stressed the importance of the messenger when building trust – the messenger can help to build trust through honesty, integrity, consistency and frequency, and it is here that the importance of recognizable brand icons comes into play. For more on that, we recommend reading Vallance's article entitled 'Distinctly different: unique brand assets are the first step towards a sale'.[13]

The short-hand version is that he believes the future of successful branding is consistently recognizable brand icons and assets, distinctive in their own right and fully integrated into all contact points from the brand to build saliency through familiarity and constancy.

One example of this is the Meerkats for Compare the Market, which took the brand from fourth in a category of four to the number one price comparison website for motor insurance, according to GlobalData's 2022 UK Insurance Consumer Survey, with a 54.5 per cent market share[14,15]

Whilst stressing that advertisers have to earn attention in a noisy world, Vallance highlights the inherent risk should brands try to borrow influence – it is dangerous to be dependent on others for people's trust in your own brand. For this reason, a strong brand icon allows you to build your own influence through entertaining content. At this point, Vallance cited #MeerChat, a short-form content series on TikTok where the Meerkats engage millions of viewers through quirky, chat-show themed videos, a form of brand content that people seek out, precisely because it is entertaining in its own right.

The counterpoint to all of this is to beware of advertising that is, as Vallance describes, mechanistic, when there is no obvious value exchange. This is just noise, it wears the audience down and should be seen as a missed opportunity to build trust in that constant campaign to be the brand that people vote for. Dismissive of advertising that isn't useful, informative or entertaining, describing it as communication rubble, he argues the best brand advertising shouldn't need to interrupt. Instead, it should attract attention.

THREE KEY TAKEAWAYS

1 Build trust in your brand through advertising by showing how you can help make people's lives a bit better – optimism and positivity are key!

2 Your brand is in a daily battle for trust; consistency is paramount.

3 Create your own brand properties that convey and reinforce trust directly, don't rely on third parties to build it for you.

Community built on trust

Georgina Bramall, Marketing Strategy Director, and Lisa Boyles, Head of Go To Market and Media, giffgaff

In 2024, a fifth of giffgaff's new members came from referrals, possibly one of the most commercial proof-points we came across of the value of being trusted in terms of customer growth.

How they have achieved this level of advocacy and recommendation begins with understanding the origins of giffgaff, a company born by O2's former Global Director of Brand Innovation, Gav Thompson.[16] As a disrupter to an established market, and as a newcomer, it needed to build trust fast. It focused from the outset on growing a community of people that understood there could be a different way of 'doing mobile', and Bramall says that community is the yardstick today; if the brand does something wrong, they will make it known very quickly. The team talk about giffgaff's history as 'the mobile network run by you' and explain that the openness of how the network is run is essential to building and maintaining trust.

What struck Matt during the interview was how Bramall and Boyles always referred to the people that spend money with giffgaff as members, never customers.[17] This choice of term is deliberate, because they don't view the relationship as purely transactional. With a legacy of being a 'pay as you go' network, there is high risk of people leaving; there is no tied 'loyalty', so giffgaff must find a way of making people part of something, hence the openness, the trust and the importance of the community.

The success speaks for itself – giffgaff's mission is to become the UK's most recommended connectivity provider and it currently enjoys the highest net promoter score in the category, one generally low in trust. They were also voted Uswitch Mobile Network of The Year 2025.[18]

And that trust helps when the brand runs into problems, as it did when it was discovered to be overbilling people by mistake. In 2019, giffgaff received an Ofcom fine for accidental overbilling, but there was also credit given to the brand for reporting it to Ofcom themselves, reimbursing people and providing the option for people to donate the missing pounds and pence to charity as an alternative.[19]

To keep building trust, the giffgaff team places a high importance on partnerships with agencies and media brands, and for many of the latter, they hold direct relationships. Boyles uses a Responsible Reach Matrix to add rigour to the media plan and regularly speaks with media partners one-to-one about areas where the giffgaff team believe improvements can be made by a media brand to be more responsible and so trusted as a brand partner.

Bramall and Boyles take the responsibilities they carry for the brand's advertising very seriously. As we finished this book, they published the second iteration of their Responsible Marketing Manifesto, in collaboration with MG OMD.[20] This manifesto of principles and practical action is open source for any advertiser to review and adopt and covers responsibilities that brand owners and their media agencies can assume on sustainability, inclusion, and 'doing the right thing'. That giffgaff can stand by such a principled stance of openness and trustworthiness speaks volumes for the brand and its leadership.

THREE KEY TAKEAWAYS

1   Strong levels of trust can be gained through building a community.

2   Trust can help protect a brand when it runs into trouble.

3   To be trusted, take a responsible approach to *all* elements of your advertising work.

From controlling to conducting trust

By Jessica Tamsedge, UK CEO, dentsu Creative

We conducted a written Q&A interview with this agency leader who steers the business to build brands through what the company describes as 'Transformative Creativity'.[21] Tamsedge also sits on the UK's IPA Council and the Industry Advisory Panel to the Advertising Standards Authority, offering a perspective on how to uphold industry regulation in a way that is both fair and progressive.

How has dentsu's approach to building trust through advertising campaigns on behalf of its clients changed over the years?

Traditionally, we built brands on broadcast and one-way narratives, assuming this would build connection, relevance and ultimately trust. This was followed by an era of hyper personalization, with endlessly versioned stories and messages to meet customers' every move, moment and need. We then came to realise that trust is more of a social construct, built through community and co-creation, not top down or even one to one. We are now in what we call the age of algorithm and influence, where every piece of content we see has reached us through social signals or through the endorsement of trusted voices. It's why investment in influencer marketing is seeing so much growth and creates a tension for advertisers in how they control vs conduct their brands, building trust through their own actions as well as through others' voices.

What does conducting trust mean for a brand – what are they in control of, and what are they relinquishing control of?

We talk about brands moving from controlling to conducting. There are simply too many ways in which consumers today engage with brands that the legacy approach of 'launching and leaving' a campaign no longer holds. We are navigating paid, owned and earned environments, reliant on partner voices, creators, even brands' own audiences to determine brand perception. As customer complaints letters become social posts, the distance between product experience and brand trust has collapsed. As brands entrust 'influencers' with their key messages, even the most paid and choreographed of stories must be told in the influencer's own voice. And the rise of UGC (user-generated content) brings with it such unpredictability that only the most iconic and 'culturally understood' of brands can hope to benefit. Launching Hilton's 'Like a Winner' campaign with Lando Norris as part of our McLaren sponsorship was the perfect example of brands conducting. After a series of videos in which Lando goes about ordinary (sometimes surreal) tasks 'like a winner', we saw the internet explode with people blitzing their inboxes, clearing up after their toddlers and beating the traffic... all like a winner.

And so, the importance of brand distinction has never been greater for brands. What is the intangible glue that holds the brand together and ensures recall and attribution? We talk about this as a brand's 'body language', creating consistency in attitude and tone. Clients of ours like Ronseal have done this powerfully and consistently over time. 'Does Exactly What it Says on the Tin' is more than a line. It is a no-nonsense attitude to getting things done. We know exactly what voices to enlist on behalf of a brand like this and how to tell its stories beyond advertising, as we did with the Great Garden Revolution in partnership with Channel 4.

How do you go about identifying how and where a brand can now confidently and credibly build trust with its target audience?

For a long time, social campaigns were treated with a degree of mystery. Will this speak to the cultural zeitgeist? Will this transcend organic to achieve the much-coveted realms of viral success. The past 10 years have also seen brands chase every major news story, every cultural topic, racing for a point of view that connects their brand to the conversation. This isn't the fault of advertisers, in fact customers would often call out brands for not showing up with an appropriate point of view quickly enough. Black Lives Matter saw a flurry of ill-advised and tenuous 'activations' from brands. A number of brands were called out for tokenism, having been nearly cancelled for not showing up quickly enough to begin with.

For many reasons, the cultural tide has turned, and we have the opportunity to get back to basics. Does this brand have a right to show up in a particular cultural space? Is it additive, useful… entertaining?

At dentsu, we believe in science as well as creativity to credibly connect brands with audiences. We use a methodology called the Attention Gap, identifying where our audiences' interests lie, including topics that are adjacent to the brand we are looking to activate, but relevant to its broader category. For example, in activating Hilton's McLaren sponsorship, we saw stronger interest in the F1 drivers' own wellness and pre-game rituals than the races themselves. Live race viewing audiences had dropped 16 per cent over the past two years, while F1 social communities and fandoms have grown exponentially. Campaigns like 'Race Ready Yoga' and 'Vroom Service' allowed us to lead with Lando Norris and share stories of his experience around the race through social and content, connecting the brand to the moments that matter most to our audience, in the spaces where they were spending their time.

Can you tell us more the role of the fan and 'fandom' now in building trust for a brand, and how a brand can harness this?

We have a model called 1:9:90 which inverts the traditional mass media model and represents a powerful and efficient way to build brand trust at scale. With the rise of smaller online communities (nano influencers represent 65 per cent of the industry), we start with the 1, the influencer who holds greatest credibility with a given audience. The 9 then represents the influential voices in that community, i.e. influencer 'peers' who build advocacy, ultimately driving the 90, i.e. broader conversation and reach. Working with 7-Eleven, we identified conversations around the brand often centred around 7-Eleven's forecourts as it was the perfect backdrop for photographing cars. Cars of 7-Eleven emerged as a fan first community conversation that we subsequently gamified using fan language 'Where Car?' and activated in Fortnight.

THREE KEY TAKEAWAYS

1   The way brands are able to build trust is changing to reflect the broader changes noted earlier.

2   Build trust by identifying where your brand can fit into people's areas of interest and be a valued participant in the conversation.

3   One of the most powerful advocates for trust in your brand is your customer (or fan)

Trust, reputation, risks and opportunities

Murray Bisschop, UK Marketing Director, Tesco

Rewind the clocks back to 2016 and the Tesco brand was at the outset of a reputation recovery mission, following an industry scandal over horsemeat and also accounting issues. An example of the early pressures was when a product performed well in a blind quality test, but once revealed as a Tesco product, the customer rating went down, something Bisschop describes as 'a net brand drag'.[22] It was clear that it would take more than just advertising for the company to rebuild its reputation with customers, it was going to have to 'behave its way out of this', an approach led successfully by then new CEO, Dave Lewis.

As the behaviour of the company changed, a slew of successful advertising campaigns followed through things like 'Food Love Stories' through to the latest food advertising platform, 'It's Everything'. Early testing for the new campaign is strong, and Bisschop believes the proposition that you can have the experience you deserve is working with people because it is true. Even the style of the advertising is real, human, deliberately not over-produced, to show how the company is in lockstep with the customer experience.

We asked Bisschop how advertising and marketing has changed since he first joined his previous company, Unilever. There's no doubt in his mind: things have evolved. It's more data-led, sophisticated and changing faster; there's more to stay on top of and the half-life of interest in things is shortening.

Bisschop stressed it was impossible to understate the value of where your brand turns up, but controlling that was getting much harder. The priority was to work as closely as possible with partners to reduce risk and address any concerns over the brand appearing in unwanted places.

This understanding of context requires constant maintenance and, like other marketers we spoke to, there has been a growth recently in Tesco's use of influencers in its campaigns. He thinks this is happening for two reasons. Firstly, the channel of influencers is proving to be a viable route to building trust. Secondly, there are structural changes taking place, away from big, high-level brand partnerships to a range of influencers across a variety of topic areas.

While he insists you can't cede your customers' trust to others, once you're confident in your offering, you can talk with authority through them. He cites the example of Tesco's 'Free From' range where influencers in the celiac community, for example, can provide great credibility to the products on offer. He notes that this structural change is one where the focus is moving away from reach and follower numbers to one around relevant content topics.

For this reason, Tesco, with its partners, EssenceMediacom and Goat, is consistently trying to ensure it is listening to the right people across all relevant content areas. Then, with its creative partner, BBH, it considers if it wants to say something about the issues.

Bisschop describes how the down elevators – the things that pushed trust to low levels – used to be glacial, as were the up elevators, but this up/down dynamic has accelerated.

An example is how Tesco, like the other supermarkets, helped feed the nation during Covid and Tesco staff showed up instore to make that happen. A boost in reputation and trust levels followed, but 18 months later, inflation and pressures on cost-of-living meant trust levels for supermarkets were hit once again. Tesco must turn up ready for competition every single day, says Bisschop, people know and compare prices and quality millions of times over daily. If you behave well and do the right thing, the reputational benefits follow.

THREE KEY TAKEAWAYS

1 It takes more than advertising to rebuild trust after a crisis; it is first about the way your brand responds and behaves.

2 Maintaining trust in a brand is of growing complexity; levels of trust can rise and fall faster than ever before.

3 Influencers are useful as trusted advocates for what you and your brand can offer to people, especially in identifiable interest communities.

The importance of being liked

Lucy Jameson, founder, Uncommon Creative Studio

Campaign named Uncommon 'the most exciting start-up of their generation', which was demonstrated when the studio won the coveted title of 'Independent Agency of the Year' at Campaign's annual Agency Awards in 2021.[23]

You trust people that you like, so it's logical that to succeed in advertising, says Jameson; you need to make ads that people like. Better ads, she said, create better relationships. In a conversation for this book, she pointed to homophily studies, a sociology concept which, when you look at the Ancient Greek structure of the word, means 'same, common' (homos) and 'friendship, love' (philia).[24] Many studies in the area of homophily highlight the tendency of people to associate and connect with those similar to themselves. Jameson describes how this works in advertising, for brands to present themselves as for 'people like you, from people like you', underlining that it's important to be liked as a way of building a connection of trust with the audience. When it comes to trust itself, there's little point in talking about that directly in the work, but there are different ways that likeability can be built to support that sense of trust.

This is supported by data we have seen from Credos which shows there is a close relationship between positive attitudes towards advertising and people's trust in it.

Jameson pointed to the importance of where you advertise. The impression of size, commitment and accountability that buying a presence in mass media can give a brand matters. In this sense, 'the sheer act of doing advertising at scale' has an important significance when it comes to building trust.

She also talked of the trust equation that every brand needs to consider when planning what relationship it wants to have with its customers. There is a necessary give and take in the transaction between the two. Is the brand sacrificing something for the customer? Moving from just selling to them, to helping them with something that is important to them? This switch from a self-oriented approach in the relationship between the brand and customer to where the brand's social contribution is also considered is a critical part of the trust equation. It moves trust to a different level, making it not just about trust in competence to deliver a product or service at a particular price point or quality but trust built through an authentic connection with the brand's values.

THREE KEY TAKEAWAYS

1   Make your advertising campaigns something that people like and enjoy.

2   Think about how and where your advertise your brand; 'big media' status can help build people's trust in it.

3   A trust equation to consider is how your brand makes a positive contribution to people's lives; feature that in your advertising.

Trust matters at every touchpoint

James Murphy, CEO, Ogilvy Group UK, and formerly of New Commercial Arts and Adam&EveDDB

Trust in advertising is a foundation of what agencies are trying to deliver for every business, says Murphy, pointing out that not every advertiser automatically commands trust; some businesses have a stronger perceived moral fibre than others.[25] He also highlights that advertising is not there to make up any deficit in trust in a company's behaviour; it is there to promote excellence in a particular product or service. In that sense, it is there to amplify positives, not hide negatives.

Murphy was part of the team that was instrumental in the resurgence of John Lewis, the UK retailer, in particular with its campaigns during the Christmas advertising season. He explains that this is an almost perfect example of where a brand had a strong history in the public consciousness with its business model of a partnership, virtuous in many ways and so when the advertising began, the brand started from a point of inherent trust. However, just because a business does good things doesn't necessarily mean people will shop there, and so the advertising was tasked with adding desire and excitement to the idea of shopping at John Lewis, in particular gifting at Christmas. The work had, he said, 'a multiplier effect' on the business, with its series of much-loved campaigns over the course of a decade twice winning the Grand Prix in the IPA Effectiveness Awards, plus a Gold in 2020 for its long-term business success.[26]

Thinking about the role of advertising, Murphy quoted William Morris,[27] the celebrated 19th-century designer, saying we should reflect on his advice to 'Have nothing in your houses that you do not know to be useful or believe to be beautiful'.

Advertisers can earn trust by not polluting, but instead turning up in funny, beguiling and compelling ways. Don't be crass, shrill or misleading. Certainly, don't think your ad should say 'trust me' but instead make sure it gives rational or emotional value to the consumer.

When you get it right, says Murphy, trust can reinforce a brand's performance with a positive impact on price elasticity: people will pay a reasonable price, even at a premium to competitors, if they believe in you and the value you offer.

As he reflected on the changes in advertising, Murphy highlighted how the target customer is surrounded by a constellation of touchpoints. It is vital to get every one of those touchpoints right. Businesses operate now in what he describes as the 'vigilante economy' – people can research whether that price reduction you're promoting is genuine, whether your supply chain is as sustainable as you claim it is, whether you pay your staff a living wage and treat them well. If you get one part of the advertising mix wrong, you can prompt a 'pile on', where people who might or might not be your target customers protest vocally online, ultimately leading to a collapse in trust.

This constellation of touchpoints requires something Murphy referred to as a cloud of kinetic assets. He referenced the 2024 Sainsbury's Christmas campaign which featured the BFG as one recent example.[28] The team produced a high quality, much lauded 90-second advert but the questions were then, ok, where do we put it, what do we do with it? How is it used instore, around the store or live in real time online across social media platforms? The task of the marketer and their advertising team is to create and manage those kinetic assets, all delivered correctly.

At the heart of this dynamic shift in advertising, made possible by the rapid growth in digital media options, is the vital importance of quality control to ensure trust is built and not damaged. The advertiser and agency team must be fully equipped to produce the volume of quality assets needed at the right pace, and to distribute them effectively.

THREE KEY TAKEAWAYS

1 Not all brands start with the same levels of trust and advertising cannot hide problems with what your brand offers (or fails to offer).

2 The quality of *every* advertising asset matters when it comes to building trust with people.

3 There can be a financial benefit to increasing trust in your brand, allowing you, for example, to sustain a price premium.

Conclusion

In this chapter, we have heard directly from advertising leaders at brands, advertising agencies and media owners, all sharing how they think about trust when it comes to the advertising work they and their teams deliver.

We have seen a range of considerations if you are to truly put trust at the heart of your brand's advertising, some of which reinforce insights we have identified in earlier chapters and more that we will build on in the coming chapters.

First, we have been reminded by Ogilvy's Bennett of the basic human need to trust and of just how important it is to understand how trust is constructed when it comes to setting your campaign strategy.

We have heard how critical it is for a retailer (Boots) that sells all kinds of products to be trusted to provide what people really need in their lives, and how increasingly sophisticated its advertising campaigns are becoming to fully connect in trusted ways with customers of all generations.

Jackson at Channel 4 showed the value of you and your team truly knowing your brand inside out and being able to make the right call on what type of advertising messages and activities will generate increased trust with your target audiences. This goes beyond the tangible and on to the 'gut feel' of knowing what will really make your brand stand out against the competition.

VCCP's founder, Vallance, highlighted the importance of positivity in your advertising to show how you can help people make things better in their own lives, and to do this in a way that is distinctive and consistent. This, he says, is how you can build trust in a constant election-style battle to secure the vote of your customer.

Bramall and Boyle's approach at giffgaff has elevated the customer to a member of their community and has reaped the commercial benefits that extra level of trust engenders. They protect this trust by ensuring what, how and where they advertise is as responsible as it can be in the eyes of their members.

Meanwhile Tamsedge at dentsu shared just how much has changed in recent years in how you can build and manage trust in your brand. This includes how important 'others', such as your most valued, passionate customers, are in the advertising mix to shaping the perceptions of whether your brand can be truly trusted.

Another big brand advertiser, Tesco, echoed this rapid pace of change in how trust is won and lost, and the growing complexity of tracking and managing where the brand shows up for your audience in a daily battle for attention.

Jameson at Uncommon talked of a trust equation between you, your brand and your customer, challenging you to ask what you are giving your customer in return for their trust and whether it is truly of the value to warrant that trust.

Finally, Ogilvy's Murphy reminded us that advertising is there to make the positives of your brand famous, and to give it the rational or emotional value that supports trust. He reminded us of the business value of trust in justifying a price premium and he, too, pointed to the growing challenge of managing an ever-wider range of brand assets to connect with your customers.

So, each of these top players in the business of advertising, brands and marketing, had something different to say, their own take on the topic that stemmed from their own experience, role or market. Yet all of them were keen to stress the significance of people's trust to their work. All of them sought to enhance it in the ads they made and for the brands they nurtured. All of them recognized challenges along the way, changes occurring in society and media that impacted their efforts, and the imperative to really understand their customers or audiences if they were to earn their trust.

Finally, there were two areas concerning trusted advertising to which our interviewees kept returning: the rising importance of influencers and the trust value in how and where your brand appears to your customers. We will explore both of these topics in greater detail over the coming chapters.

Notes

1 Author interview with Dan Bennett, March 2025

2 D H Maister, R Galford and C Green (2001) *The Trust Equation. The Trusted Advisor*, Simon & Schuster

3 BrAIDS for AIDS, https://braidsforaids.com/ (archived at https://perma.cc/UU59-EHC5)

4 'Say Maaate to a Mate', Mayor of London, Ogilvy, July 2023, www.ogilvy.com/work/say-maaate-mate (archived at https://perma.cc/FWX8-KQA7)

5 Author interview with Pete Markey, March 2025

6 Boots unleashes the magic of beauty this Christmas with the launch of festive campaign, Boots, November 2024, www.boots-uk.com/newsroom/news/boots-unleashes-the-magic-of-beauty-this-christmas-with-the-launch-of-festive-campaign/ (archived at https://perma.cc/8ZJF-5Y3H)

7 Author interview with Katie Jackson, March 2025

8 Channel 4, About Channel 4, Channel 4's remit, www.channel4.com/corporate/about-4/what-we-do/channel-4s-remit (archived at https://perma.cc/4WJQ-BTUF)

9 M Innes, 10 years of 'Superhumans': Inside Channel 4's transformational Paralympics campaign, Marketing Week, March 2022, www.marketingweek.com/super-humans-inside-channel-4-paralympics-campaign/ (archived at https://perma.cc/94KH-X9X6)

10 Channel 4, 4creative campaign tees up climate change programming with carbon skid marks, November 2023, www.channel4.com/press/news/4creative-campaign-tees-climate-change-programming-carbon-skid-marks (archived at https://perma.cc/XC2X-25A8)

11 Channel 4, Everything you need to know about Channel 4's Black to Front Project, September 2021, www.channel4.com/4viewers/black-to-front-project (archived at https://perma.cc/5Q8R-UM4K)

12 Author interview with Charles Vallance, January 2025

13 C Vallance, Distinctly different: unique brand assets are a crucial first step towards a sale, Campaign, February 2023, www.campaignlive.co.uk/article/distinctly-different-unique-brand-assets-crucial-first-step-towards-sale/1814130 (archived at https://perma.cc/4NLE-GBQ5)

14 Meet the Meerkats, CompareTheMarket, www.comparethemarket.com/meerkat/meet-the-meerkats/ (archived at https://perma.cc/J5CN-8B87)

15 R Shotton, Why it works: How two meerkats made insurance memorable, Marketing Week, August 2024, www.marketingweek.com/why-it-works-meerkats-insurance-memorable/ (archived at https://perma.cc/EP4J-SE8G)

16 About giffgaff, www.giffgaff.com/why-giffgaff (archived at https://perma.cc/WK49-E8TS)

17 Author interview with Georgina Bramall and Lisa Boyles, April 2025

18 Uswitch Telecoms Awards 2025, www.uswitch.com/telecoms-awards/#top-mobile-awards (archived at https://perma.cc/6WZK-5KFL)

19 M Sweney, giffgaff fined £1.4m for overcharging millions of mobile customers, *The Guardian*, July 2019, www.theguardian.com/media/2019/jul/30/giffgaff-fined-overcharging-mobile-phone-customers-ofcom (archived at https://perma.cc/ZZE6-2YN9)

20 giffgaff's Responsible Marketing Manifesto, giffgaff, July 2025, www.giffgaff.com/blog/giffgaff-news/responsible-marketing-manifesto/ (archived at https://perma.cc/XWG8-QDVE)

21 Author Q&A interview with Jessica Tamsedge, March 2025

22 Author interview with Murray Bisschop, March 2025

23 Campaign, Independent Agency of the Year 2021: Uncommon Creative Studio, www.campaignlive.co.uk/article/independent-agency-year-2021-uncommon-creative-studio/1740696 (archived at https://perma.cc/H5MU-6SN3)

24 Dictionary.com, 'homophily', www.dictionary.com/browse/homophily (archived at https://perma.cc/S5LB-EQNW)

25 Author interview with James Murphy, February 2025

26 L Aitken, 'An amazing decade' for John Lewis makes it IPA Gold, WARC, October 2020, www.warc.com/newsandopinion/opinion/an-amazing-decade-for-john-lewis-makes-it-ipa-gold/en-gb/3890 (archived at https://perma.cc/8YT4-KQFA)

27 Introducing William Morris, V&A, www.vam.ac.uk/articles/introducing-william-morris (archived at https://perma.cc/F2Q4-QHYZ)

28 Sainsbury's, Sainsbury's & the BFG launch their phizz-whizzing new Christmas campaign, https://corporate.sainsburys.co.uk/news/press-releases/sainsbury-s-the-bfg-launch-their-phizz-whizzing-new-christmas-campaign/ (archived at https://perma.cc/WSN4-XT9Z)

06

Trust in the age of
the influencer: Part 1

Introduction

There's little doubt in our minds that one of the most dynamic factors in trust and advertising is the advent of influencers. The role they are playing in campaigns for brands looking to establish trust with their audiences has created an entire new advertising channel. Its development reflects the very changes in trust across society that we have already discussed: from hierarchical to distributed, vertical to horizontal, corporate to personal. And it's growing fast around the world.

A phrase that often cropped up when we discussed this new phenomenon with people was a dichotomy we observed – that 'nobody trusts influencers, but everybody has an influencer they trust'. Why is that, and what is going on? What can we learn from the evolution of the influencer, the impact of this role and the even newer development of the content creator as advertising messenger?

So, in this chapter, the first of two where we consider influencers, we are going to review the sector and its potential impact, good or bad, on trust in advertising.

We're going to take an 'industry' view first by covering the work of a new trade body setting professional standards to protect and build trust in influencers' work, and we'll look at the issue of ad disclosure by influencers, as seen by the ASA.

In the next chapter (Chapter 7), we'll take a 'practitioner' view, with insights from practitioners from agencies, brands and influencers themselves.

Let's be clear, in the context of this book and the formation of the Advertising Association a hundred years ago, this is a new, still nascent sector of advertising. Part of its newness is the evolution of the language used in it, especially relating to 'influencers' and 'creators'. They are not the same thing. Influencers are not necessarily creators; creators are not always influencers. However, in the context of their work for marketers, it is their 'influence' that matters, whether that is generated by their creativity or other skills. So, we will use the word influencer as the generic term, with 'creator' being used only where that is relevant to the context or individual and interviewee concerned.

Things are moving fast. A global survey by Statista asked marketers and industry leaders how much of their marketing spend was being committed to influencer marketing campaigns. There were a range of responses - 14 per cent said 10 to 15 per cent of their budget, while 12 per cent reported a commitment of more than 50 per cent.[1] A second report by Statista showed ad spend in the 'Influencer Advertising' segment of the UK advertising market was forecast to increase between 2024 and 2030 to reach an estimated £1.4 billion per annum.[2]

With that sort of investment, the need for public confidence in the ad-funded content presented to audiences is ever more important to brands and influencers alike. So, the role of expert agencies in helping companies navigate a new, complex advertising landscape full of both risks and rewards is vital.

A new trade body for the influencer sector

The Influencer Marketing Trade Body (IMTB) is a relatively new organization in the advertising ecosystem.[3] Set up in 2021 by Scott Guthrie, IMTB's Director General, it counts Dentsu Creative, Goat, Ogilvy and Whalar among its agency membership.

The IMTB's remit is wide. It works to represent influencer agencies and marketing platforms, to promote their role and to encourage the businesses in this fast-emerging sector to adopt and promote professional standards. Doing so will help formalize the work of thousands and thousands of people, some working full time, some working part time, all striking up individual commercial relationships with advertisers across all kinds of areas of common interest. Note, it is the first new member of CAP (Committee of Advertising Practice) for over a decade, becoming one of UK advertising's rule-makers.

The role of the agencies here is critical in supporting advertisers to identify and manage the many relationships they need in this space. IMTB's focus is the UK market, and it is seeking counterparts in international markets, with a European alliance of fellow trade bodies in France and Germany and alignment with practitioners in Australia.

We asked Guthrie to help set the scene for this fast-developing channel for marketers – and it's all about trust.

INFLUENCERS: THE IMTB VIEW

By Scott Guthrie, Director General, IMTB

Within a single decade the influencer marketing industry has transformed from impish fad to juggernaut, and today it is larger than either the recorded music industry or cinema's box office.[4,5]

Worth around half a billion dollars in 2015, the influencer marketing industry's global value jumped to $6.5 billion in 2019. By 2024 the industry had reached $35 billion, marking a fivefold increase in five years. By the end of the decade, forecasts put the sector's value at $56 billion.[6]

As visually driven industries, fashion, beauty and travel were early adopters of Instagram influencers and continue to invest heavily, but today influencers exist in every niche, on every social media platform, and work with brands throughout the product lifecycle from product development to co-ownership of new brands as well as in their best-known role: product promoters.

Influencers drive trends. They nurture communities of interest, becoming guardians of consumer trust. Critically, influencers propel decision-making. The key to influencer marketing's power is its ability to over-index in earning consumer trust compared with other marketing channels, particularly with younger consumers. That trust in influencer content converts into a positive impact on buying decisions.

Influencer marketing's effectiveness through the whole sales funnel has enticed marketers to devote more of their budget to the channel. Around 9 in 10 marketers (88 per cent) who have run influencer campaigns intend to increase or at least maintain their spend.[7] More than half (54 per cent) of multinational brand marketers plan to boost spend in 2025 and 61 per cent agree that influencer marketing will become more important in the future according to a survey of marketers.[8]

Unilever is a prime example of this shift for multinational brands. CEO Fernando Fernandez said in early 2025 that his company's marketing shift to social first, with influencers at the fore, will probably be the company's biggest change and one he will push forward fast.[9] Why? Fernandez explains that messages coming from brands that are corporations are seen as suspicious, so a marketing activity system where others speak on your behalf at scale is vital.

The relatable, authentic brand advocacy which influencers lend has helped embed influencer marketing within cross disciplinary, integrated marketing programmes. Mark Read, CEO of WPP, talks of influencers as part of every big campaign these days.[10]

Consumer purchase figures underline these marketing decisions. A study showed that 47 per cent of British adults had made purchases based on influencer recommendations.[11] In the US 57 per cent of Gen Z trust influencers when deciding whether to purchase a product.[12]

People trust influencers and that trust is on the rise. The share of Gen Z and millennials who trust influencers grew from 51 per cent in 2019 to 61 per cent in 2023.[13]

As a consequence of this trust bond, social media users now follow influencers in ever-greater numbers. Some 88 per cent of US Gen Z adults follow at least one influencer on social media, and nearly one in four (22 per cent) follow more than 50.[14] In the UK, 55 per cent of 18–29 year olds follow more than 21 influencers, 26 per cent follow more than 50 and 17 per cent follow more than 100.[15]

Our appetite for influencer content is growing: 70 per cent of adult Gen Zs say they want to keep seeing the same quantity of influencer content in the future or even more of it.[16]

Estimates of the global number of active influencers vary widely. Goldman Sachs puts the figure at 50 million.[17] Linktree says it is four times that at 200 million.[18] Kellery Advisory's nationally representative study in the US estimates there to be 27 million paid influencers there – equating to 14 per cent of 16–54 year olds.[19] However, Keller notes the majority (56 per cent) are part time or hobbyist influencers leveraging their social media presence for supplemental income. This is reflected in their earnings: 52 per cent of influencers in the US earn less than $10,000 a year. Tapping into this long tail of side hustlers often makes for highly relatable, highly representative content, but comes with the risk that they are not always fully cognizant of requisite rules and regulations, including on advertising disclosure.

Influencers have emerged in the evolving landscape of digital media and content creation as a powerful new voice shaping how we experience, connect with and interpret the world.

An explosion in interest

Certainly, more of the conversations we had for this book surfaced influencers as a topic of attention and investment than we had initially expected. This was supported by a general belief that the influencer channel offers a different, perhaps more nuanced way of building trust between the advertiser and customer. That, and experience of a compelling ROI from spend with influencers. We spoke with people who referenced particularly powerful sales results in fashion and beauty, where an individual recommendation can cause a product line to sell out.

The sense we have gleaned from our research is that this growth has been developing steadily for the past decade but took on greater significance for advertisers during the pandemic years (2020/21), accelerating from 2022 onwards. Nobody we spoke to suggested reducing spend in this emerging channel, despite their recognition of challenges to identify, manage and work effectively with influencers.

The strategic shift of Unilever's marketing effort toward influencers that Guthrie referenced earlier has big implications.[20] The company will need to work with a very large number of influencers and produce a much higher volume of social posts, meaning that it will have to operate in a very different way to create and distribute content for its brand. Fernandez' policy appears to be driven by two things – a view that audiences are becoming more suspicious of traditional advertising and a return on investment from influencers that provides compelling evidence to spend more there. How much more, though?

Fernandez noted how there were 19,000 zip codes in India alone, and that Unilever will require an influencer in every single one of these; in some circumstances not just one, but perhaps a hundred.

This is a big signal of change and genuinely marks an explosion of interest in the influencer sector, but it doesn't come without risks to trust. In the same *Times* article, the IMTB's Guthrie highlighted how Unilever's ambition will bring a hidden management cost in ensuring the tens of thousands of selected influencers understand the company's brands, their aims and values, as well as that they are working properly within the regulations of each country. Adherence to regulations is integral to ensuring the work can be trusted. With different rules around the world, you can understand the challenge that lies ahead.

What will also be interesting to see, Matt suggests, is the shelf-life of a typical influencer, and how regularly the list of individuals your brand is working with will need to be refreshed. There's a great difference between a media brand staffed by a range of editorial and commercial talent and an individual, when it comes to capabilities and long-term stability as a brand partner. Particularly the range of influencers in play, stretching as far as those defined as micro, even nano. Time will tell.

Tackling trust in the influencer sector

It's fair to say the IMTB is acutely aware of the importance of trust in its sector, from a regulatory point of view as well as building confidence in the use of influencers by brands. It has put in place the standards that advertisers need for their work to be considered as legal, decent, honest and truthful.

We're going to take a closer look at those standards now.

The Influencer Marketing Code of Conduct

First, the IMTB has worked in partnership with the UK advertisers' trade body, ISBA, whom we've mentioned before in this book, to set up an Influencer Marketing Code of Conduct that aims to:[21]

- Ensure compliance with the regulatory framework set out by the Advertising Standards Authority (ASA) and Competition and Markets Authority (CMA), as well as with the CAP/BCAP Codes.
- Raise standards of conduct in influencer marketing and advertising.
- Improve the relationship between brands, talent agencies and influencers, including promoting a genuine alignment of values between the influencer and the advertiser.
- Enable advertisers to employ authentic and effective influencer marketing.
- Seek to prevent harm which might be caused by the content or placement of influencer ads.
- Deliver the transparency that consumers expect and deserve.

Signatories of the code range across advertisers, agencies and influencers themselves.

This code was first published in 2021 by ISBA and underwent a fundamental revision in 2024, dividing commitments into sections on best practices for brands, agencies and influencers themselves. It covers key elements such as proper ad disclosure and measurement, health and wellbeing and the prevention of harm.

ISBA and IMTB, as joint owners of the Code, describe it as 'a living document' which may undergo further iterations given the pace of change and growth in this sector. However, both trade bodies stress the goal for the Code is to be a baseline for legal, decent, honest and truthful influencer advertising.

Like the Codes of Advertising Practice, we highly recommend making sure you are familiar with this Code. Compliance is a backstop to ensure advertising produced with influencers and content creators is work that can be trusted.

Free advice service

Second, IMTB offers a service called REASSURE to its members.[22] This is free at the point of use and offers advice to ensure content is compliant with the regulations. It's comprehensive – covering everything from CAP Code and consumer legislation to prize draws, competitions and promotions, and from protecting the young and vulnerable to disclosure rules across platforms.

A quick glance highlights the range of possible pitfalls, and the damage to trust that a brand risks if an influencer produces commercial content on your behalf that is not in line with the industry's standards. These all apply to other media channels, but perhaps the people working in those are more familiar and compliant with the rules because of the maturity of their channel and the professional training in place. The role of the agencies that manage clients' relationships with individual influencers is, as the IMTB's work is showing, critical to the sector's standing as a responsible advertising environment.

Certainly, when you look at recent ASA cases, the rulings against influencers breaking the rules are significant. Of the 15,327 complaints about online advertising to the ASA in 2024, 3,484, nearly a quarter, were against influencers.[23] This is an area of advertising which needs help to ensure all campaigns meet the standards needed to retain public trust and confidence in it.

Understanding hidden advertising

Third, the IMTB has published a detailed explainer for all working in the sector to help identify and understand Hidden Advertising.[24] Again, this Guidance is worth a close read to ensure work can be trusted. An example of advice is for content creators who want to make sure they are not misleading their audience:

All commercial content must be correctly labelled and clearly identifiable as an ad. This also includes where you post about any gifts you've received, even if there's no obligation for you to do anything with it.

To do this, all labels must be clear, prominent and easy to understand. It is not enough just to tag a brand in your post, use discount codes or affiliate links.

The IMTB's work has just begun, and it is looking for allies, not just in the UK but around the world, to help as the influencer sector grows and matures.

We're some way off full disclosure of ads by influencers

That the IMTB's and ISBA's Code is needed was shown by the ASA's second Influencer Ad Disclosure report,[25] published in 2025. The ASA's AI-powered system analysed over 50,000 pieces of content including Stories, Reels, and posts across Instagram and TikTok, from 509 UK-based accounts and 390 individual influencers. The sample included influencers previously flagged in the ASA's first Influencer Ad Disclosure report (2021), influencers brought to the attention of ASA/CAP in the year prior to the 2024 monitoring, and a random selection of influencer accounts to reflect what the public may typically see on their feeds. This approach was deliberate to track persistent issues and spot emerging trends in how influencer ads are being disclosed – or not.
Key findings:

- Approximately 57% of the influencer ads analysed stuck to the rules on ad disclosure.
- 9% of advertising content did attempt to use a disclosure label, but the language used ('Link in bio', 'Gifted', 'Thank you', 'Aff' or 'Affiliate', 'Collab', 'PR' or 'PR Trip' and 'Personalized discount code') failed to make its commercial nature clear.
- 34% of the influencer ads viewed included no disclosure at all.
- More than half of influencer ads in the fashion and travel sectors were either undisclosed or poorly disclosed.

The ASA reminded people that transparency is important – people should always know when they're being advertised to. Without clear disclosure, ads can mislead and risk undermining trust in influencer content. It reiterated its role to help influencers and content creators to get it right when it comes to featuring ads on their profiles, but that it also wouldn't hesitate to act against repeat offenders.
CAP has an excellent cheat sheet on its website that makes the rules simple and clear to influencers, reproduced in Figure 6.1.

FIGURE 6.1 The influencer's cheat sheet to declaring ads on social media

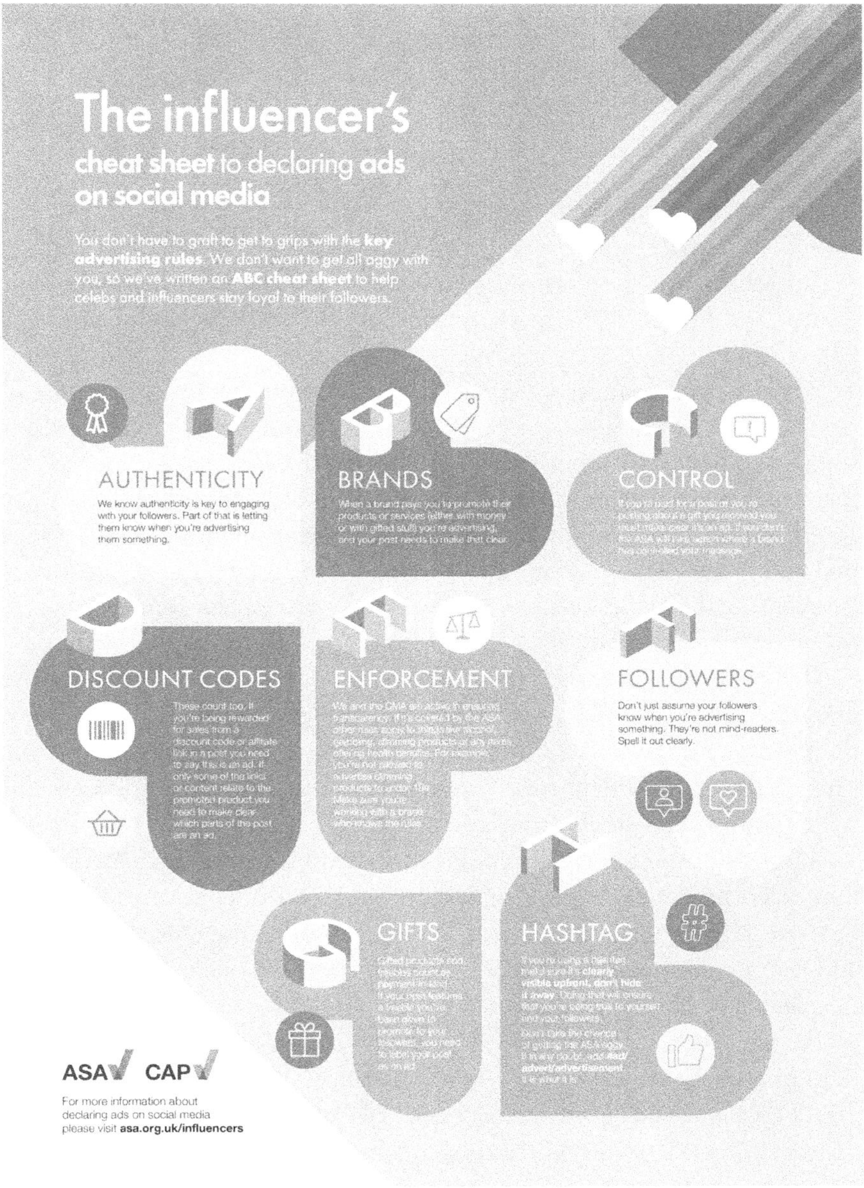

There is also a multiple-choice questionnaire that influencers can run through as part of a very comprehensive section of advice and guidance to help people understand and follow the rules.

CAP's advice for anyone operating in this channel is simple – if it's an ad, make it obvious: that's how to build public trust and confidence in this new form of advertising.

Conclusion

Influencers (and content creators) are not going away. They are growing fast from their current levels of a 2–3 per cent share in the media plans of most big advertisers and far more of many newer brands in, for instance, fashion, beauty and health. How much more they will grow across sectors and advertisers is hard to say but grow they will.

If Unilever's Fernandez is right, and global advertisers join him in boosting their influencer budgets twentyfold in the next few years, then demand, supply and prices will all increase. So will criticism, examination and regulatory probing. Just as the success of social media has brought political and media scrutiny to bear on the platforms and players involved, so the rise of the influencers is attracting the attention of legislators and regulators. Establishing the habits and guardrails of trustworthy behaviour is critical to the sector's long-term health.

The decision to deal with thousands of suppliers when advertising your brand, rather than working with a handful, brings a greater range of opportunities to make trusted connections with customers, current and new, but also greater management time, costs and risk of something going wrong. Intimacy and authenticity come at a price.

Standards around influencer content funded by advertisers are essential. Influencers need these to be credible (the content creators we interviewed for the next chapter are acutely aware of this), and advertisers need them to be adopted whole-heartedly to be confident in the investment they make and the plans they have to increase it.

The work both of trade bodies like the Influencer Marketing Trade Body, ISBA and of the self-regulatory system is critical. With the funding to back the development of professional standards with an agreed cross-border approach, there's no doubt this hugely exciting and innovative space will offer new, trusted storytelling opportunities to advertisers that deliver compelling returns.

If this is an area of interest to you, and you value trust in any work you commission (which we hope you do), stay close to developments like the ISBA and IMTB Code of Conduct, the Codes of Advertising Practice and the CMA's work.

Notes

1 Share of marketing budgets spent on influencer marketing according to marketers and industry leaders worldwide as of January 2025, January 2025, Statista, www.statista.com/statistics/268641/share-of-marketing-budgets-spent-on-digital-worldwide/ (archived at https://perma.cc/Z5C4-W37E)

2 Influencer advertising spending in the United Kingdom from 2019 to 2030, Statista, February 2025, www.statista.com/forecasts/1445521/influencer-advertising-spending-uk (archived at https://perma.cc/AH3A-YAY6)

3 About the Influencer Marketing Trade Body, https://imtb.org.uk/ (archived at https://perma.cc/K77P-3VEJ)

4 M Stassen, Global recorded music revenues hit $29.6bn in 2024, up 4.8% YoY; users of paid music subscriptions reach 752m, Music Business Worldwide, March 2025, www.musicbusinessworldwide.com/global-recorded-music-revenues-hit-29-6bn-in-2024-up-4-8-yoy-users-of-paid-music-subscriptions-reach-752m/ (archived at https://perma.cc/QM2P-T9UF)

5 Box Office Mojo, IMDb Pro, www.boxofficemojo.com/year/?area=XWW&grossesOption=totalGrosses (archived at https://perma.cc/X2CQ-AXMB)

6 Statista, Influencer Advertising – Worldwide, 2025, www.statista.com/outlook/amo/advertising/influencer-advertising/worldwide (archived at https://perma.cc/XDN5-E3AC)

7 M Iskiev, The 2025 State of Marketing & Trends Report: Data from 1700+ global marketers, Hubspot, June 2024, https://blog.hubspot.com/marketing/hubspot-blog-marketing-industry-trends-report (archived at https://perma.cc/U3G3-HYYC)

8 WFA, More than half of multinational brands plan to boost influencer market spend, March 2025, www.wfanet.org/knowledge/item/2025/03/27/more-than-half-of-multinational-brands-plan-to-boost-influencer-market-spend (archived at https://perma.cc/9NK3-B4R6)

9 Barclays: Fireside chat with Fernando Fernandez, CEO, Unilever, March 2025, www.unilever.com/investors/results-presentations-webcasts/barclays-fireside-chat-with-fernando-fernandez-ceo/ (archived at https://perma.cc/3RJZ-EZMJ)

10 The Economist, Too many people want to be social-media influencers, October 2024, www.economist.com/business/2024/10/29/too-many-people-want-to-be-social-media-influencers (archived at https://perma.cc/SQR2-LDWK)

11 Mintel, Personal connections on social media drive more consumer purchases than influencers, Mintel research reveals, September 2023, www.mintel.com/press-centre/personal-connections-on-social-media-influence-consumer-purchase-mintel-research-reveals/ (archived at https://perma.cc/L44P-6MKR)

12 GoDaddy, End of word-of-mouth advertising? GoDaddy data shows Gen Z trusts influencers more than friends, October 2024, www.prnewswire.com/news-releases/end-of-word-of-mouth-advertising-godaddy-data-shows-gen-z-trusts-influencers-more-than-friends-302279022.html (archived at https://perma.cc/R824-PHWZ)

13   Morning Consult Pro Report: How brands can succeed at influencer marketing, September 2023, https://pro.morningconsult.com/analyst-reports/influencer-marketing-trends-report (archived at https://perma.cc/7VP8-F7JH)

14   Morning Consult Pro, Influencers aren't going anywhere, and their power is expanding, October 2024, https://pro.morningconsult.com/analysis/influencers-content-creators-evolving-power-2024 (archived at https://perma.cc/B8T5-J3Y3)

15   Izea, UK Trust in Influencer Marketing, June 2024, www.dropbox.com/scl/fi/9t5xc98ufla0lzgl303zu/IZEA-Insights-Trust-in-Influencer-Marketing-UK-2024-1.pdf?rlkey=jsenj6qbx02ak1qc9vjrruqpe&e=1&dl=0 (archived at https://perma.cc/92E5-X3VU)

16   Morning Consult Pro, Influencers aren't going anywhere, and their power is expanding, October 2024, https://pro.morningconsult.com/analysis/influencers-content-creators-evolving-power-2024 (archived at https://perma.cc/B8T5-J3Y3)

17   Goldman Sachs, The creator economy could approach half-a-trillion dollars by 2027, April 2023, www.goldmansachs.com/insights/articles/the-creator-economy-could-approach-half-a-trillion-dollars-by-2027 (archived at https://perma.cc/A4HS-MH69)

18   Linktree, The 2022 Creator Report, https://linktr.ee/creator-report/static/Linktree-CreatorReport-2022-02f3aa05a27be6fecb3537b13d5ec9de.pdf (archived at https://perma.cc/449G-CR99)

19   The Keller Advisory Group, Creators uncovered: Insights from a nationally representative study of us creators, November 2023, www.keller-advisory.com/creators-uncovered-insights-from-a-nationally-representative-study-of-uscreators (archived at https://perma.cc/4WPJ-A5Q9)

20   'The voices that matter': Unilever recruits an army of influencers, Rupert Neate, *The Times*, 17 March 2025, www.thetimes.com/article/f117e467-f21f-4b9c-8806-6e74e0238fae (archived at https://perma.cc/W7PP-NJEG)

21   ISBA/IMTB Influencer Marketing Code of Conduct, March 2025, https://imtb.org.uk/influencer-marketing-code-of-conduct/ (archived at https://perma.cc/S3UU-ENF7)

22   IMTB, Reassure, https://imtb.org.uk/reassure/ (archived at https://perma.cc/K587-GUSD)

23   IMTB, REASSURE, https://imtb.org.uk/reassure/ (archived at https://perma.cc/K587-GUSD)

24   IMTB, Hidden advertising, https://imtb.org.uk/hidden-advertising/ (archived at https://perma.cc/53CD-MSQS)

25   Influencer Ad Disclosure on Social Media: Instagram and TikTok Report (2024), Advertising Standards Authority, May 2025, www.asa.org.uk/news/influencer-ad-disclosure-on-social-media-instagram-and-tiktok-report-2024.html (archived at https://perma.cc/6N4Z-6NSQ)

07

Trust in the age of the influencer: Part 2

Introduction

While regulators, trade bodies and business leaders seek to ensure the burgeoning influencer marketing sector develops responsibly, the people making it happen are moving ahead.

In this chapter, we're going to share our conversations with people from three agencies operating in this sector and with two creators, and consider work by leading brands demonstrating the benefits of trusted influencer campaigns.

Their experience, views and policies are forging the new world of influencer advertising at speed and, as we learned, they have strong and valuable perspectives on trust.

Nurture trust with content creators like you're a gardener

Emma Harman is President, EMEA, of Whalar Group, a global creator company, and Co-Chair of the Influencer Marketing Trade Body (IMTB).[1] With a background in the music industry, where she worked with talent including Amy Winehouse, Girls Aloud and Craig David, she is now a passionate advocate for the UK's creator economy.

She describes content creators as world-builders and believes that this growing group of talents are distinct from influencers and celebrities. To Harman, content creators are constantly building their audiences, forever exploring new ways to connect and engage with them, and she advises brands 'to leave their shoes at the door' when considering how best to work with them.

Central to the 'trust' offered by content creators to brands is that often these people are customers themselves, says Harman. Their own experiences of a brand help shape the content they can produce about it to connect in authentic ways to its audience. Accessing this 'trust' requires a specific approach and Harman likens it to gardening. 'You have to nurture it,' she explains, clear that brands can't just sponsor culture, they have to be in it. The best analogy, she says, is to think about how you might integrate a product into a TV show for it to appear in a meaningful way. You achieve this by building true partnerships, she advises. Meet with content creators and work with them in collaborative ways to help decode your brands' big idea into social media channels.

Harman is dismissive of those who lament the passing of advertising's 'golden age' of the big idea, arguing that the most exciting, culturally resonant creativity is now happening on social media. In response, Whalar is expanding its bench of creatives and cultural strategists to help brands harness this momentum, embedding them deeper into creator communities and culture at large.

She points to how social media platforms – TikTok, Instagram, YouTube, Snap, even LinkedIn – are rapidly recognizing and encouraging content creators because of the engagement power offered by the entertaining content they bring to the platforms. All the platforms are waking up to creators, she argues; marketers need to invest in the creator economy, which she describes as the future of content, commerce and search.

MAKING THE CASE FOR CREATORS AND TRUST

By Emma Harman, Whalar Group

These research papers and reports help Whalar make the case for content creators as an increasingly important part of a trusted purchasing journey for today's customers.

ENDERS ANALYSIS: CONSUMERS, CREATORS, AND BRANDS – REWRITING THE MEDIA PLAYBOOK, (2025)[2]
This report speaks directly to the topic of trust and creators. In particular we note:

- The rise of creator-led media is not just a result of format innovation (e.g. TikTok-style short video) – it's a product of a multi-dimensional trust economy.

FIGURE 7.1 Enders analysis: multi-dimensional trust economy model

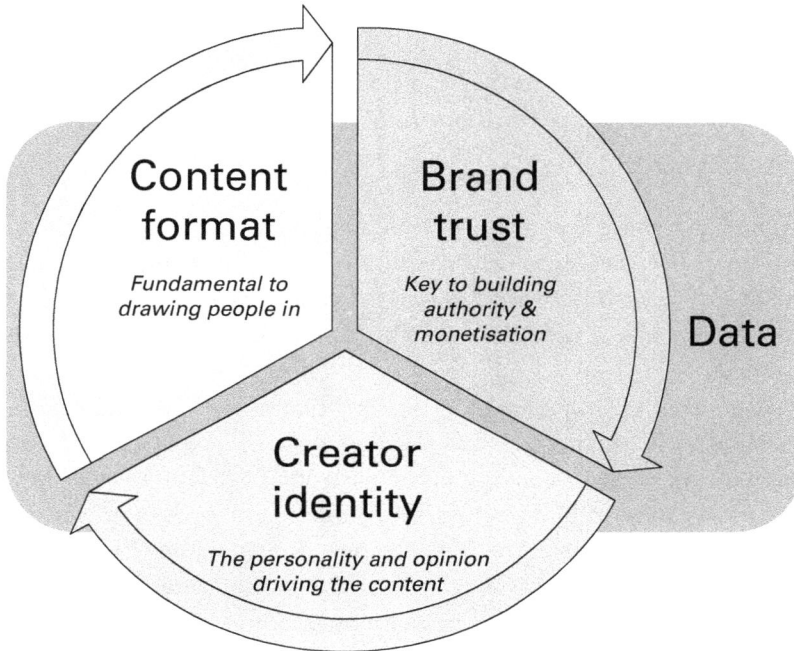

- At its core are four interdependent pillars:

  o **Content quality:** high quality, relevant and original content earns credibility even when people are unfamiliar with the brand, acting as a point of entry to trust.

  o **Creator identity:** relatable, consistent and opinionated voices create para-social relationships with their audience to build trust.

  o **Brand trust:** if a brand is already trusted, it helps a creator grow faster and audiences are more open to trying content when they know where it's coming from.

  o **Smart use of data:** all of this is underpinned by data and audience understanding which is critical for a sustainable content strategy.

2022 EDELMAN TRUST BAROMETER: THE NEW CASCADE OF INFLUENCE[3]
This global research report looked at the impact of creators on consumer behaviour, including that:

- 67% of consumers trust the creators they follow that talk about, review and recommend brands and products.

ARCHIVAL X VOUGE: GEN Z BROKE THE MARKETING FUNNEL (2024)[4]

This US market report explored how brands can cut through the noise online, in particular with younger customers, and found:

- The research phase is crucial for brand trust: 70% of Gen Zs and 69% of millennials only trust a brand after carrying out their own research.

Harman believes we are only just beginning to realize the size, significance and potential of the UK's creator economy. Whalar's clients are allocating from 2–5 per cent of ad spend to content creators and she expects budget levels to increase by 15–20 per cent in 2025, with spend on an upward trend from there.

The content creator economy works because we trust humans, and humans are at the heart of this development, she concludes. Harman's passion for the creator economy, particularly for UK talent, extends beyond her work at Whalar. She believes much more can be done to champion content creators as part of the UK's creative industries and that we need to move fast to keep pace with the US. This growing collection of UK talent is forging new ways to build 'soft power' on the world stage, drawing in big international viewing figures for UK creative content. A new export sector, it needs the backing of marketers and the UK government to fully deliver on its potential.

THREE KEY TAKEAWAYS

1   Nurture your content creators as you would your most important customers.

2   Properly invest in partnerships with the content creators most important to your brand.

3   Ask how can your brand be a valuable part of the world they are building.

The rising importance of authenticity

In the age of the influencer, trust is synonymous with authenticity, according to Dafydd Woodward, Global Chief Operating Officer, Goat, a global influencer marketing agency acquired by WPP in 2023.[5,6] That trust factor is challenged every day by clients who seek influencers to make content for them, because the content must be true to the influencer themselves, as well as to the brand. Woodward stresses that if the brand/influencer/content relationship doesn't fit, it won't appear authentic, and then it won't work.

He observes that protecting this authenticity is hard, that there have always been grey areas of trust in advertising, and that this is due to the constant evolution of advertising and media. Changes in the way people consume media, increasingly on social media platforms from influencers, brings different grey areas for trust in advertising.

To tackle that problem, every influencer that Goat works with is contracted to ensure content is properly disclosed as advertising and meets regulatory standards. His team is seeing increasing success with what he describes as influencer-first content, advertising produced and published by the influencer, then supported through paid promotion to bring it to a bigger audience. The influencer's number of followers, which once drove client selection, is now a secondary consideration to the quality of their content.

Goat has worked with tens of thousands of influencers using a range of tools to filter them for its client portfolio, which numbers in the hundreds. Woodward's view is that brands used to be wary of influencers, wary of platforms and wary of brand safety issues, but the sector has now moved beyond the point of no return as an effective channel. With AI-assisted discovery platforms filtering the millions of influencer profiles in their databases, and with the ability to better verify authentic creators, the guardrails are in place.

He described the agency's role as ensuring that the influencer environment is a safe place, so although the risk of using influencers may be 'non-zero' when compared to other channels, the return on investment is worth it as regulation and standards worldwide improve. As we looked ahead, he described what he sees as the next frontier for trust as to how the industry deals with AI-generated content, and the threat of bad actors undermining the credibility of real profiles and real content. It is possible for bad actors to game the system, he suggested, to build a community for the sole purpose of selling around it, but if there is a sniff of inauthenticity, it simply won't work.

The days of celebrities posting pre-scripted promotional messages are long gone, with that approach providing zero value for brands. He warns it is still easy to get it wrong, to produce something that is blatantly inauthentic, but then beware the size of the subsequent PR job to unwind that damage to trust.

To protect against this, he sees a pyramid developing, with more and more influencers working through talent management companies. At the apex, the most successful will have managers and lawyers, too, while micro-influencers (50,000 followers or fewer) will require more direct management, and the broad base of nano-influencers will deal as individuals. Risk-averse brands will choose to work with influencers that are established and have built trust with brands.

As our conversation drew to a close, Woodward returned to the crucial importance of human authenticity for brands when developing their advertising campaigns: content that genuinely delivers on that human-to-human connection. While he acknowledges a position of bias, he believes the industry spends way below the level of investment warranted – if you were to map spend against the attention levels influencers now receive, the investment is in the wrong places.

He argues that brands will shift more and more money to invest in authentic connections, and that budgets for influencer marketing will continue to increase as influencer-first content grows in wider advertising campaigns.

THREE KEY TAKEAWAYS

1 Authenticity is everything when it comes to trust, influencers and how your brand benefits from the human-to-human connection.

2 Using influencers isn't 100% risk-free; knowing and following the regulations and standards is essential.

3 The most important consideration is the quality of an influencer's content, not necessarily their audience size.

The influencer marketing equation doesn't work without trust

People trust people more than they trust advertising. For Ogilvy's Global Head of Influence, Rahul Titus, this sweet spot of trust in people is clear, with influencer content consistently outperforming brand-made content.[7] When we spoke to him, he was quick to point to case study after case study of this; the underlying reason for Ogilvy's influencer division being the fastest growing part of the business.

Perhaps the most surprising example of this was work the team did for Google around the launch of its Pixel 9 phone.[8] This was a social-first campaign, backed with ad spend featuring content from creators unboxing their new phones. The team spotted one lone TikTok creator – @new4andy – posting about how she was alone with her noodles watching everyone else unbox their phone and quickly responded. Her subsequent post featuring the new phone in a custom-designed instant noodle box generated 40 million views in three days and led to significant brand uplift.

Coca-Cola's 'Recipe For Magic' campaign was built around a 30-second TV ad spot just three years ago.[9] Now, the stories of enjoying a meal with a Coca-Cola are told by thousands of influencers worldwide, with a majority of the ad spend on this theme going to them. Titus points to L'Oreal, too, which works with tens of thousands of influencers in the UK alone, and to how the Cannes Grand Prix winning campaign for CeraVe, with Michael Cera, was built as a social-first, influencer-driven campaign.

One of the key reasons for this, he argues, beyond the clear trust difference, is the speed of production, the possibility to respond to what he describes as 'the speed of culture'. His advice to any brand looking to engage in a popular culture moment is to act within 24 hours or move on. By then, it's too late and won't look authentic.

This pace demands new ways of working with clients, Titus says, requiring a different kind of trust between advertiser and agency with faster response times and more fluid budgets to make advertising work. All informed by a sophisticated 'social intelligence engine' which understand cultures and can identify the next viral moment to make the most of. He stresses the importance of craft, but says advertisers need to be open to what he describes as 'lo-fi content', where the brand isn't necessarily apparent, templates are deployed, big ugly fonts are writ large, because all these elements make this the content that works the best. Remember, 80 per cent of the content on platforms is by creators, Titus points out, with most of it in this lo-fi style – it is this type of advertising content, one to one, that appears to be a POV from a friend which makes that all-important connection. Again, Titus returns to the word 'craft' but says this is now about beautiful thumb-stopping content that works in a one-to-one environment, and points to brands like Burberry as leading the way.

We asked Titus about the risks involved for advertisers when it comes trust and, like others, he admitted brands are not as in control, but that Ogilvy (and WPP) has strict contracts in places with all the influencers involved, with ID, background and even compatibility checks around world view, to mitigate and manage the risk. To him, this is already a highly regulated sector, because trust is so intrinsically important.

If you remove trust from the influencer marketing equation, it won't work, he says; trust is that fundamental. It's why AI disclosure is so important, and it's why Ogilvy has always made sure influencers they work with do not digitally distort their body or face. For the same fundamental reason: trust.

If you want to win in today's culture, this is how, concludes Titus. He sees a fundamental change in the business model of advertising as we know it, with the democratization of creativity at the centre, a revolution fostered by the success of TikTok. With rapid measurement of results, testing and boosting the most effective, performance can be dramatic. At the same time, anything inauthentic is called out in what Titus describes as our industry's fast feedback loop. He goes as far as to say that 'Authenticity is the one thing we have to sell' and urges clients to 'let go' and trust the creators. They know their communities – not followers any longer – and know a wrong choice by them for a brand will antagonize the community. Ogilvy, he said, is like a WeWork for entrepreneurs, connecting the dots to the brands.

THREE KEY TAKEAWAYS

1 Working with influencers requires a much faster pace of content creation and approval from you and your brand.

2 Full and proper disclosure is essential to maintaining trust, including any use of technology to change body or face.

3 The lo-fi 'craft' of influencer content may differ in perceived quality to that for your brand in other advertising channels.

Advertising in the influencer age

Billion Dollar Boy is a global creator agency offering data and insight, strategy, creative, social content production, paid media and campaign management. We spoke with Thomas Walters, founder and CEO, Europe, about how the company was formed in 2014, at the outset of this new evolution for advertisers.[10]

Companion, its AI-powered creator marketing platform, is central to Billion Dollar Boy's offering. It helps the company discover and vet new creators, track influencer content and generate instant campaign reports for clients. The team draws information from its database of more than 130 million influencers around the world, and curates their own detailed databases to help pre-qualify influencers likely to be compliant with the requirements of the advertiser. It is critical, for example, if you are an alcohol brand, to know that any influencer you partner with will follow the rules of alcohol marketing set by the industry and regulators in any given market.

While the company originally managed influencer talent, that service posed a perceived conflict of interest with their responsibility to make impartial recommendations for client campaigns. Now, in addition to working directly with brands to deliver influencer marketing campaigns, it bridges the gap with talent through its Talent Partnerships team, which focuses on building and maintaining creator relationships.

Walters noted that avoiding advertising is increasingly easy, so the job is to create content that people really want to watch.

The challenge here is to get the balance right between people watching creators' content because they love their work and ensuring that any commercial content feels natural and authentic so it can be trusted. When it comes to trust, there are regulations in every market and he believes the standards for influencers are often higher than they are for celebrities who use their fame to promote products and services, something we are going to explore further through interviews with content creators.

He shared more about the Companion platform and how it helps to ensure the agency recommends the right influencer(s) for client campaigns. Key criteria fit into three areas: cultural fit between brand and influencer and community; safety over sensitive areas, for example profanity, nudity or political views; and effectiveness, i.e. the scale and reach that the influencer offers.

All of this then helps shape a list for client review, flagging any risk factors.

Such due diligence is central to the selection of influencers the advertiser can trust to communicate on their behalf to their communities.

As with any media partner, a successful campaign by an advertiser which enlists the support of one or more influencers will be built on a relationship of trust between the two parties. Billion Dollar Boy, like other agencies in the sector, seeks to aid that process to deliver a trusted and successful relationship.

To help us understand that process more, we spoke to Sophie Crowther, Billion Dollar Boy's Talent Partnership Director, who has worked at the heart of the creator economy for more than 10 years, about what she has learned when it comes to trust, advertising and content creators.[11]

INTERVIEW WITH SOPHIE CROWTHER, TALENT PARTNERSHIP
DIRECTOR, BILLION DOLLAR BOY

*How do you ensure that the brand-funded content (advertising) that you
commission as an agency from creators can be trusted?*

Transparency in posts is not only important for building trust but also required.
Billion Dollar Boy has contracts in place with every single content creator that
we work with for client campaigns. The contracts state that creator partners will
always disclose when a social post is paid for by a brand. In addition to this, the
creator must follow local laws and regulations set by the industry in whatever
territory the content is running. This might be the UK's Advertising Standards
Authority or similar bodies elsewhere. Sometimes the standards we must set go
further. For example, when it comes to advertising alcohol brands, content
must be appropriately age gated to ensure audiences are of the legal age to
view alcohol advertising; this varies across markets, but it is our responsibility
to adhere to these laws and ensure our creator partners do the same. In
addition to advising our creator partners on regulations, our team also closely
monitors content output to ensure everything is fully compliant.

*Can you share your views on how this sector of the creative industries, which
is competing hard for a share of advertising spend, has evolved?*

Let's remember it's still a very young and quickly maturing business sector. The
content creator, a term that evolved from the broader, catch-all term
'influencer', is perhaps even more nascent. On top of that, there is no union
representing creators in the sector, but it is fast-growing, and the career is
becoming more professionalized. It's a hugely important and credible way for
people to find informative and entertaining content about all kinds of things.

A decade ago, brands leveraged creators more as a media channel – a way to
directly access their loyal audiences with their messaging. Today, with the true
establishment of the creator economy, creators have expanded far beyond content
creation. They're launching their own brands – our own research has found that
the vast majority (88 per cent) have already launched their own product or
service.[12] They're also breaking into entertainment, with creator-led productions
on the rise and rivalling some of the biggest TV shows. This is especially true as
YouTube now holds the second-largest share of viewership compared to other
major media conglomerates like Netflix and Hulu. The line is blurring between
YouTube influencers and traditional entertainers. Take for example The Sidemen's
charity football match held at Wembley Stadium, which garnered 90,000
attendees, 2.5 million live viewers and £4.7 million raised. All of this shows how
much the creator economy has evolved and is shaping mainstream culture.

Additionally, the standards set by regulators, like the ASA in the UK, are strong but there's a need to regularly update the guidelines as the industry evolves, and everyone, including content creators, brands and agencies, should hold a responsibility to follow those standards. There are also challenges with different standards depending on the part of the world that you are making content for, with different regulations around advertising needed in Asia than, say, for the UK. Or some gaps in what is deemed as an ad, for example the payment for music clips to be used in the background of content, without a declaration that the music company is paying for the content creator to do that. Technically this is a paid promotion, but it isn't transparent with audiences.

What more should the advertising industry do to build trust in content creators and the work they produce for brands?

We need to establish infrastructure to protect all major players in the creator economy, and support the fact that creator careers are becoming more professionalized. The more the industry invests in creators' growth, wellbeing and professional development, the more their careers will be respected, taken seriously and trusted. But it takes the whole industry to lift them up. There are so many diverse, talented content creators, but not a clear path forward for growth or a solid infrastructure to guide them, which is difficult to navigate. We need to do more to support their work, and the industry is slowly shifting in this direction. Instead of one-off creator campaigns, we're seeing more long-term partnerships with creators, and brands are joining in to invest in their profession. For example, our FiveTwoNine business – a community designed to support creators in business – is gaining a ton of interest from creators across the UK and the US. Creators crave support as they navigate this role and look to grow, and more brands are beginning to contribute through FiveTwoNine – offering expert consultations with creators, insights, educational materials, and more.[13] Creators crave support as they navigate this role and look to grow, and more brands are beginning to contribute through FiveTwoNine – offering expert consultations with creators, insights, educational materials, and more.

The content creator view: tips on building trust through advertiser-funded content

In our journey to understand the dynamics of trust for content creators in the advertising that they make, we also interviewed two creative professionals established in the UK: Keith Afadi and Em Wallbank, who both work with Billion Dollar Boy.

Keith Afadi, Content Creator

A triangle of trust

Keith Afadi, a content creator with a passion for the art of filmmaking and a background in advertising, believes that trust is an integral part of his work: "I am putting my reputation on the line with every post, so any content must be about things I believe in. If a creator doesn't trust the brand itself, it becomes very obvious very quickly.'[14]

He described a 'triangle of trust' which exists between him, his community and the brand. Any content must respect that. Afadi believes this is a new form of advertising, where the brand-funded content that he makes must be content that is catered to the community and is content that they're interested in consuming.

There is a fundamental difference between audience and community for Afadi. Brands aren't 'buying my audience', they are working with him to create content that is in tune with his personal values and the values of his community. He is not interested in doing anything which could diminish the trust his community has in him. He knows that people will tell him straight if he gets it wrong.

He cited an example of an alcohol brand that approached him, though he rarely drinks alcohol. It was a high-end champagne brand, and the subsequent storytelling technique was not about the taste or quality but about integrating the brand into his routine, preparing for a glamorous night out, something true to his own lifestyle. Due to the focus on incorporating the brand into his lifestyle, the collaboration was a success.

His approach is to try to always connect with people as individuals; they're not just a name and a location. He described the difference as always seeking to have a conversation with his community, rather than simply having an audience that responds with a comment, good or bad, and the craft is in how he involves the brand in the conversation.

To a large extent, his ask to brands seeking to work with him is 'let me do what I want', as that will probably work best. Creators know their community best and having creative flexibility will help the creator marry the brand with the audience in an authentic, successful way.

He stressed the importance of being aware of, and adhering to, the guidance set by the advertising regulator, in his case the UK's ASA, but observed that levels of compliance vary across different categories of advertising. For example, there is high compliance in the tech sector but, he believes, much lower in fashion. His take was that, because the content is obviously marked as 'advertising', the content has to work harder, be more creative, and catch and hold people's attention even more. And his experience is that people hold creators more accountable than other forms of advertising like TV, with the authenticity of the storytelling paramount.

He also shared the view that 'anyone can speak to anyone now'. This is a powerful encapsulation of the new advertising world we see emerging, a world in which the power to communicate has been democratized. We are living through a period of rapid evolution for the content creator, which as a profession may still be very much in its infancy, but whose impact is increasingly apparent.

Emma Wallbank, Content Creator

The more you share, the more trusted you are

'People aren't stupid. Content creators aren't beamed down from space to make ads. We need to treat consumers like geniuses.' Em Wallbank is a content creator known for comedic content, including her impersonations of famous characters like Harry Potter's adversary Draco Malfoy.[15] At the time of writing this book, Wallbank was marking two years working as a full-time creator in the sector. She described being a content creator as someone who occupies the middle ground between celebrity and the public, offering accessibility into their life. With that accessibility comes huge accountability. Her followers are not shy in criticizing content not deemed to be authentic or genuine – content that isn't trusted.

Her view is that social media is generally used as a billboard right now, in limited ways, and there is massive untapped creative potential. She points to some of her favourite TV commercials – Sheila's Wheels, Cadbury's Gorilla – as examples of ads that are more than just a straight branded sales message. Made by content creators, they have the potential to create the same impact with the communities they serve. However, to get the creative right, the content must be believable, something that people will genuinely trust. She fears for the credibility of a creator who confesses to making a piece of content just for the money, no matter how competitive things might be or how tough it is to generate a regular income.

For Wallbank, previously a care worker, becoming a content creator after the Covid lockdown was her way of entering the creative industries. She views herself as working at the nexus of the media, entertainment and advertising sectors. She's a one-person content production studio who has gone as far as making her own sets and costumes in order to make content that will entertain her community. In just two short years as a content creator, she has self-developed skills to feedback on brand briefs and write scripts. Her understanding is that the major tech platforms are looking for ways to answer the growing demand for short-form video content, which, in part, explains the rise of content creators.

Unlike an established media owner, she has no limit on ad content versus editorial content. There are no scheduled ad breaks in her content, signalling when to expect a brand message. Instead, her view of ad-funded content is that it must always be genuinely entertaining, to keep that trusted connection with her community. There's no gain making a piece of ad-funded content that isn't up to her best standards.

She also talked about the need for maximum self-awareness to protect and maintain the trust that people have in her. Her advice is that content creators have to be aware of the news, now and in the future, and always be forward-thinking to 'protect the future you'. A view expressed in a post in 2025 might just be used against you in 2027.

When Wallbank gets a brief, her starting point is to ask, 'what is the most creative thing I can do while achieving the client's goals?' In her case, as a comedian, she also asks, 'how can I use humour to maximize effectiveness?' In return, she asks brands to remember why she has the followers that she has, to trust her curation of that relationship and to believe that the content she makes on their behalf will resonate.

When it comes to trust, she believes the more you share, the more trusted you are. She has been offered (but turned down) all kinds of health and beauty treatments offered for free in return for posts, not only because it's against the rules to post without promotional disclosure, but more importantly because it would undermine the trust her followers have in her. She warned against difficulties content creators are facing generally. Firstly, that regulatory standards vary for content creators around the world, and secondly the risk of some content creators not meeting the standards needed to maintain trust in this newly emerging profession.

Building trust with influencers and new audiences

Finally, we're going to turn to a brand and look at its work with influencers.

TUI, the travel company, has been steadily increasing its investment in influencers, most notably through its work with TV presenter Davina McCall to promote TUI BLUE.[16] We spoke with Hayley Shortman, Senior Influencer Marketing Manager, about the company's most recent work with influencers to help build trust and engagement with disabled customers and, by doing so, increase accessibility to holidays abroad for this customer base and help open up a bigger market for the company.[17]

Shortman shared how the use of influencers helped the company show through lived experience what the holidays were truly like and that, while the campaign had less reach in terms of audience size, it provided much more powerful results in terms of customer trust and engagement.

REAL-WORLD EXAMPLE
TUI accessible holidays influencer campaign

Navigating the world of disability can often feel daunting and the fear of 'getting it wrong' has often held TUI back from publicly discussing the company's capabilities for disabled customers. With 24 per cent of the UK population classified as disabled, TUI set out to drive awareness and consideration of its accessible holiday offering whilst supporting the disabled community to feel more confident when they travel.[18] The TUI customer experience team had recently launched a partnership with AccessAble, providing hotel guides to support the decision-making process for disabled customers and it was now time for a campaign to take the proposition further.

TUI's creative briefs were built on insights from a survey conducted by Purple Goat, aiming to understand the barriers to travel for people with disabilities, both for TUI and the overall industry, and addressing these with the social media content produced. TUI chose relevant influencers for the story to be told as authentically as possible, documenting their experiences and sharing more personal and emotive stories that would resonate and build trust amongst disabled communities. The influencers selected represented a variety of accessible needs (wheelchair users, deaf/hard of hearing, blind/visually impaired, neurodivergent, diabetic/chronic illness) who TUI then paired with the most suitable hotels to accommodate their needs and ensure they had positive and memorable experiences.

TUI ensured that the influencers experienced the same level of service as other customers. Each influencer had a call with TUI's assisted travel team ahead of their trip to ensure their needs were catered for and they experienced elements such as TUI retail stores and its partnership with SignLive to see how customers would go about booking a TUI holiday with assisted travel requirements.

Each influencer posted one Reel focused on their holiday highlights, and one Reel on how they booked their holiday through TUI. The videos were placed in this order so the viewer could connect to the happy moments first, leading to learning how to book an accessible holiday with TUI in the following Reel. Content was posted ahead of the summer holiday period to place TUI front of mind for both new and existing customers for booking their next accessible holiday. Influencers also posted on Instagram Stories throughout their trips, a natural placement to share updates and daily moments on holiday, as well as highlighting some specific accessible features. TUI chose Meta as its preferred posting channel due to its larger existing audience base and their high awareness of TUI.

The campaign's performance was outstanding, generating high levels of engagement and positive sentiment, doubling the rate of searches for TUI accessible holidays and driving up TUI's ratings and consideration scores across all ages.

It's a great example of an influencer campaign of genuine authenticity and empathy. It brought a particular audience with complex needs into a new understanding of TUI's carefully designed proposition, combining the qualities of competence, integrity and benevolence to build overall trust.

Trust, mobile phones and intimacy

Meta, along with CreativeX and Kantar, published a new report which used AI to understand how to best achieve creative effectiveness on Meta's main platforms.[19] The research reviewed three years of data; 56,984 creatives, 1,295 campaigns, 13.1 billion impressions from five countries across three continents on Facebook and Instagram advertising for apparel, automotive, beauty products, food and beverage, and restaurants.

What's pertinent about this report is how it began by considering the uniqueness of the mobile device as a platform for commercial messages. The researchers described an interpersonal environment which has profoundly altered the way an advertiser can strike up intimacy and immediacy with individuals.

The research goes into more detail about intimacy and that human connection – the power of what they describe as the 'human vibe' to connect.

When we reflect on earlier areas we've covered in this book – that people trust people, the movement of trust from top-down to sideways, the thirst for 'authenticity' – it's clear how the strength of the influencer channel is enabled by this one-to-one, hugely personal mode of communication.

Also, it's a reminder of how important it is that people delivering advertising messages as influencers can be trusted to declare commercial interests and ensure what they are promoting is legal, decent, honest and truthful.

Conclusion

We've seen that the influencer – and of course creator – sector is growing fast. And it's growing up fast, too. It was heartening to hear from our interviewees just how seriously they take the maintenance of hard-earned trust, for the benefit of both advertisers and the influencers themselves. They appreciate the value of the authenticity, affinity and strong personal relationships that they bring to their communities and so to advertisers. As agency or individual professionals in the new space, they are well aware of their responsibilities.

Of course, our interviewees are at the pinnacle of the business. Their sense of – and focus on – their responsibility to be trustworthy is something that needs to become the norm for the millions of influencers across the world, many of them younger, newer to the business, less familiar with the needs of audiences and business partners, or less caring.

Without that security, brands will not continue to grow their investment as scrutiny and regulatory pressures increase.

This growth in interest in influencers seems central to the whole question about what's happening to trust in the 21st century. Influencers embody the idea of distributed trust; they provide the personal affinity that leads people to feel their content is authentic. Creators, more and more, also illustrate the first driver of trust we saw in Chapter 4 – the power of enjoyable, relatable, engaging advertising content.

There is a lot of work still to be done for the whole market to be as worthy of trust and respect as those to whom we spoke (remember the ASA stats we shared in the previous chapter), but the future of the channel depends on it.

For you, and your brand, it's almost certain that you will be engaging with influencers as an important way of building business based on trust in your brand.

We hope these two chapters have helped to set the expectations of how you manage that important relationship with an influencer to ensure the unique trust benefits offered by this channel are fully protected and realized.

Notes

1 Author interview with Emma Harman, Whalar Group, April 2025
2 Consumers, creators, and brands: Rewriting the media playbook, Enders Analysis, May 2025, www.endersanalysis.com/reports/consumers-creators-and-brands-rewriting-media-playbook (archived at https://perma.cc/23P4-EVCU)
3 2022 Edelman Trust Barometer: The New Cascade of Influence, Edelman, www.edelman.com/trust/2022-trust-barometer/special-report-new-cascade-of-influence (archived at https://perma.cc/9QTD-EJC4)
4 Gen Z broke the marketing funnel, Vogue Business, 2024, www.voguebusiness.com/story/consumers/gen-z-broke-the-marketing-funnel (archived at https://perma.cc/THJ6-QPQE)
5 Author interview with Dafydd Woodward, Goat, April 2025
6 WPP acquires data driven influencer marketing agency Goat, WPP, March 2023, www.wpp.com/en/news/2023/03/wpp-acquires-data-driven-influencer-marketing-agency-goat (archived at https://perma.cc/X6XD-PA5G)
7 Author interview with Rahul Titus, Ogilvy, March 2025
8 Jennifer Adetoro, LinkedIn post, September 2024, www.linkedin.com/posts/jenniferadetoro_google-pixel-just-helped-a-creator-go-viral-activity-7236644173041274882-KbK_/ (archived at https://perma.cc/M89Z-UTAB)
9 Coca-Cola Recipe for Magic, www.coca-cola.com/xe/en/offerings/coke-with-meals-recipe-for-magic (archived at https://perma.cc/W5FK-FNVS)
10 Author interview with Thomas Walters, Billion Dollar Boy, January 2025
11 Author interview with Sophie Crowther, Billion Dollar Boy, February 2025
12 Billion Dollar Boy, Creator Entrepreneurs on the rise with two-thirds of consumers buying creator-founded products and services, October 2024, www.billiondollarboy.com/news/creator-entrepreneurs-on-the-rise/ (archived at https://perma.cc/ZU8R-SHVF)
13 About FiveTwoNine, www.fivetwonine.com/ (archived at https://perma.cc/T9L5-97LA)
14 Author interview with Keith Afadi, February 2025
15 Author interview with Em Wallbank, February 2025
16 TUI, Davina McCall suns herself in Turkey whilst road testing Tui Blue's new Wellness menu, June 2022, www.tui.co.uk/press/davina-mccall-suns-herself-in-turkey-whilst-road-testing-tui-blues-new-wellness-menu/ (archived at https://perma.cc/4QSJ-TVMC)

17 Author interview with Hayley Shortman, May 2025

18 TUI Accessible Holidays Case Study, provided by TUI

19 A new era of storytelling: Inspiration for today's brands, AdAge, November 2024, https://adage.com/white-paper/new-era-storytelling-inspiration-todays-brands (archived at https://perma.cc/R7GL-A4LM)

08

Can advertising generated by AI be trusted?

Introduction

This is probably one of the hardest, if not the hardest, chapter to write in this book.

AI's impact on our lives generally is yet to be fully understood. Views lurch from Terminator-style doomsday predictions to a world where all problems are solved, from health to climate change, and nobody needs to work anymore. Whatever the outcomes, there's no doubt this is another revolution, though, akin to the industrial revolution, with the potential to eclipse the revolution of the internet and mobile we have already lived through. That said, society does have a track record of panic when a new information technology arrives in our lives, dating back to the printing presses, the advent of radio and the 'magic' of TV in our homes, let alone the internet, so we shall try to take a cool, considered look at AI.

What it means for advertising and the people who work in it is still to be determined, but transformative uses of AI to plan, create, distribute, track and measure advertising are emerging, along with a new set of challenges in ensuring it can be trusted.

What we write is very much based on the knowledge we have now. Things will change, fast, even between finishing this book and when it hits the bookshelves. But some of the implications of its development are becoming clear.

So, to help us consider what trusted advertising means in a time of AI, we're going to review research findings, look at some early public reactions to advertising generated by AI, share interviews with experts and cover suggestions for generating trust in the use of AI across the advertising ecosystem, as well as possible techniques to help people have confidence in the ads they see. We will also explore how AI is being deployed to ensure that advertising can be trusted and consider the work that has been done on this by a global thinktank.

What we haven't done is asked AI to write this chapter for us. That would be cheating.

But it has been very useful for research purposes… Humans + AI, that's the future…

Is a tsunami of ads headed our way?

It is highly likely the adoption of AI by the advertising industry will lead to an increase in the volume of ads produced and distributed to people around the world.

There are a number of reasons for this. It will be cheaper to create ads; it will be easier to personalize ads to individuals; it will be simpler to manage campaigns and fine-tune them; the AI machine itself will need feeding more ads to learn what works best, and there will be increased competition for content to attract people's attention.

The thought of this fills Matt with dread – an ever higher volume of poor-to-average quality advertising bombarding people won't help build people's trust in advertising. Being optimistic, James counters that it will mean fewer badly put together, inaccurate or clumsily targeted ads, and enhanced policing, so improving people's experience and, ultimately, trust.

Remember the issues we ran through back in Chapters 3 and 4? The new challenge is how to unlock the full potential of AI in advertising to help keep advertisers and their work focused on quality, effectiveness and improved customer experience.

Let's look at Amazon Ads as an example of a large tech platform which is increasingly offering AI-powered solutions to advertisers of all kinds. For SMEs, they offer access to image generation capabilities previously only available to larger organizations, while for big brand advertisers, there are cost efficiencies to be had from using AI to create the extensive ad inventory needed to personalize ads for hundreds, thousands, even millions of customers.

In a blogpost, Kelly MacLean, Vice President of Amazon DSPs, Ads Technology, shared how the company uses billions of different signals to inform its ad delivery system, and while this volume might seem overwhelming to an individual, it is the opposite for the machine because more is better, acting as fuel to feed insights and learning.[1]

Every tech platform is developing its own AI-powered services. Microsoft Advertising talks about content creation at scale as part of an article about three GenAI trends shaping the future of marketing.[2] Agency groups like WPP, Omnicom and Publicis are developing their systems, and advertisers are building their own inhouse.

There's a tsunamAI of personalized ads heading the public's way.

How might this impact trust in advertising and what needs to be done to ensure the public can remain confident in the advertising that they see, knowing – or suspecting – that it's been created by machines?

Early controversy of the use of GenAI in fashion ads

In March 2025, H&M announced plans to work with models and their agencies to create digital replicas of 30 different individuals to use in AI-generated images for social-media posts and marketing campaigns.[3] The story was quickly picked up by international news outlets, with a range of concerned reactions from influencers like American celebrity Morgan Riddle, to unions like Equity which represents UK fashion models.[4]

H&M made clear that models own the rights to their 'twins' and will be allowed to let other brands use them, including its competitors. The company also acknowledged it doesn't know the repercussions on the wider fashion advertising industry – the stylists, make-up artists, photographers – but believes models in ads must take part in the AI revolution.

H&M isn't the only fashion brand running into controversy over the use of GenAI in ads. Levi Strauss & Co trialled using AI-generated model images as a way to increase diversity and then had to clarify it would not be scaling back live photoshoots.[5]

AI will be used in fashion ads. The question is how best to ensure that the way this is done is acceptable to the fashion industry and the wider public.

Public attitudes towards the use of AI-generated content in advertising

But where is the general public on the use of AI-generated content in advertising?

In a recent paper by Konrad Shek, Public policy and regulation director at the Advertising Association, Shek first summarized how the public feel about the increase in AI-generated content in ads.[6]

While it's too early to make final conclusions, Shek noted growing evidence that people are sceptical about AI generally and would prefer for its use to be transparent.[7]

He cited YouGov surveys demonstrating geographical region variations in attitudes toward AI in advertising, ranging from widespread discomfort to acceptance as long as brands make it clear if they have used AI in various advertising scenarios.[8]

The demand for transparency could also be seen in a Getty Images study, where nearly 90 per cent of consumers globally wanted to know whether an image had been created using AI. Similar numbers wanted to trust that an image or video was 'authentic'.[9] The same study found that nearly half (47 per cent; up from 41 per cent in 2022) of people worldwide were nervous about AI. However, younger people, especially men, were more open-minded about AI being incorporated in brand communications, seemingly because of their greater (claimed) familiarity with AI and its perceived benefits.

Shek also noted results from Edelman's 2025 Trust Barometer, which we reviewed in Chapter 2.[10] The point he highlights is how there is a striking correlation between people's sense of political and social grievance (i.e. mis/distrust in the establishment/government/business) and their attitudes towards AI. The higher the levels of grievance, the lower the levels of trust.

Further evidence of public attitudes came from the Advertising Association/Credos' quarterly trust tracker, which revealed significant concerns about its use and transparency.[11]

Nearly half of respondents (46 per cent) believed that using AI-generated adverts was unacceptable, compared to just 31 per cent who found the practice acceptable. The remaining 22 per cent expressed uncertainty on the matter, suggesting the UK public remains divided but leaning towards scepticism, at least at present.

When it came to transparency, an overwhelming majority (77 per cent) believed that AI- generated adverts should be clearly labelled as such. Only 13 per cent disagreed, with 10 per cent undecided. This figure is highly consistent with an Institute of Practitioners in Advertising (IPA) study, conducted by Opinium, which quizzed 2,000 people in the UK aged 18+ on the ethics and etiquette of using AI. The IPA study found that 74 per cent of consumers believed that brands should disclose the use of AI-generated content.[12]

In the same study, when asked whether knowing an advert was AI-generated would affect their trust, 37 per cent reported they would be less likely to trust it, while 47 per cent said it made no difference and only 16 per cent indicated they would be more likely to trust it.

Over 80 per cent of respondents expressed some degree of concern when asked about a future with increased AI-generated advertising in media.

Shek concluded that the public remains wary about the role of AI in creating advertisements and strongly favour transparency through clear labelling. An interesting thing to note is that none of these studies gauged attitudes towards editing practices commonly used now and not labelled. Whilst labelling might have some merits, as explored later in this chapter, it may also generate concern that could undermine transparency goals. Shek also suggested further research into the relationship between the lack of understanding of AI among the public and mistrust of AI – which is possibly driving alarm and the requirement for labelling.

Let's turn to the views of two leading practitioners from advertising agencies…

AI, advertising and trusted information

How can we ensure people trust advertising that is created and delivered by GenAI?

This is a question we posed to Alex Dalman, Managing Partner and Head of Social Innovation at faith, an agency within the VCCP Group launched in May 2023 to pioneer work in the AI space.[13,14] Her telling answer was that 'we debate these things all the time'; it matters.

We started by discussing the labelling of ads and what might be required to ensure advertising could still be trusted as the use of GenAI accelerates across the industry. Dalman first outlined the importance of maintaining the standards already in place: the CAP Codes, the work of the ASA, and respecting the safeguards of copyright and IP.

She went on to express the view that there is a clear delineation between the representation of real-looking human beings, famous or otherwise, and other forms of advertising. She believes that any representation of a 'human' which could be passed off as real should be labelled as generated by AI to protect people from being misled or mis-sold to. However, it shouldn't be necessary to label every use, particularly because much of the software being used to enhance backgrounds, landscapes, and sets is just like CGI, which people know and can see as such. She pointed to the examples of a huge home furnishings business which has an entire catalogue of AI-generated product imagery, and the application of AI by fashion brands to create unlimited photos of 'models' wearing the complete range of their clothing portfolio for websites and ecommerce sites.

As an aside, Matt discussed this with his teenage daughters who disliked the idea of AI-generated models placing pressure on body image but did like the concept of AI presenting models that matched their own body shape and size.

One of the biggest potential applications of AI to enhance the advertising experience, according to Dalman, is around information. We know from Chapters 3 and 4 that the public value advertising for the information that it provides. In theory, GenAI should be able to turbo-charge the delivery of accurate and personalized information in the ads that are served.

However, Dalman highlighted the challenge all brands will face to ensure that the information provided is accurate and up to date. As we write, brands are introducing AI-powered chatbots, trained on their own copyrighted content to advise consumers, but is the content flawed? Financial advice site, Moneysupermarket, is one such example.[15] However, it carries a very clear disclaimer that the information may be inaccurate.

Dalman said this was typical of many brands and that there is going to be an intense, ongoing requirement for them to manage their digital footprint carefully. Anything online about your brand could potentially inform large language models (LLMs) collecting data to provide answers, but if it is based on old web pages, perhaps even websites that the brand hasn't created itself, there is a risk the information will not be correct. And, if incorrect information is presented to people in advertising, this will impact trust.

She concluded that marketers will need to train AI very well about the brands they are responsible for. The maintenance of an accurate representation will be an ongoing job, as the information becomes out of date, tone of voice changes, brand imagery is updated, and products and services are launched or dropped.

She cited an example of a brand that faith works with where the best way to train the LLM to produce materials with the correct tone of voice was actually to write new copy, rather than rely on it being able to do this with old, out-of-date copy in the mix.

She also pointed to another by-product of the prevalence of AI-generated ads, the ubiquity of the ordinary, and believes this will place an even greater premium on genuine, human-made creativity.

Perhaps the most relevant example of AI being used by VCCP and faith in a campaign to build trust was when mobile telephony brand O2 unveiled the newest member of its fraud prevention team, 'Daisy', in November 2024.[16] This human-like 'AI granny' answered calls in real time from fraudsters, keeping them on the phone and away from real customers for as long as possible. It was trained using cutting-edge technology and real scam-baiter content. Daisy combined various AI models which worked together to listen and respond to fraudulent calls instantaneously. It was so lifelike it successfully kept fraudsters on calls for 40 minutes at a time. As 'Head of Scammer Relations', Daisy's campaign successfully highlighted the need for customers to remain vigilant, and report suspected fraudulent calls and texts. All of this was timed in the run-up to International Fraud Awareness Week and is a strong example of how a brand can create a trusted messenger to build on its relationship with customers.

Dalman shared with us the care taken to make Daisy very obviously 'not real' (in the ads), but real enough to hoodwink the scammers as audio only. Firstly, the quality of information in her backstory was vital for her to be credible in any conversation, so an entire storyline about her life was written, covering everything from hobbies to family, her working life to her (incorrect) bank details. Then her voice, convincing enough to work on telephone calls. However, the video of Daisy was deliberately hyper-real, so that people weren't fooled and could see, trust even, the trick that was being played on scammers.

As an example of AI in advertising deployed to not just build trust, but to tackle one of the most damaging things for people's trust in advertising – scam ads – it doesn't get much better than this.

THREE KEY TAKEAWAYS

1 The existing rules of advertising apply to ensure your work can be trusted, even if you use GenAI to make it and distribute it.

2 Do you have a plan to ensure information generated by AI about your brand – the language and visuals, and its character or tone of voice – is accurate and up to date?

3 AI threatens us with the 'ubiquity of the ordinary'; human creativity will remain at a premium.

Transparency is essential for AI in advertising to be trusted

Sean Betts is Chief AI & Innovation Officer at Omnicom Media Group UK and leads the group's AI Centre of Excellence.[17] He is also an independent AI researcher and developer, and we started by talking about how a conversation about trust in AI and advertising at a macro-level is incredibly hard to do, simply because of its scale and breadth.

Whether we are talking about the relationship between agency and advertiser, between agency and tech platforms, between agency, advertiser and AI builder, between company and staff, or between the advertiser and the public, all roads, for Betts, lead back to transparency. The relationship dynamics though, he explained, are very different with specific and unique elements of trust and transparency at play.

He started with the relationship between agency and client, and the need for transparent agreement upfront on the use of AI in the service provided, whether that is to transcribe a meeting or to provide a response to a creative or media brief. The use of AI should always be declared, he argues.

He contrasted that with the relationship between agency and tech platform, where there is more work to be done on the transparency around the AI-powered services on offer. This will allow an agency and its clients to have a fully informed view of how performance is being driven in the platforms and optimize campaigns accordingly.

Things become even more complex for brands when you consider the relationship between advertiser, agency and AI builder. With multiple companies building different AI services, all in a race to deliver market-leading solutions, there is currently no mechanism, says Betts, to understand how brands appear in these AI models.

You can build an analysis based on share of brand by measuring how often a brand is mentioned vs other brands and where it ranks from model to model, but there is simply no way to transparently influence what is being presented about your brand, he explains. For example, if you were to ask the question 'what is the best SUV for a young family of four with enough boot space for camping gear' 100 times via the API you will get 100 different responses that mention different car models. This data can be used to create a 'share of model' metric that tells you how often a car brand is mentioned for that particular prompt, but lack of transparency on how these answers are arrived at could lead to issues for people's trust in brands, he argues.

From there, he turned to the challenges of trust in the way a company uses AI with its employees, highlighting how, for example, the conversations between staff or with clients recorded in AI tools such as Microsoft Copilot could be logged and then referenced. As mentioned earlier, transparency about how these are used is key when it comes to trust in AI.

Finally, we turned to the relationship between the advertiser and the public and how, at these early stages, differing levels of trust are emerging in different business sectors. For example, the use of AI in advertising for film and entertainment brands is frowned upon in many instances, given the sensitivities about the broader use of AI in the creative industries and the perceived threat to jobs and livelihoods. In comparison, fast fashion and consumer goods companies like Temu and Shein are 'embracing AI to drive innovation', he says.

The use of AI by advertisers can be transparent and still prompt a negative public reaction though, Betts highlights. He pointed to the examples of the Toys 'R' Us ad which prompted a backlash after using OpenAI's video generation tool, Sora, and a similar backlash experienced by Coca-Cola's AI-generated Christmas ads.[18,19] In both cases, Betts observes, the issue wasn't a lack of transparency but brands misjudging people's potential reactions to the resulting campaigns.

Betts remarked that AI is a constant in conversations now with every client, whether about advertising strategy, creative work or commercial considerations. He finds questions asked about AI can be focused on automation, speed to market, creative personalization at scale and cost efficiencies. How we use AI as an industry to build greater trust isn't a question he gets.

In Betts' personal weekly newsletter, The Blueprint, he cites a social post by OpenAI's Sam Altman suggesting AI's impact will be more like the Renaissance than the Industrial Revolution.[20] Here's how Betts reflected on that comment:

> It's an interesting analogy and comparison. The Industrial Revolution was defined by a shift in productivity, but the Renaissance was about rediscovery, creativity, and human potential. I really like this framing and its optimistic tone and it's absolutely something I think we should be aiming for.
>
> If we let AI take us down the route of the Industrial Revolution, we'll be trying to automate everything and there is the potential for huge economic disruption. If we're able to steer AI down the route of the Renaissance, we'll be using AI as a catalyst for a new era of art, science, and thought. Much more exciting and hopeful!

Betts' optimism for the use of AI in advertising, and more widely, is infectious, but he highlights just how fundamental transparency is to make sure that there is full trust in the way advertising is made in the coming years.

THREE KEY TAKEAWAYS

1   AI is already everywhere in the advertising process; ensure you can trust its use in your advertising supply chain by requiring openness on how, where and when it is used.

2   Trust in AI's use in your advertising isn't just about how the public react; it is about the partners you work with and the people who work on your brand.

3   Will your use of AI in advertising just be about cost-savings and economies of scale, or about making even better work that builds people's trust in your brand?

Now for a look at a couple of key developments in the UK industry in how AI can be best used to build, not undermine, trust in advertising, whether that is with the public or within the advertising ecosystem.

It's still important to note that like all things AI-related, this is a moving picture.

Defining the responsible use of AI in advertising

In September 2023, the Advertising Association set up a new task force to define the responsible use of AI in advertising.[21] With the support of experts from across the industry (including Alex Dalman and Sean Betts), the aim was to build a coordinated policy approach in recognition of the rapid need to establish ethical safeguards and develop industry guidelines. The task-force would also work with the Advertising Standards Authority (ASA) where appropriate, to ensure the use of AI in advertising campaigns will continue to be transparent and legal, decent, honest, and truthful. All about trust once again…

It was first chaired by Google and advertising agency VCCP, and met regularly to share best practice examples and explore how to ensure the advertising and marketing industry is a responsible user of AI. Also on the agenda were the productivity and creativity gains for the industry and wider economic benefits for the UK, following AI's increasing prominence as a transformative technology.

Just under a year later, the AI Taskforce published a report called 'Advertising and AI: Showcasing applications and responsible use'.[22] The word 'trust' appears regularly in the report, with one of the key findings specifically stating:

> Responsible and ethical AI adoption is not optional. Nor should AI be used in a manner that is likely to undermine public trust in advertising. This requires careful navigation around issues such as privacy, IP, fairness, bias, accuracy, transparency and sustainability.

Contributors included ISBA who were clear that 'this includes preventing the use of undisclosed deepfakes – or fake, scam, or otherwise fraudulent advertising'.

An additional view on the importance of trust was expressed by Clear Channel and the Data Marketing Association (DMA): 'we need to create AI models that are fuelled by a values-driven data ecosystem – embracing transparency, accountability and the responsible use of data to build and maintain consumer trust as outlined in the DMA Code'.

The report concluded with a 12-point checklist for responsible AI adoption:

1 Implement robust ethical frameworks prioritizing consent, accountability, and core industry values.

2 Develop high-quality prompts and curate rich training data for AI models.

3 Consider the implications around intellectual property, privacy, fairness, bias, accuracy, and sustainability.

4 Implement human oversight and fact-checking for AI-generated content.

5 Foster transparency about when and how AI is being used.

6 Protect creative rights and negotiate fair compensation for artists when using their works in AI training.

7 Ensure compliance with all applicable laws and regulations.

8 View AI as a collaborative partner to enhance human creativity and ingenuity, not replace it entirely.

9 Establish clear guidelines and best practices for prompt engineering.

10 Provide education and dedicated resources for exploring AI capabilities responsibly.

11 Continuously re-evaluate AI adoption practices as the technology evolves.

12 Collaborate across the industry to develop standards and share learnings.

It noted that 'by thoughtfully combining human and AI, as a form of co-intelligence, we can reshape what is possible in creativity, business impact, and social good'.

Around the same time, UK advertising trade bodies ISBA and the IPA announced 12 guiding principles for agencies and advertisers on the use of generative AI in advertising, with a focus on the creative process.[23] They embrace the ethical use of AI to protect the public and people working in the creative sector and cover transparency, intellectual property rights, human oversight and more.

There was consistent messaging again on the importance of protecting public trust and confidence in advertising, and also the need for transparency around AI usage between advertisers and their agencies, which promises to remain a major focus for the advertising industry's trade bodies, and other leaders in this space.

Be prepared for the rapid mass normalization of AI usage

We spoke with Venya Wijegoonewardene, Chief Strategy Officer, Spark Foundry, who cautioned us to be ready for how quickly human relationships with AI will become normalized, and for brands to accelerate further in using AI to facilitate relationships with their customers.[24] Here's what she said to us.

The phrase 'transformation' is often overused and can feel dramatic and unprecedented. But I think the biggest transformations are happening right in front of our noses and we don't even realise it. AI is weaving itself into our daily lives, we barely notice it's happening. And slowly but surely, we're fundamentally rewiring how we relate to information and each other.

Think about it: when did you stop being amazed that Netflix seems to read your mind and suggest a film that is exactly what you were in the mood for? Or when you strike up a friendship with ChatGPT since it's now the go-to for planning your holidays.

Slowly but surely, we are becoming more accustomed to using AI to optimize our lives. As the technology becomes better, the relationship becomes more human. Brands are building human tone and empathy into chatbots that may have been colder and more transactional in the past. It's less transaction, more conversation. And because we've normalized AI relationships in one part of our lives, we naturally extend that trust when it appears somewhere else.

For planners, this throws up several challenges to contend with: how do you face into a world where agentic recommendations disrupt decision-making? There are technical shortcuts like making sure your content is optimized to feature in recommendation engines. But there are bigger questions: building a truly distinctive brand so that you're already on the shortlist before consumers turn to AI to help them make the decisions.

The real challenge isn't the technology itself, it's that we're building intimate relationships with entities designed to influence our choices, often without realizing it. We need to get better at recognizing these dynamics and perhaps engage with them more consciously. Our ability to navigate this new landscape with both openness and a healthy dose of scepticism will define how trust evolves in our AI-integrated world.

So, what does our industry need to do to make sure that people can continue to trust advertising in the AI era?

How AI is being used to effectively regulate advertising

In November 2023, the UK's independent advertising regulator, the ASA, launched its five-year strategy – AI-assisted Collective Ad Regulation – which covers the period 2024–28.[25] The new strategy explained how the organization was increasingly using AI to identify ads that may be problematic and to support its compliance work, the bedrock of ensuring the public can trust ads to be legal, decent, honest and truthful.

This new strategy was formulated to respond to the challenges of effectively regulating advertising in the ever-evolving media landscape by increasing investment in AI to have 'more impact online'. At the time, the ASA revealed it was on course to process more than 3 million ads through its Active Ad Monitoring system in 2023 with plans to scale significantly, enabling it to take down more irresponsible ads in high priority areas. This would protect everyone, but particularly vulnerable people, from misleading, harmful or offensive ads. Importantly, the system would also allow the ASA to provide more and better reporting on areas where there is high compliance in online ads, including after its interventions. In other words, to provide data on just how much advertising is within the rules and, as such, can be generally trusted by the public.

It's important to remember that all of this work is done with the backing of government and statutory regulators to ensure ad regulation is effective; and that the ASA shares progress across national borders through membership of EASA and ICAS, the European and Global trade organizations for advertising self-regulatory bodies and industry.

The ASA's 2024 Annual Report provided an update on how this strategy was progressing and, as it was launched, we spoke with the ASA's Chief Executive, Guy Parker, about the results and the ASA's plans to ensure advertising can remain trusted by the public during this period of AI-powered transformation.[26,27]

Parker started by reflecting how the big game changer for the ASA in its regulatory role was the advent of the internet and the subsequent developments in ways to access it, most significantly mobiles. For him, this was both much more challenging and made the job much more interesting, particularly as the ASA's role extended in 2011 to covering non-paid advertising claims on websites and social channels. On top of this has come the rise of influencers and content creators, throwing up further challenges and making it clear that the ASA's old way of operating simply couldn't meet these new demands.

That old way was about mostly acting as a reactive complaint handler. For context, 95 per cent of complaints come from the UK public and they total around 35,000–40,000 per year (in comparison to a total of around 60,000 across Europe including the UK!). It's clear that people in the UK care very much about their ads being trusted and trustworthy, with two-thirds of complaints from all Europeans coming from people in the UK.

In a world of finite resources and an increasing volume of advertising (and possible complaints) something had to change. It is also important, Parker points out, not to view complaints as a perfect proxy for how the public view advertising generally, as there are demographic differences between complainants and the general public (they trend older and more upmarket than most).

Hence the shift to proactive regulation and the use of AI to gather intelligence to inform action. In simple terms, this means identifying an issue causing harm and then thinking creatively about ways to tackle it, from raising awareness of the rules, to enforcement notices to sectors, media publicity or a set of rulings as the basis to issue further guidance to a particular sector.

It was clear to Parker and the ASA team that there would be severe limitations on this proactive approach if they relied on humans alone to deliver results. They needed to introduce the use of AI to manage the rising volume of online ads. The ASA's AI workstream was established in 2018/19, and

2020 saw the introduction of an AI strategy to build an inhouse data science team. By 2021, the ASA had appointed a Data Science Lead, who oversaw the building of its Active Ad Monitoring System technology from 2022.

This system captures online ads of all kinds from across the open web, social channels, influencers and content creators, and company websites. The predictive machine models that the ASA's team have built make sense of the ads, predict likelihoods of interest for further review and draw attention to ads that may be breaking the rules. This information is then served to an internal portal where humans review reports. Parker talks enthusiastically about how this is being adopted across the ASA, allowing more and more ads to be proactively reviewed.

The numbers involved reflect this.

From 40,000 ads captured and reviewed in Q4 2022, the number grew to 3 million in 2023 and nearly 29 million in 2024. The target is circa 50 million ads in 2025, which should be made possible by ever closer links through APIs to platform ad libraries like Google's (with Meta committing to a similar tie-up during 2025).

Parker acknowledges that gaps remain, but conversations continue to try and reduce these and he's confident of good coverage to secure what he describes as 'an industrialized scale of ad reviews'. This will allow the ASA to proactively review and identify offending ads in problematic sectors – ads for things like dubious health products, potentially dangerous weight-loss remedies or bogus unauthorized investment opportunities. All similar things, notes James, that caused concern to the AA's founders a century ago.

As such, Parker believes the ASA is in a strong position nationally and globally, with a clear determination to be a leader in the use of AI for regulatory purposes. The outcome he is aiming for is 'more responsible ads and less dodgy ones', a sustainable improvement in compliance through clear guidance. He expects that the total of around 50 million ads a year, checked by a combination of AI and humans, should reach its natural plateau, with it being unlikely that the number will increase much beyond that.

Parker wants people to be able to trust advertising on the basis that it deserves people's trust. He says that we could just try to tell people that advertising is trustworthy, but what matters most is that ads are worthy of people's trust and do not lead to real world harms. He stressed how much it matters to the ASA that responsible advertising can flourish and deliver on its important economic and social role, supporting jobs and competition and communicating vital public information when needed, as during Covid-19.

He called for even greater collaboration with tech partners to help establish best practice internationally, with the ultimate goal of alignment of the big global players distributing ads to users of their platforms.

Back to that 2024 annual report from the ASA which shows how AI-based tools are now used in most of its projects, including its work on climate change and environmental claims, influencer marketing, financial advertising, prescription-only medicines, gambling, e-cigarettes and cosmetic surgery clinics based outside the UK. Some 94 per cent of the ads it had amended or withdrawn last year came from its proactive work using the Active Ad Monitoring system. That system is now making use of LLMs to speed up review of content in increasing numbers of projects, with plans to increase the number of topics it can monitor and to work with industry to fill gaps in the visibility of all ads online.

At a time when AI is being increasingly adopted by the industry to help with the production and distribution of ads, it seems only right that AI is smartly deployed by the regulators to ensure all ads online follow the rules and can be trusted.

Balancing transparency with practicality is key to trust

We return now to Shek's paper cited earlier in this chapter; produced for the ICAS Global Think Tank, it argues for a nuanced approach that balances transparency with practicality.

He cites how the public have long been protected through the ASA's core principles of advertising regulation, that the work should be legal, decent, honest and truthful. These, he argues, remain as true now in the AI era as they have ever been.

He presents his conclusions as follows:

1 Existing consumer protection frameworks already provide robust mechanisms to address misleading or deceptive advertising, regardless of whether AI was used in content creation. The issue is not the technology itself but whether the advertisement has the potential to deceive or mislead consumers.

2 Public attitudes toward AI-generated content reveal significant scepticism and a strong preference for transparency. However, the research also indicates that indiscriminate labelling may trigger unintended consequences, including the 'implied truth effect' and a general aversion to AI-generated content, potentially undermining trust in advertising more broadly.

3   Regulatory approaches to AI-generated content vary significantly across jurisdictions, with some implementing comprehensive labelling requirements while others adopt more advisory approaches. This fragmentation complicates the development of consistent global standards.

In the paper, Shek proposes a risk-based framework with labelling requirements for high-risk applications where AI-generated content has significant potential to mislead consumers. At the same time, he advocates avoiding unnecessary labelling that might create consumer confusion or devalue creative content.

As he points out, the goal should not be to simply label every piece of AI-generated content but to prevent consumers from being misled (about the nature, claims and other content of the ad) and preserve people's trust in advertising. He argues that through careful consideration of context, risk and consumer understanding, the advertising industry can make the most of the creative potential of generative AI while maintaining the trust that underpins its relationship with people.

But just how disruptive might AI be to advertising? And what might the public be asked to trust instead?

Which AI agent will you trust?

We could well be in danger of ending up with egg on our faces now, but (deep breath) here goes.

As we write this book, the next wave of developments centres on AI agents.

For the layperson, an AI agent is a software system or program that can act independently, meaning it can make decisions and take actions to achieve a goal without direct human intervention. These are already being developed by the major GenAI companies and, aside from presenting major changes to the business world, also promise a transformation in the way people shop and build shopping lists.

A *Guardian* journalist, Victoria Turk, trialled a new AI 'agent' from OpenAI, the maker of ChatGPT, in March 2025 to do her shopping for her.[28] The agent made her brand choices from her generic shopping list with Ocado and then made a food order for her from a local restaurant of its own choosing. So it, not she, was the decision-maker on what she might buy and where her meal came from; she was putting her trust into AI to make the choices that advertisers spend millions prompting us humans to make!

This type of support for shopping could be applied to every area of our economy, something that is being tracked by researchers and industry media commentators to try and understand the implications for advertising as we know it. On what grounds did the agent make its decisions? What role might advertising play in that, if any? Where will brand-owners need to direct their funding to influence AI agents if humans remove themselves from everyday choice-making? Are we moving from SEO to Large Language Model Optimisation (LLMO)? In April 2025, eMarketer published a post considering how machine-to-machine (M2M) marketing will work, where an AI agent for a brand negotiates with an AI agent for a customer, and how marketers will need to understand how best to influence that decision-making process. According to eMarketer, AI agents could cause a 38 per cent drop in ad exposure during discovery, 47 per cent during consideration, and 30 per cent at conversion.[29] Meaning? If AI agents will change how people search for products and services, how do you make sure your product or service is on the AI agent's list of recommendations? Equally, how do you as the customer know you can trust your AI agent to give you a list of the best choices? This new dynamic promises to further upend the way people encounter brands and their advertising in all its forms, including paid-for recommendations.

This is happening now. Bain & Company report that around 80 per cent of US consumers are using AI-generated content for at least 40 per cent of their searches, but their trust in what the AI provides appears to vary based on the use case.[30] For example, the survey showed 56 per cent of respondents trust AI for learning and 51 per cent for shopping, but that number falls to 34 per cent for health advice, 32 per cent for financial guidance and 29 per cent for news. The numbers are even lower for legal advice, major purchases and information around mental health. The more complex and personal the search topic, the less AI is considered trustworthy.

Meanwhile, Digiday reports that companies like Visa and Mastercard are allowing AI agents make purchases for customers – Visa with its new 'Intelligent Commerce' system and Mastercard with 'Agent Pay'.[31] Also, that ChatGPT and Shopify have announced new in-chat shopping capabilities.

Aside from the impact on how the current advertising ecosystem works, there's a big question here which centres on transparency in the AI and advertising ecosystem. How will customers know they can trust the answers that AI agents provide them with? Who will regulate that information to ensure it is legal, decent, honest and truthful?

Only time will tell, as AI systems become ever more sophisticated and people become more adept at – or complacent about – their use.

Trust is all about intent

For the final contribution to this chapter, we spoke with the Chief AI Officer at WPP, Dr Daniel Hulme.[32] He joined the advertising industry when his company, Satalia, was acquired by WPP in 2021 and openly admits he is not from an advertising background, but instead is focused on the impact of technology on society and principally how AI can help to solve frictions in the marketing supply chain.[33] He envisages a future where ads are enjoyable, and people truly value them.

He described the approach at WPP with AI adoption through WPP Open as helping to solve a series of challenges for the advertising industry. The first is around creative quality and whether AI can be creative… his answer is yes, but principally by creatives using the technology to push the boundaries in their work. The second concerns content creation, recognizing the growing need for accurate, brand-specific content, and the approach of using AI to create and test it. The third is about the audience, where AI can test how people think and feel about ads, replacing identity data by instead modelling human behaviour to design ads. The fourth is in machine learning to predict performance outcomes; the fifth in channel optimization for best returns; and the sixth is where AI will become a channel, providing dynamic advertising in its own right. The final use of AI will be in the 'moment', knowing how and when to capture the right product at the right time with the right message.

All of this leads to his expectation of both more, and more relevant, ads for people than ever before.

However, at the heart of all this technological change is a fundamental question for an advertiser when it comes to trust, argues Hulme – what is your intent? He stresses AI doesn't have intent. Humans do.

He provides a thought experiment as an example. A taxi company has a wealth of data on its customers as they book taxis through their mobile devices. One such data point is the device's battery level. It could be possible to connect price to battery charge; the lower the remaining charge, the higher the fare. Or it could be providing customers who need it most with cars complete with chargers to collect them. The first favours the taxi company's profit, the second benefits its customers. Which might build more customer trust? Hulme stresses the most important thing will be to make your brand's AI's decision-making process explainable to people so they understand what you are doing and why: good intent will build trust.

Hulme flags a couple of watchouts for the future. He asks us to think about what might happen if AI in advertising for a particular product or service goes very right; what might be the knock-on effect elsewhere? He sees a world where brands will sell based on a purpose, not just on 'faster and cheaper', because people will be able to use AI agents that find the products they want based on their own values.

He reminds us that there is no such thing as AI ethics, there is just ethics applied to the use of AI, and for this next wave of advertising to be trusted and trustworthy, everything begins and ends with the intent you have for you, your brand and your customer.

THREE KEY TAKEAWAYS

1   Ask yourself what is your intent with the use of GenAI in the advertising for your brand?

2   Test ways you can build increased customer trust in your brand through GenAI.

3   Be prepared to be tested by people's AI agents on the legitimacy of your brand's claims (especially around values or purpose); you could lose trust if you come up short.

Conclusion

How to ensure advertising that features AI-generated content can be trusted is one of the biggest questions now facing our industry. Industry leaders around the world are focused on how to answer it.

It's clear the volume of ads (and content created by brands) is going to increase. There will be a growing battle to be the first choice from negotiations between machines that will be deployed to provide answers to people's questions about their lives, including their purchasing decisions.

All of this is transformational for advertising as we know it.

Early indications are that the impact of AI in the advertising workplace will be disruptive, in particular to the agency business model and jobs. The 2025 All In Census, a study of over 14,000 practitioners from across the UK advertising and marketing industry, led by the Advertising Association, ISBA and the IPA, and conducted by Kantar, found the majority of respondents (63 per cent) felt enthusiastic to use AI more in their roles, with only 15 per cent feeling the opposite. Forty-four per cent of respondents agreed that AI has made them more effective in their job, whilst 22 per cent disagree. However, the use of GenAI by advertising professionals as of March 2025 is far from ubiquitous – 41 per cent of respondents used it regularly vs 39 per cent who don't, with the remainder using it some of the time.

Dalman and Betts helped us to understand the range of areas we will need to consider, from how brands manage their content, which is feeding the AI machines, to the relationships between areas of the advertising ecosystem using AI in producing and distributing advertising. The work by ISBA, the IPA, the Advertising Association and others is laying down what responsible advertising looks like. And Hulme makes the point very clearly – the responsibility for trusted use of AI in advertising lies with the people behind it.

Parker and Shek both point to the past – the importance of principle-based regulation that has ensured advertising is legal, decent, honest and truthful – and look to the future, both in harnessing the capabilities of this new technology to help achieve that objective and considering how signals of when and where AI is used to create advertising could help, not harm, public trust and confidence.

Finally, this topic is the fastest moving of all those we've covered in this book. By publication, there will certainly be new examples of good and not so good use of AI in advertising, its use and public awareness will have grown again and the discussions of how best to deploy this transformational technology will have moved on again.

Understanding the role of AI in the advertising industry has just begun, but the principles of its use are nonetheless clear, as they have been for every transformative technology the industry has adopted over the past two centuries: use it with honesty and care to help people in their lives and the choices they make, so that they welcome it and trust it.

Notes

1 Amazon Ads, From under the hood to front and center—how AI is changing the ad experience, September 2024, https://advertising.amazon.com/library/news/ai-advertising-benefits (archived at https://perma.cc/V87T-R6EA)

2 P Longo, Three generative AI trends shaping the future of marketing, Microsoft Advertising, March 2025, https://about.ads.microsoft.com/en/blog/post/march-2025/three-generative-ai-trends-shaping-the-future-of-marketing (archived at https://perma.cc/LN93-SP8X)

3 M Bain, H&M knows its AI models will be controversial, business of fashion, BoF, March 2025, www.businessoffashion.com/articles/technology/hm-plans-to-use-ai-models/ (archived at https://perma.cc/D7Y3-EAVE)

4 L McMahon, H&M to use digital clones of models in ads and social media, BBC, March 2025, www.bbc.co.uk/news/articles/c3vwg73xndeo (archived at https://perma.cc/MK4M-YF4Q)

5   Levi Strauss & Co., LS&Co. Partners with Lalaland.ai, March 2023, www.
    levistrauss.com/2023/03/22/lsco-partners-with-lalaland-ai/ (archived at https://
    perma.cc/HQY2-RKRK)

6   ICAS, Beyond Simple Labelling: A nuanced approach to transparency in
    AI-generated content in adverts, prepared by Konrad Shek, Public Policy and
    Regulation Director, Advertising Association, for the ICAS Global Think Tank,
    May 2025

7   S Tan, AI-generated advertising: How do consumers around the world feel?
    YouGov, June 2024, https://business.yougov.com/content/49622-artificial-
    intelligence-ai-generated- brand-advertising-how-do-consumers-around-the-
    world-feel-comfortable (archived at https://perma.cc/AYW5-9YFC)

8   S Tan, Artificial Intelligence for marketing: When should businesses disclose AI
    use for brand advertising? YouGov, June 2024, https://business.yougov.com/
    content/49623-artificial-intelligence-for-marketing-when-should-businesses-
    disclose-ai-use-for-brand-advertising (archived at https://perma.
    cc/6HPY-QYRY)

9   Getty Images, VisualGPS – Building Trust in the Age of AI, 2024, http://reports.
    gettyimages.com/VisualGPS-Building-Trust-In-AI.pdf (archived at https://
    perma.cc/T365-WC3M)

10 Edelman, 2025 Edelman Trust Barometer Global Report – Trust and the Crisis
    of Grievance, Edelman Trust Institute, www.edelman.com/sites/g/files/
    aatuss191/files/2025-01/2025%20Edelman%20Trust%20Barometer%20
    Global%20Report_01.23.25.pdf (archived at https://perma.cc/82XU-SVVH)

11 Credos Quarterly Tracker, Advertising Association, April 2025

12 IPA, Three-quarters of consumers want brands to disclose use of AI, IPA &
    Opinium, June 2023,https://ipa.co.uk/news/ai-attitudes-report (archived at
    https://perma.cc/5D5A-FMHJ)

13 VCCP UK, VCCP launches AI Creative Agency, faith, May 2023, www.vccp.
    com/news/2023/may/vccp-launches-ai-creative-agency-faith (archived at https://
    perma.cc/93E2-V47G)

14 Author interview with Alex Dalman, faith, January 2025

15 MoneySuperMarket: Meet Fin: Your MoneySuperMarket AI Support Agent!
    https://support.moneysupermarket.com/en/articles/11469722-meet-fin-your-
    moneysupermarket-ai-support-agent

16 Virgin Media O2, O2 unveils Daisy, the AI granny wasting scammers' time,
    November 2024, https://news.virginmediao2.co.uk/o2-unveils-daisy-the-ai-
    granny-wasting-scammers-time/ (archived at https://perma.cc/MRW4-87WU)

17 Author interview with Sean Betts, OMG UK, May 2025

18 D Di Placido, Toys 'R' Us AI-generated ad controversy, explained, Forbes, June
    2024, www.forbes.com/sites/danidiplacido/2024/06/26/the-toys-r-us-ai-
    generated-ad-controversy-explained/ (archived at https://perma.cc/V6UF-VY2M)

19 D Di Placido, Coca Cola's AI-generated ad controversy, explained, Forbes, June
    2024, www.forbes.com/sites/danidiplacido/2024/11/16/coca-colas-ai-generated-
    ad-controversy-explained/ (archived at https://perma.cc/V6UF-VY2M)

20 S Betts, A week in Generative AI: OpenAI, Flash & Research, The Blueprint, 2024, www.the-blueprint.ai/p/a-week-in-generative-ai-openai-flash (archived at https://perma.cc/3EAT-AFE7)

21 Advertising Association, AA convenes UK advertising industry AI taskforce, September 2023, https://adassoc.org.uk/our-work/aa-convenes-uk-advertising-industry-ai-taskforce/ (archived at https://perma.cc/Y4TA-QT6P)

22 Advertising Association, Advertising Association publishes inaugural report from AI Taskforce, August 2024, https://adassoc.org.uk/our-work/advertising-association-publishes-inaugural-report-from-ai-taskforce/ (archived at https://perma.cc/W2RR-M7J6)

23 ISBA, ISBA and The IPA launch industry principles for use of generative AI in advertising, November 2023, www.isba.org.uk/article/isba-and-ipa-launch-industry-principles-use-generative-ai-advertising (archived at https://perma.cc/MZS8-YJ6X)

24 Author interview with Venya Wijegoonewardene, May 2024

25 ASA, AI-assisted, collective ad regulation – our new strategy, November 2023, www.asa.org.uk/news/ai-assisted-collective-ad-regulation-our-new-strategy.html (archived at https://perma.cc/7X3Q-2HH5)

26 Author interview with Guy Parker, ASA, April 2025

27 V Turk, Who bought this smoked salmon? How 'AI agents' will change the internet (and shopping lists), *The Guardian*, March 2025, www.theguardian.com/technology/2025/mar/09/who-bought-this-smoked-salmon-how-ai-agents-will-change-the-internet-and-shopping-lists (archived at https://perma.cc/Y5VT-ZPY5)

28 E Leiderman, AI agents could shrink ad opportunities at key stages of the consumer journey, eMarketer, April 2025, https://content-naf.emarketer.com/ai-agents-could-shrink-ad-opportunities-key-stages-of-consumer-journey (archived at https://perma.cc/8XYS-T5QY)

29 N Sommerfeld, Consumer reliance on AI search results signals new era of marketing, Bain & Company, February 2025, www.bain.com/about/media-center/press-releases/20252/consumer-reliance-on-ai-search-results-signals-new-era-of-marketing--bain--company-about-80-of-search-users-rely-on-ai-summaries-at-least-40-of-the-time-on-traditional-search-engines-about-60-of-searches-now-end-without-the-user-progressing-to-a/ (archived at https://perma.cc/MVJ9-ZPEY)

30 M Swant, In graphic detail: How AI is changing search and advertising, Digiday, May 2025, https://digiday.com/marketing/in-graphic-detail-how-ai-is-changing-search-and-advertising/ (archived at https://perma.cc/CBR8-5JVW)

31 Author interview with Dr Daniel Hulme, June 2025

32 WPP, WPP acquires leading AI technology company Satalia, August 2021, www.wpp.com/en/news/2021/08/wpp-acquires-leading-ai-technology-company-satalia (archived at https://perma.cc/X4PE-VMZZ)

33 All In, All In Census, Advertising Association, ISBA, IPA & Kantar, May 2025, https://advertisingallin.co.uk/all-in-census-data/ (archived at https://perma.cc/6JGH-SNBY)

09

Does it matter
where you show up? Part 1

Introduction

As we have seen already in this book from the leaders we have spoken to, marketers and their agency partners care about where their brand appears and are acutely conscious of the impact that this can have, good or bad, on how much people trust their brand and advertising message.

Some of this 'trust' is explicit in the advertiser's media choice, such as the decisions by online-only brands to invest in TV and Out of Home (OOH) to be 'trusted' as concrete brands in the real world; some is implicit, for example the choice to align with world views, in particular media titles, aligned with those of your customer. Either way, the decisions you make about where you want your brand to be seen can have a telling effect on how much you are trusted by your target customers.

We are going to dedicate the next two chapters to this important and complex subject. In the first part, we are going to look at the world of media planning and buying and will begin with the view of a senior journalist who works on the front line of media and advertising... it's a great scene-setter.

Trust is about how brands show up

Gideon Spanier has been writing about the business of media and advertising for more than a decade. He joined Campaign magazine as Head of Media in 2015 with a remit to cover media owners, agencies and brands and started writing at a time when ad spend was shifting away from print and moving largely into the big tech businesses. He became Editor-in-Chief in 2020 and was Chair of the British Society of Magazine Editors (BSME) in 2024, providing him with an extensive perspective across the publishing ecosystem.

Spanier believes that trust has always been an issue for everyone working in media, but particularly so since the rise of social media. This is because the media provide information and suddenly people had a choice of many more sources of information, with social media helping to aggregate 'relevant' news for individuals. That this happened at the same time as the advent of advertising through search and social on the tech platforms was essentially a double whammy for the business models of publishers.

He described trust in advertising as 'a fragile commodity', something that has been under pressure for a long time. For brands, trust is inherently important, he says, foundational, but with the massive increase in advertising inventory available to advertisers and the accompanying fragmentation, it is much harder to control where brands show up. As such, Spanier suggested, perhaps brands have been prepared to compromise on the environment in which they appear, in terms of content and audience, a little too much.

During his time as a journalist, various media channels have had their own crises of trust, whether the UK tabloid press with the phone-hacking scandal or tech platforms with problems around 'hate speech' or content linked to terrorism. These moments have led to temporary suspensions of advertising, and he observes that when advertisers move as a pack and withdraw spend it can have a powerful effect. However, a single advertiser with just their own budget has limited impact, especially in the context of a global mega-platform, and most are reluctant to 'take a stand'.

His view is that where you choose to advertise is more important than where you don't and that advertisers have a responsibility to know where their money is going and what it is funding. We asked him if he believes advertisers do enough to support a trusted media environment and he replied he wasn't sure that it's really their job. The easiest way instead is for them to choose not to spend money where there might be content – toxic or hateful – that they would rather their brand isn't associated with. It is the government's job to regulate the media.

The structure of media choices has changed greatly during his time covering media. He has witnessed the globalization of ad spend – the tenfold increase in spend with four or five tech platforms, while the spend with the media buying agency groups has stayed largely flat. A real concentration of power has resulted.

In this sense, the owners of today's tech companies are much like the press barons who founded the Advertising Association a century ago, wielding huge influence across editorial and advertising content. He cites that one significant difference between President Trump's two election campaigns is that the second has closer alignment with the major tech platforms because of the influence they offer. Where US advertisers choose to advertise has become more politicized as a result, with impending US regulation also a factor.

Meanwhile media buying groups, even as they have globalized, have less control over total ad spend compared to 10 years ago. They haven't grown at the same rate as the tech companies and through financial representation of a collection of advertiser clients, their motive is economic, not ethical, he suggests. There is also a strong advertising ecosystem built around collaborations and partnerships, leading to a reluctance to rock the boat.

The nature of supply and demand has changed forever as the world's advertising industry has moved from serving thousands of companies to millions in the 'long tail'. Even big brands on the major platforms have a small share of spend compared to what they might have with other kinds of media owners. The world's biggest brands, however, still carry weight because their advertising is held to a higher standard by the public. Spanier believes top advertisers (famous companies) must make much more careful decisions about where and when they appear, because of the general scrutiny they are under.

Spanier looks positively on the fact that younger generations understand brands more and appear to trust them more. They are more likely to call brands out, and 'cancel culture' is a threat, but in their chosen media where brands can provide entertaining content, 'brand and editorial content feel like they have parity'. It's clear to Spanier that entertaining and engaging content still drives the best results for advertisers, but he does believe that the fragmentation of media has led to a reduction in big, stand-out brand campaigns.

When it comes to trust, Spanier says we are now living in a different era which brings a genuine challenge to society. We live in a 'blurred world' where the dividing lines between fact and fiction, between advertising and editorial, are not as clear as they once were. The 'collapse of consensus' can mean that more extreme positions can be popular and profitable, leading to what Spanier calls the 'commercialization of polarization' by some media owners. At the same time, as advertisers' creative palettes are expanding with the exciting prospects brought by GenAI, that same technology brings massive challenges when it comes to trust.

But trust in brands is high, says Spanier, and research like Edelman's shows they have the opportunity and the ability to lead. It's now about how they show up. This is the opportunity for advertisers when it comes to trust to build on this by appearing in the right places that appeal to them and their audiences.

He is clear that advertisers are under no obligation to support journalism but reminds us that journalists are there to find out the truth and keep hold of it in the face of those who may seek to undermine facts for their own commercial interests.

He urges advertisers to remember the importance of context when it comes to trust in their own brands. The consequence of a decline in trusted content through reduced ad spend is, in his view, a threat to democracy and, from an advertiser perspective, will result in a diminished choice of trusted environments for brands to enjoy.

The role of the trusted media advisor

It's a big business, planning and buying media on behalf of advertisers in the UK and around the world. Spanier has highlighted just how big and important that role is within the advertising ecosystem both in helping advertisers to build trust through the correct media choices for their brand, and in supporting trusted media environments through where their spend goes. We will discuss the moral obligations of that spending power at another point in this chapter, but for now let's be clear about the role of the media agency in the mix – they are there to help their clients deliver effective returns on their investment in media and also return a profit to owners or shareholders.

There's a tension here – how important is trust against results when it comes to the relative performance of investment in different media channels? Hence the work by commercial media channels to explain how the effectiveness of your advertising is intrinsically linked to how trusted the media environment is where your advertising runs.

In this next section, we're going to hear views from specialists in media planning and buying, one who works at a global agency group and one at a UK independent agency.

Does where you place your ad really matter?

Will people have different views of you, critically trust you more or less, depending on where you run that advertising campaign? This is a question that has been at the heart of media planning and buying for decades.

For Luke Bozeat, GroupM UK Chief Operating Officer, 'the type of environment you appear in reflects the type of brand you are'.[1] He points to sponsorship as the simplest articulation of that premise in practice. As a brand, you select a sponsorship because you want to borrow some of the trust that exists in that property. Say you choose to sponsor a major film awards ceremony, such as the BAFTAs. That says a different thing about your brand than if you choose to sponsor a prime-time TV show like ITV's *Love Island*. They both lend your brand something that comes from the property's connection with the audience.

Bozeat shared the view that there has been a decade or more where the focus within media planning has been on audience-based buying, but that there has been a recent shift back towards context. Clients are increasingly aware of the effect of contextual relevance and are placing greater importance on the environment in which their advertising is appearing.

For this reason, it's important to consider the audience that you are targeting and their views on the range of media environments open to you. This is a fast-changing landscape and Bozeat stresses the need to understand the advertising environment that you as a client are considering for your brand. Ask yourself, will it reflect your values correctly and authentically? After all, you're spending money with a business partner, and you need to have confidence in them that the money will be safely and effectively deployed for your brand and contribute positively to the trust you seek to build with your audience.

Turning to influencers, for example, Bozeat pointed to the increasing choices open to advertisers and their agencies. Instead of the attraction of a macro-influencer, a Cristiano Ronaldo, if you like, with several million followers, GroupM's clients may be steered toward partnering a selection of micro-influencers. Each may only provide a small audience, but their relationship with that audience is strong and taken together the impact of their recommendations means that the results are impressive. In that context, it seems that the bond of trust between influencer and audience can be powerful.

Perhaps as importantly though for Bozeat was the use of first-party data to inform media planning. He argues that such data should be used to deliver ads well and that the responsible and ethical use of data is integral both to trust and to delivering a relevant and satisfying advertising experience. Take an example of where it goes right: new parents receiving ads about products to help them with looking after a baby – well-targeted information and ideas they will appreciate. But if that ad targeting goes wrong, and someone who isn't a new parent starts receiving those same ads, it throws up all sorts of questions beyond their irrelevance, annoyance or irritation.

Questions like why are you following me, did I give you permission to follow me and how have you got my data? He suggested that the industry has more to do on helping people understand what the advertising industry does with their personal information.

One brilliant example of the intelligent use of data by a large business to communicate at a local level is Tesco's campaign for Ramadan, delivered on Out of Home sites by Smartly and GroupM.

More than 4 million Muslims observe and celebrate Ramadan in the UK every year, but the festival can be largely absent from mainstream British media. With many fasting from sunrise to sunset in Ramadan, food and drink play a central role and Tesco uncovered a frustration with food advertising unknowingly tempting Muslims to break their fast early, rather than supporting them. So, smart data was used to precision plan east-facing sites within Muslim hotspot areas. The creative used the latest day-and-night digital technology to display a fasting and non-fasting message. The resulting campaign generated a huge uplift of Tesco and Ramadan mentions on socials, with applause from Muslims and the wider public.

Trust and transparency in media planning and buying

For Jenny Biggam, owner of the7stars, one of the UK's biggest independent media agencies, ensuring trust in where your advertising appears depends on the business model of media planning and buying.[2] Biggam is very clear that the best approach is to 'plan before you buy', to first understand client objectives, develop the strategy, agree the approach with the advertiser and then buy the media that is genuinely needed.

This is a challenge to the approach offered by other agencies that buy volume-based media deals and sell space on to clients – 'inventory media' – which, in Biggam's view, fundamentally changes the business model of media planning and buying. For her, the inventory model means the agency is moving from a consultant about, to a retailer of, media. In return for what is perceived as cheaper media space, advertisers waive their rights to audits, instead accepting that they will receive reports on where their ads have appeared but not necessarily how much they paid for the space they appeared in.

Biggam has a view on the role of the media agency in helping advertisers understand where and when they show up. She wants clients to trust the advice that her agency offers and says there is always a need to interpret the data provided by tech platforms and others about the performance of advertising on individual channels. She believes it's important to take a healthy, fully rounded view of advertising effectiveness and reporting when it comes to considering the results of a media plan.

Ultimately, as a specialist in media planning and buying, trust for Biggam comes down to the approach you take and the transparency in the business model you choose to implement. She refers to the famous study by the *Guardian* which bought its own ad inventory and discovered that for every pound an advertiser spent programmatically with the title, only 30 pence reached the publisher, the rest being extracted by different ad tech companies in the supply chain.[3] That said, more recent studies by PwC and ISBA, specifically the Second Programmatic Supply Chain Transparency Study has noted improvements in return of spend to publishers since then.[4]

Trust problems lie in the business models, she notes, with our industry advising clients on significant ad budgets with no regulation of how the advice and service is paid for. This, she argues, is in stark contrast to an industry like finance where, for example, a pensions advisor must provide complete transparency on charges and fees earned for the advice given.

She is sympathetic to those in the news media landscape who believe that advertising revenues have suffered as action on brand safety diverted funds from news content and quality journalism, inadvertently damaging both. It's for this reason that the7stars are supporters of the News Alliance, an initiative to encourage advertisers to support trusted journalism.[5] Biggam refers to the unintended consequences caused by keyword blocking which she suggests is 'lazy planning', citing an example where restrictions of the word 'shoot' means advertising wasn't appearing alongside coverage of football matches. In her view, content that has gone through some form of editorial control to reach an audience has to be more trusted.

Biggam acknowledges it is harder to build trust now through media than it once was. Broadcast media was a shortcut to building brands, she says, and there are fewer big signalling moments for advertisers to communicate to audiences. Viewing is split, with more blurred lines across devices and people viewing more than one piece of content simultaneously, but she reminds us of the 'value of wastage', of people overhearing your message and the amplifying effect in fame and saliency that can come from that. She shares that for some clients; trust is an important metric in brand health. Trust is, for example, important to finance brands, even more so to a start-up in the finance sector, where the question facing the media planner is about what channels will drive the biggest and fastest brand trust with customers. This is why the bigger stature formats such as large, extensive, OOH advertising sites are business critical to some advertisers. For others, such as a company selling sweets, trust is implicit, so this is something that is not so obviously needed to be built through the signalling of where you show up.

For others, where perhaps the ad is for an item that is more of a one-off, or impulse purchase, like a meal deal or a low-cost fashion item, trust is implicit. As such, something that is not so obviously needed to be built through the signalling of where you show up but more about appearing at the right time in the buying journey. Trust remains important though, in that what's promised in the ad can be trusted by the customer to be delivered.

Always though, as a planner, Biggam notes, you should be asking what you want the public to trust you for and find the best media choices to help build that trust.

Advertising: who cares?

One new initiative worth tracking, led by advertising industry veterans Nick Manning and Brian Jacobs, is Advertising, Who Cares (AWC) as the industry consider ways to make sure there is trust within the advertising ecosystem and the work it produces can be trusted by the public.[6]

AWC launched in September 2024 with the objective of finding ways to create better advertising through smart thinking. It cited issues impacting upon trust that we have covered earlier in this book, problems such as bombardment, excessive frequency, the dangers of poor creative work, fraudulent/scam advertising and the broader issue of brand safety online.

AWC launched with a manifesto including the goal of tackling problems around trust between agencies and their clients, which AWC states is driven by a lack of transparency and an increasing practice within the largest agencies to make up revenue and margin shortfalls by fees from media vendors.

We asked Manning, co-founder of Manning Gottlieb Media (now MG OMD), formerly chief strategy officer at Ebiquity and now owner of Encyclomedia, to share more about what he thinks could help to rebuild this important element of trust in the advertising ecosystem.

He began by talking about how the widespread lack of agency honesty in media buying is well-known and the subject of several studies by advertiser trade bodies, most notably the US Association of National Advertisers in 2016.[7]

Manning believes advertisers can rectify this situation in three relatively straightforward ways:

- They can insist on contractual terms that oblige their media agency and associated parties to only ever act in the advertisers' best interests.
- They can require their commercial partners to provide all money and data needed to track all advertising delivery and performance.
- They can reward their media agencies correctly for the work they perform, with incentives for incremental business uplift that is measurable due to transparency.

He continued by saying it is important that advertisers revise their procurement practices and cease looking for 'savings' that perpetuate the current state-of-affairs that lead to today's problems. They should instead emphasize business results that are a direct result of the advertising their partners create.

He concluded that the industry needs media transparency to happen if it is to demonstrate its worth in a complex, dynamic and unstable world.

Conclusion

There's a tremendous amount of money invested in advertising inventory with media owners and tech platforms around the world. One trillion dollars of it.[8]

There are different ways of buying it, and different views on how this works and the impact the different approaches have on trust within the advertising eco-system; trust between advertisers, agencies, media owners and tech platforms. Advertisers appear to be increasingly concerned about the implications for their brands' reputations of the media context in which they are seen.

At the heart of the debate is a growing complexity in tracking how and where your money is spent and with whom, but the sage advice is to do everything you can to secure full transparency on how your money is invested and full visibility of where your brand appears.

Why? Because it matters to your audience, your customer(s), your staff – all of which plays back into the trust you are building for the long term in your brand. In that very pure sense, the money you spend on where you show up is an investment in trust to help your brand succeed.

Notes

1 Author interview with Luke Bozeat, GroupM, February 2025

2 Author interview with Jenny Biggam, the7Stars, April 2025

3 D Pidgeon, Where did the money go? Guardian buys its own ad inventory, The Media Leader, October 2016, https://uk.themedialeader.com/where-did-the-money-go-guardian-buys-its-own-ad-inventory/ (archived at https://perma.cc/U4FR-BCJ7)

4 ISBA & PwC, Second Programmatic Supply Chain Transparency Study, January 2023, www.isba.org.uk/knowledge/second-programmatic-supply-chain-transparency-study (archived at https://perma.cc/54V8-9N6E)

5 B Jackson, The News Alliance launches to encourage advertisers to support trusted journalism, Campaign, March 2025, www.campaignlive.co.uk/article/news-alliance-launches-encourage-advertisers-support-trusted-journalism/1910962 (archived at https://perma.cc/GB56-9RD3)

6 Advertising, Who Cares?, www.advertisingwhocares.org/ (archived at https://perma.cc/YN2M-VCD4)

7 An Independent Study of Media Transparency in the US Advertising Industry, ANA & K2 Intelligence, 2016, www.ana.net/content/show/id/industry-initiative-media-transparency (archived at https://perma.cc/9JH3-B8Z9)

8 WARC, Global advertising spend to pass $1 trillion for the first time this year, November 2024, www.warc.com/content/feed/global-advertising-spend-to-pass-1-trillion-for-the-first-time-this-year/en-GB/10119 (archived at https://perma.cc/UCR4-DQGD)

10

Does it matter where you show up? Part 2

Introduction

We're now going to consider the evidence presented by different media channels about how the unique environment they each create for advertisers offers benefits of greater trust through association.

Matt has worked in media and advertising communications for closing on four decades and handled briefs for different commercial media owners (and their marketing bodies) to advance their unique attributes as places for advertising that will be trusted and effective. He is well aware of the strong competition between commercial media who present 'trust' as one of the key reasons for the effectiveness of advertising campaigns running with them. This is particularly true of commercial media channels, but perhaps less so of the more recent options for marketers provided by the global tech platforms. The latter have had different challenges to deal with when it comes to 'trust' and brand safety, principally because of the difference in their business models in how content is created and published, and the way in which advertising appears alongside it.

For this reason, we are going to concentrate on long-established commercial media channels in this chapter and then review the work of the tech platforms in the next. Woven through both is the work of the self-regulatory system. Led by the ASA in the UK, it sets standards to keep work 'legal, decent, honest and truthful' for people to be able to trust the advertising they see.

The great trusted media battle

A quick backstory. In the late 1990s and early 2000s, there emerged in the UK a series of media marketing bodies, each with a remit to champion their own channel. First up was the Radio Advertising Bureau (RAB), followed by

Thinkbox for TV, and then others appeared – the likes of Outsmart for Out of Home (OOH) advertising, Magnetic for magazines, Newsworks for newsbrands, and more, while brand leaders like Royal Mail made the case for direct mail.

Confession from Matt: he was involved in the launch communications for three of them: Thinkbox, Outsmart and Magnetic. Their remits were similar: to market the power of their medium's advertising effectiveness to advertisers, highlighting each channel's unique attributes and demonstrating its strengths through research and thought leadership. Their objective was to either protect share of ad spend or grow it as part of a marketer's choice of media, in the face of emerging competition from the new world of search, then social.

The notion of a 'trusted environment' became increasingly important, particularly as 'trust' and 'brand safety' began to emerge as a dividing line between commercial media and tech platforms.

As the competition intensified, we began to see collaboration across media channels to show the halo effect of appearing in a particular combination, which has led to an excellent set of research papers and studies, enriching our understanding of the different roles that channels can play in building trust through advertising. We're going to review a selection of those in this chapter.

The focus for these media marketing bodies has been unrelentingly on the effectiveness of advertising in their channels, not to be confused with making the case for trust in their editorial content. Nonetheless, occasionally this has been a factor and, in the latest research, how brands benefit from association with trustworthy content appears to be a theme of growing importance.

Your media choice sends 'trust' signals to people

Signalling Success (2020) was a ground-breaking study developed by researchers Ian Murray and Catherine Heaney of house51 for UK TV marketing trade body, Thinkbox.[1] It helps us understand how the choice of media is linked to 'trust' that people place in your brand.

The research was an experimental design, inspired by academic research from Duke and Stanford universities. House51 created a fake brand (TIXE) and used a generic description of the service it offered in ads to isolate the effect of different media channels on people.

A nationally representative sample of people in the UK were presented with a description of a fictionalized brand in either online retail, FMCG, mobile phone networks or the home insurance categories, and given a brief outline of its launch advertising campaign. In each case, all the information was identical except the medium being used in the campaign.

The study showed evidence of how media channel 'signalling' acts on the way people perceive:

1 product or service quality
2 your company's confidence in itself and its financial means
3 your company's likely success, popularity and favourability with other people in society

So, what do the researchers mean by signal strength? Essentially, this is described as a product of our collective consumption of media and our collective understanding of media price, leading people to place differing levels of confidence or 'trust' in brand advertising depending on the channel.

The researchers found no correlation between the signal strength of media and its actual price per person to an advertiser. However, there was a much stronger relationship between people's estimates of how much a medium costs and the signal strength it possesses. Ultimately, therefore, the research concluded that a media channel choice can inform how much trust people will have in the claims you make.

The results showed that brands advertising on TV, magazines and radio were perceived as most trusted to deliver on promises made. A third (30 per cent) trusted promises made in TV advertising to be delivered, making TV the most trustworthy medium, just ahead of magazines (29 per cent) and radio (28 per cent).

The original study took place during the Covid-19 lockdown in 2020 so it covered TV, newspapers, magazines, radio, social media and video sharing sites but not cinema and OOH, as the social situation meant it wasn't credible to include these channels in the experiment.

Four years later, Everyday People (Murray again, but this time with Andrew Tenzer) collaborated with EssenceMediacom on a second report. Signalling Success 2 built the signalling story by connecting the original research design to Essence Mediacom's econometric database.[2] Nine channels were tested: TV, cinema, newspapers, radio, content creators, OOH, video-sharing sites, social media and podcasts. The report's author, Richard Kirk, EssenceMediacom's Chief Strategy Officer, went as far as saying that this report is 'more proof that the media is the message'.[3]

The researchers used the database of econometric studies behind EssenceMediacom's Media Mix Navigator to show that while a channel's signalling strength has no relationship to short-term return on investment (ROI), it is a good predictor of long-term ROI and a very strong way of explaining the halo effects the channel can have on other media investments, as we can see in Figure 10.1.

FIGURE 10.1 Signalling Success 2, media signalling strength by channel

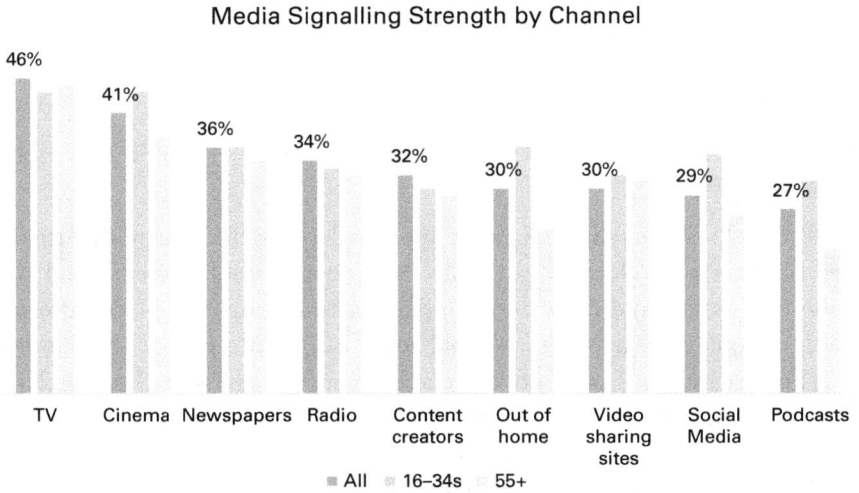

Media Signalling Strength by Channel

46%

41%

36%

34%

32%

30%

30%

29%

27%

TV   Cinema Newspapers Radio   Content   Out of   Video   Social   Podcasts
                                   creators   home   sharing   Media
                                                       sites

All   16–34s   55+

FIGURE 10.2 Signalling Success 2, price estimates and actuals vs signal strength

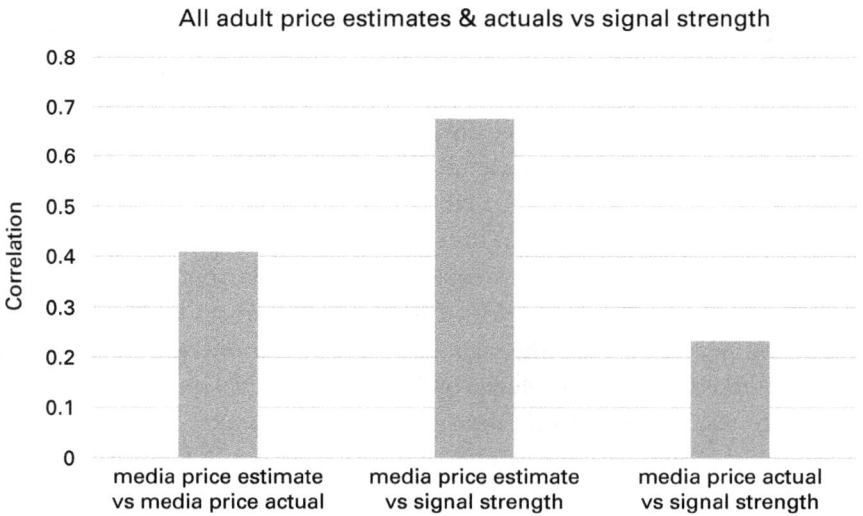

All adult price estimates & actuals vs signal strength

0.8

0.7

0.6

0.5

Correlation 0.4

0.3

0.2

0.1

0

media price estimate   media price estimate   media price actual
vs media price actual   vs signal strength   vs signal strength

FIGURE 10.3 Signalling Success 2, signal strength correlation

All Adult Signal Strength correlation

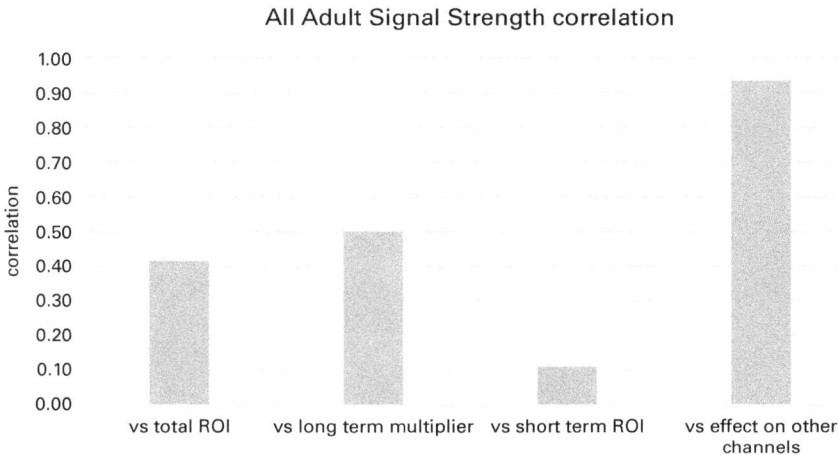

The researchers found that media choice generally informs people's perceptions of a brand in similar ways across all age splits. Younger consumers were more responsive in general to the proposed advertising, but across channels responses were broadly the same whichever demographic was isolated.

Let's consider those results back in that first chart.

Big, public, shared media elicited the strongest brand response from people – cinema, TV, news and radio tended to perform best. That echoes some of the things we have been told by marketers about the importance of being 'seen', being 'visible', 'public' and 'shoulder-to-shoulder' with other 'big' companies, particularly your competitive set and critically at peak times during your marketing calendar, such as the Christmas gifting period for retailers.

Signalling Success and Signalling Success 2 help us understand how media choices can help you say something about your brand and build greater trust with people as a result.

Now let's hear from specialists in this area...

The trust case for pre-clearance

One way of adding an extra layer to whether you can ensure your advertising will be trusted, as according to the rules set by the industry, is to use an organization that clears them before they go public. This is the case for all

UK advertising on TV, cinema and radio where ads are generally pre-cleared by the commercial media companies responsible for them.

In the case of TV, this is done by a company called Clearcast. Originally the compliance department for British broadcaster ITV, Clearcast has since been funded by ITV, Sky and Channel 4 and is there to help advertisers check that their work is fully cleared and compliant before they go on air.

The challenge ahead is how to put this standard of pre-clearance in place in a world where there is an increasing volume of video advertising appearing on all kinds of devices. We spoke with Sam Smith, Managing Director of Clearcast, about the company's ambition to spread the Clearcast 'gold standard' of clearance beyond traditional linear TV, to help build trust in advertising across all platforms.[4]

Smith explained how the Clearcast team's goal is to help build trust in advertising everywhere and applies its expertise every day to help advertisers understand the rules and work through what's possible. A quick visit to their site will present you with reams of examples of guidance to advertisers, depending on different seasons and times of the year. Matt is particularly fond of the guidance offered up for advertisers considering their Christmas ads, such as the importance of making sure you never suggest Father Christmas might be a myth to younger viewers and avoiding the hazardous portrayal of flammable decorations hanging above lit fires.[5]

Clearcast's work is effective. Smith cites the 'clearance effect' where the goal is to constantly reduce the number of TV ads that are judged to have broken the rules. While roughly a third of complaints to the ASA are about TV ads, the actual case numbers are around a third of that total. There were only 13 upheld rulings against TV ads upheld in 2024 (down from 19 the year before) meaning the company ensured 99.96 per cent of the more than 31,000 adverts on TV were compliant.[6]

She cites how Clearcast helps advertisers move in time with social mores, for example in the case of advertising for period products where brands moved from the use of blue ink to showing blood (red ink). This happened even though the rules hadn't changed, but what people deemed as socially acceptable had.

Clearcast also plays a role in the Broadcast Committee of Advertising Practice (BCAP), who formulate the rules and guidance which the ASA then applies. Pre-clearance is required by Ofcom under the Communications Act, as broadcasting has long been seen to hold a uniquely powerful place in the advertising landscape. But that could be changing as other audio-visual channels grow.

It's interesting to consider the future of pre-clearance for advertising, given the growth in non-broadcast video content. Clearcast suggests that the way forward will be a combination of AI and human experts, ever ready to help advertisers make work that fits within the rules and effectively builds trust with people through the reduction of complaints to the ASA that are upheld. And no longer just for linear broadcast, as was the case.

The point is to always ask what steps you can take to make sure your advertising is within the rules before it appears and, by doing so, help contribute to greater public trust in advertising.

The trust case for TV advertising

The following examples are drawn from the resource library of UK TV marketing body, Thinkbox.[7]

The first is 'The value of TV: A behavioural science perspective'.[8] Richard Shotton's 2024 paper covers five cognitive and behavioural biases that help explain how TV advertising works, with two specifically about trust:

Public promises: Our brains trust TV. We are far more likely to trust a promise if it's made publicly. We intuitively understand there will be more severe consequences if a publicly stated promise is broken, compared to a private one. TV, as a medium that reaches huge numbers of people, is a perfect fit for this.

The methodology behind this point was an experiment with a politician making promises: in the private setting, roughly 40 per cent didn't trust the promise, but in the public setting, that figure dropped to 20 per cent.

Costly signalling builds trust: Trust in a brand is connected to the perceived expense of its marketing. The psychologists argued that the credibility of a communication is in proportion to its perceived expense ('only marketers who genuinely believe in the quality and long-term success of their product would invest so heavily'). TV is perceived as having higher capital costs than other media.

The methodology of the latter was based on work by Amna Kirmani at Duke University in 1989 who gave 214 participants a magazine article describing the launch of a new trainer. The editorial included how much the brand was spending on ads. Sometimes the piece said the brand was spending $2 million, sometimes $10 million, $20 million or even $40 million.

Participants were asked to estimate the quality of the shoes on a nine-point scale. Those who read that the campaign cost $20 million rated the brand 14 per cent higher than those who saw a $2 million spend.

The second study is a piece of work called 'Adnormal behaviour' (2022).[9] This challenged the advertising community to consider how different they are from the general public ('normal' people) that they communicate to.

Thinkbox worked with Ipsos to deliver a random probability survey of 1,158 people representative of the national population, and a survey of 216 media professionals, and asked, 'In which of the following media are you likely to find advertising that you trust?'

As we can see, TV ads were most trusted by the UK public (35 per cent), with lower levels recorded for other channels.

Finally, there is work by Peter Field for the IPA. Remember him? We talked about his work in Chapter 3, and how his analysis of the IPA case study bank has identified the rising importance of trust in recent years and its link to advertising effectiveness to deliver business results.

Field published his 'TV is at the heart of effectiveness' white paper in 2024 with three key reasons as to why TV advertising's relationship with effectiveness is growing:

1 the attention brands receive in TV advertising;

2 the emotional clout that TV advertising can generate; and

3 the issue of trust in advertising.[10]

As we know, Field used the IPA databank to correlate cases with strong trust growth reporting strong profit growth over time. In this study he showed TV leading the way in achieving strong trust effects against other media.

The trust case for cinema advertising

One of the major UK cinema sales houses, Digital Cinema Media (DCM), provides a compelling case for the trust value of its channel in its 'Cinema Advertising 101' report (2024).[11]

The DCM team point to data from IPA Touchpoints (2024) which shows that cinema is the number one choice for environment where people will trust the advertising that they see.

FIGURE 10.4 Adnormal behaviour, Thinkbox

Where do 'normal' people find advertising that...

% who selected each medium

	TV	Social Media	Radio	YouTube	Cinema	Magazines	Outdoor	Newspapers	Search	Direct Mail	Websites
Sticks in their memory	57%	28%	19%	13%	12%	12%	12%	11%	10%	6%	3%
Makes them laugh	52%	35%	13%	21%	16%	5%	6%	6%	4%	2%	3%
Entertains them	51%	30%	13%	19%	21%	9%	3%	7%	9%	3%	4%
Makes them feel emotional	47%	17%	6%	10%	15%	5%	3%	9%	4%	2%	2%
They like	40%	27%	10%	12%	14%	15%	8%	12%	14%	4%	4%
They trust	35%	6%	16%	4%	9%	12%	6%	19%	11%	6%	4%

FIGURE 10.5 Digital Cinema Media, Cinema Advertising 101

MAXIMISE TRUST WITH CINEMA

Cinema is the AV channel that audiences trust the most in terms of advertising – offering brands a positive environment and inferred sense of quality, where audiences are receptive to brand messaging

'I trust the advertising in...' scores indexed vs cinema

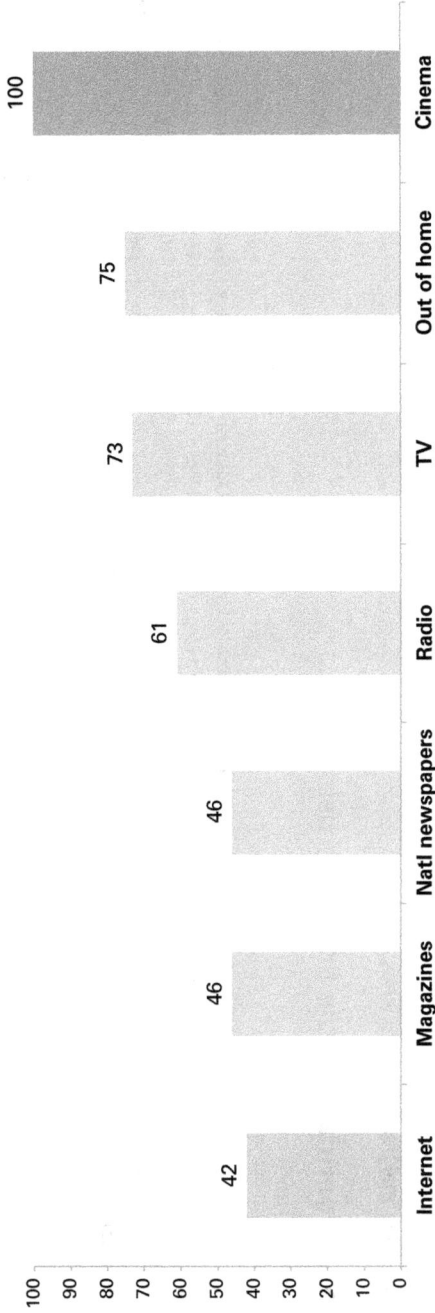

Media	Score
Internet	42
Magazines	46
Natl newspapers	46
Radio	61
TV	73
Out of home	75
Cinema	100

They remind advertisers of the value of trust and its critical connection to business growth, citing Kantar's Brand Z data, which shows brands with above average trust levels since 2006 seeing a 170 per cent increase in brand value. This is in contrast to brands with below-average trust levels which lost 13 per cent in value.

The DCM team put the effectiveness of cinema advertising down to a set of key factors which include the unique, premium impact of the big screen and immersive sound, the attention it earns from cinema goers and the shared experience of seeing the ads with others. Perhaps this is why they describe cinema advertising as 'the best seat in media'.

The trust case for radio and audio advertising

Radiocentre, the industry body for commercial radio in the UK, works on behalf of more than 50 stakeholders who represent over 90 per cent of commercial radio in terms of listening and revenue.

So, as Radiocentre itself asks, what are radio's trust credentials – and how can these help advertisers? The industry body makes a compelling and straightforward case.[12] Firstly, for its role as a trusted medium across Europe while Radiocentre's Breaking News study demonstrates how radio is the most trusted medium for news.[13]

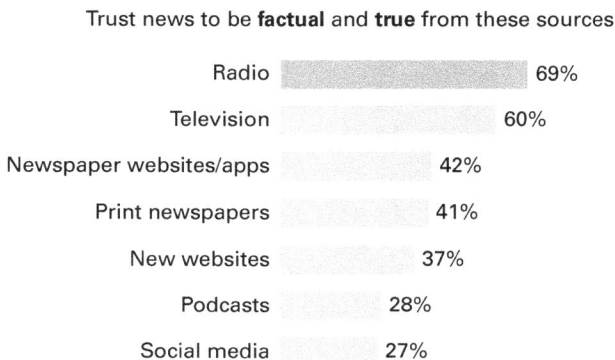

FIGURE 10.6 Radiocentre, radio and trust

Radio is the most trusted medium for news

Trust news to be **factual** and **true** from these sources

Radio	69%
Television	60%
Newspaper websites/apps	42%
Print newspapers	41%
New websites	37%
Podcasts	28%
Social media	27%

FIGURE 10.7 IPA Databank, radio and Trust

In particular, radio builds trust

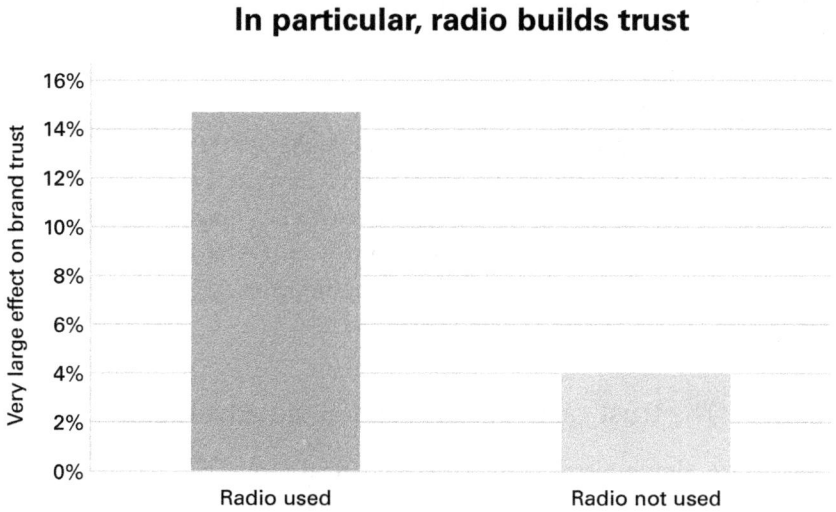

FIGURE 10.8 Radiocentre, Radioguage

Brand Trust: ALL Campaigns
Radio increases brand trust by 62%

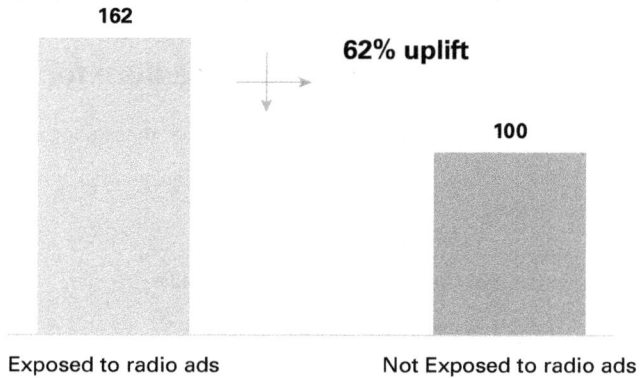

Radiocentre points to IPA Touchpoints data and measurement of how much advertising is trusted by each medium's audience. When measured in this way, the data for 'I trust the advertising… (in this medium)' reveals trust in radio advertising is higher than for other media. Furthermore, analysis of the IPA Databank highlights how campaigns that feature radio generate four times the level of brand trust as those that don't.

From a radio advertising-specific perspective, data from its own effectiveness benchmarking tool, Radiogauge, demonstrates how people exposed to radio advertising within a broader media campaign are 62 per cent more likely to trust the advertised brand.

Further insights into the power of radio advertising to help build brand trust can be gleaned from Listen Up! by Radiocentre and System 1.[14] The research study used brand and emotional data collected from over 50,000 radio listeners and non-radio listeners across a 10-year period. A key finding showed how radio ads with higher brand recognition build more trust effectively, with the highest managing to double the effect of building trust with the audience.

Audio's power to build trust extends beyond radio into podcasts too.

While the first podcast ads started to appear in the mid-2000s, it is generally recognized that the success of *Serial* in 2014 in attracting millions of listeners triggered a worldwide boom for podcast listening. Global spend on podcast advertising increased sixfold between 2017 and 2023.[15]

Much of it is radio content on demand. In the UK, for example, commercial broadcasters provide access to almost 90 per cent of commercial audio listening with an 86 per cent share of commercial audio advertising revenue, but there are other options too for advertisers.[16]

Global podcast advertising business Acast was founded in 2014 in Stockholm, Sweden. Its research, based on a sample from the US market, suggests 57 per cent of consumers trust podcast personalities the most amongst a range of other channels.[17] The company argues that hosts make genuine connections and can work brand messages into narratives, like recommendations from a friend.

Spotify also has a view on advertising and trust.[18] The company links trust to rapport, which it describes as the 'cousin' of trust and argues this underpins everything from personal relationships to global commerce.

There's clearly a power in the medium of radio and audio – sometimes known as the theatre of the mind – where people listen to a familiar voice they know and trust.

The Trust case for magazine media

The Professional Publishers Association, which runs Magnetic (its magazine marketing arm), regularly explores the topic of trust and the value it can offer to advertisers. Its work, 'A Matter of trust', in partnership with Medicom and Code, asked to what extent do people trust the published media brands vs the social media brands they consume?[19] And does this trust in the media brand translate into increased levels of trustworthiness for the brands who advertise there?

Key findings from 2017 included:

- Magazine brands are more trusted than social media brands (70% of magazine readers trust magazines, only 30% of social media users trust social media). This even holds true amongst under-35 digital natives (62% and 35% respectively).
- Magazines are also more trusted than social media when it comes to implicit measurements.
- 'Relevancy and meaning' make the biggest contribution to trust in Media brands. Magazine brands index 140 against this factor compared to just 71 for social media.
- Magazine brands inspire trust across a range of topic areas including beauty, food and motoring.
- There is a brand rub effect: trust in a magazine brand translates into perceptions of trustworthiness for brands who use this environment.

Further evidence of the value of the magazine brand on trust can be seen in the role of well-known names as kite marks – signals to people that a product or service can be trusted because it is approved by the magazine media brand.

For example, Good Housekeeping, which opened its Good Housekeeping Institute in 1924, has been reviewing products and providing customer advice for over 100 years.[20] Its own site explains how the 'tried, tested, trusted' approach for more than a century means the Good Housekeeping Institute is a widely recognized source of accurate, trusted product reviews. Interestingly, it checks everything the product claims on its packaging and in the product's advertising campaigns. And, of course, that kite mark for the Good Housekeeping Institute appears in the marketing of nearly 750 products.

The trust case for Out of Home advertising

A year on from the first Covid-19 lockdown, two major Out of Home (OOH) media owners, Clear Channel (now Bauer Media Outdoor) and JCDecaux, joined forces to try to understand what was happening to people's levels of trust during this period of huge social change. The research conducted for a report called 'The Moment for Trust' highlighted that only 34 per cent of consumers say they trust the brands they use, but 81 per cent say trust is a deciding factor in their purchase journey.[21] Nearly one in five said it was the deal breaker in their path to purchase.

The report went on to explain how OOH advertising can help advertisers build trust in their products and services.

The main premise is the importance of being public with your brand promise, and the trust benefit this brings, versus other, less visible, forms of advertising. We can see how the OOH sector makes that case in the following chart:

Another way of considering this is that it's harder to tell lies in public. This is perhaps why the researchers chose to ask the public which advertising channels they would use if they oversaw communications for government, with OOH once again performing strongly.

FIGURE 10.9 The Moment for Trust, public vs private media

Trust: Public vs private media

Level of Trust

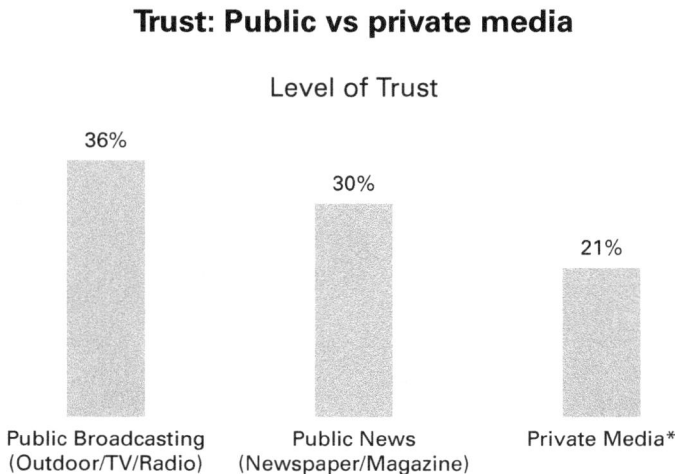

	Public Broadcasting (Outdoor/TV/Radio)	Public News (Newspaper/Magazine)	Private Media*
	36%	30%	21%

FIGURE 10.10 The Moment for Trust, OOH and government communications

Most of the public would use OOH if they were planning government communications

Preferred communication channels if in charge of communications for government / companies

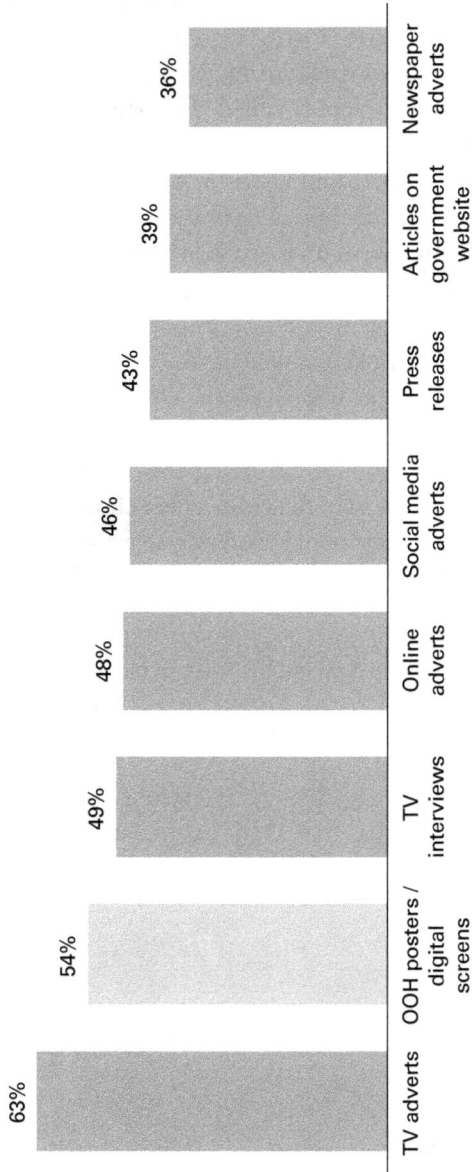

TV adverts	63%	
OOH posters / digital screens	54%	
TV interviews	49%	
Online adverts	48%	
Social media adverts	46%	
Press releases	43%	
Articles on government website	39%	
Newspaper adverts	36%	

The report concludes that advertising a product or service on OOH sites contributes to a +7 per cent uplift in perceptions of the brand, +4 per cent of trust in the claim made in the ad, and +5 per cent consideration to purchase or act.

This point about being public means the enforcement of standards leading to greater trust is made again by Outsmart, the UK trade association for OOH advertising.

In April 2025, it published analysis that while OOH ads reach 97 per cent of UK adults each week, they account for just 2 per cent of ASA complaints.[22] Tim Lumb, director of Outsmart, put this down to the uniqueness of OOH – how it only displays adverts in real-world public spaces to be viewed by the general public. This comes with a strong expectation that the adverts should not betray people's trust or sensibilities.

The trust case for direct mail

One of the strongest arguments put forward by proponents of direct mail (best described as addressed mail and door drop) is the value of being able to put your brand in tangible, physical, print form in someone's hand.

Marketreach Royal Mail, the marketing authority on commercial mail, regularly explores how direct mail provides brand and commercial benefits to advertisers. In 2023, it published a study conducted with Trinity McQueen – Customer Mail – which explored why mail is a trusted medium for people.[23] It makes a clear case for the medium's strengths as follows:

- First, say the researchers, consumers readily agree that direct mail is a trusted channel – 71% say they completely trust the mail they receive – and it's trusted across all age groups.

- Second, as the world becomes increasingly digital, direct mail offers something different. People expressed a preference for physical documents where content is important, sensitive or of a personal nature. There was also a strong sense that physical mail is private and secure.

- Third, there was much less sense of a risk of being scammed by physical mail.

As we completed this book, Marketreach was set to publish a new report, 'The Trust Factor', which explored why trust is vital to a brand's performance, commercial success and, critically, how to build trust.

We were provided with a preview of the report. Key points to note include findings about how trust in a brand is built on eight interconnected pillars: Reliability, Reciprocity, Aligned interests, Stake, Familiarity, Fame, Frequency of communication and Tenure.

This is in tune with other work we covered earlier about differing types of trust, broadly, the Rational and the Emotional.

Marketreach's work details how important it is to build trust in all of these pillars, and how loss of trust in any can impact commercial success. The report also includes a trust measurement tool, and a 'Communications Formula' to act as a guide to using communications and advertising to build trust.

The trust case for newsbrands

Heather Dansie, Insight Director, Newsworks, has been researching how trust in newsbrands works, and the value that advertisers can unlock through the association with trusted news content.[24] The Newsworks team have produced several reports, designed to help inform advertiser decisions, including 'What's the Fuss About Trust' (2018), 'Trust' (2023) and 'Youth' (2024).

Dansie talked to us about a trust crisis, one we are familiar with, where fake news and misinformation is impacting upon people's trust generally. She says at the core of this is a confidence in whether the information is true (or not), and this is where newsbrands can step forward to provide content you can trust, and that people pay attention to. This is what Newsworks has been uncovering, that people, including the younger generation, look for the source of information and ask whether this is coming from a brand that they trust. People are wise to the signals of trust, and trust is stronger with known media brands, says Dansie. People recognize the font of a newsbrand, they know where it is coming from, on any platform, and there is an inherent trust built in which advertisers can benefit from this – a halo effect for brands from being associated with trusted content.

She acknowledges that trust is a research challenge but it's one they've been tackling head-on, given the importance of trust in newsbrands more generally.

Trust (2023) sought to challenge the way trust is measured and develop a stronger metric of the true level of trust in a brand.[25] It identified two brand boosts and two brand drags when it comes to trust, as follows:

1 Familiarity: How well do I know the brand? Because trust is accrued and built up over time through repeated interactions, the more experience we have, the more confident we can be to trust.

2 Fame: This considers the cognitive bias of social proof. We draw our cues about whether to trust from others. Is the brand known to be competent? Do others regard them as such?

3 Competence: Is the brand considered good or bad at doing what it does? To ask if we trust someone (or something) is to ask what we are trusting them to do.

4 Risk: What is the general perception of risk in a category (and a brand) and what is at stake? The higher the perceived risk – financial, social, safety – of getting it wrong, the more trust matters.

This approach allowed the research team to rank brands and sectors, providing an overview of which were most or least trusted, and then to overlay the halo effect that newsbrands could add for advertisers, by also ranking newsbrands as a media channel for trust versus other channels.

What it showed is how advertisers can benefit from the halo effect of a trusted newsbrand environment. The report demonstrated stronger trust in brands when seen on a news brand, versus the same ads shown on non-news brands sites, specifically:

- 1.5 times brand trust for the following 'big advertiser' brands as part of the study: Ben & Jerrys, Tesco, Kia.
- 1.8 times brand trust for the following newer brands: Huel, Gopuff.

In addition, Newsworks published a trust calculator for advertisers and agencies to provide a more accurate overall measurement of trust in a brand which is freely available to use.

Dansie explains that trust helps us make confident predictions about others based on less information and argues that for advertisers, the media choice is paramount, that people are smart, and they know when and where they will see advertising that is regulated, within environments they can trust. This chimes with work from other media channels that offer news content to audiences.

The trust case for advertising with online publishers

To support the need for advertisers to access advertising inventory they can trust and know to be effective online, the UK's leading publishers united in 2018 to build and deliver Ozone, a technology and data-led digital advertising platform. They describe what's on offer as an easier way to access, at scale, the 'better, premium end of the web... where brands and publishers thrive online, and where consumers come to be informed, inspired and entertained every day'.

Ozone now represents 20 of the UK's most trusted and best known publisher groups, reaching 85 per cent of the population, 42.6 million people every month, with 53 per cent of that audience visiting sites daily.[26,27]

We spoke with Damon Reeve, Chief Executive, about the goals of Ozone, more than five years on since its launch.[28] He outlined Ozone's objective to create trust in the delivery of digital advertising opportunities for advertisers that harnesses 'the power of the masthead', that identifying factor which allows people to connect with a brand for entertainment, information and inspiration. This is to counter the bad behaviour that has emerged in digital advertising, says Reeve, where the placement of advertising inventory doesn't always respect the value exchange offered by the content beside it.

Reeves is on a mission to help advertisers avoid Made For Advertising (MFA) sites and instead invest in advertising around premium publishing content, content that ranges from the likes of the *Guardian* to Mumsnet. The best answer, he believes, is direct relationships between advertisers and publishers, providing a confidence that you know where the money is going, where your audience is and what you're investing in. His focus is on building a more sustainable future for ad-funded journalism, and a more sustainable future for digital advertising.

Conclusion

The argument that where you place your advertising contributes to how much you are trusted, both through context and association is, as we hope to have captured in this chapter, rich, complex and multi-layered.

The debate about the relative effectiveness and value of different media has raged for decades and will, no doubt, continue as each channel competes for ad spend. Each will continue to make the case for its role as an effective choice, including in the value it can add in building trust for your brand.

What is very clear is how important trust is to each of the media channels we have covered. The extensive efforts they put into understanding and demonstrating the role of trust in their media environments for advertising effectiveness is clear proof of its value in action.

Ultimately, you, as the advertising practitioner, can choose to be as in control as you want of how and where you show up, albeit with the logistical challenges that brings. Project Origin, which we wrote about in Chapter 4, from ISBA, should add further knowledge still to the process of making sense of the complexity of multi-media selection and balance.

Public attitudes towards media channels are dynamic, not set in stone, and they vary by age and media experience, but there is a bedrock of knowledge and understanding that can helpfully inform how your media choices will support the goal of being trusted.

Be in no doubt, the media choices you make do say things about your brand.

There is a 'trust' value in high quality creative advertising environments; there is a 'trust' value in making public promises; there is a 'trust' value in being associated with a trusted media brand; there is a 'trust' value in being seen across a range of media channels; there is a 'trust' value in signal strength from the perceived costs of what you are doing; and there is a 'trust' value to being a real, physical part of people's lives.

How you choose to build a campaign that contributes positively to your audience's trust in your brand is entirely up to you but, in a world where trust is changing and vital to how competitive your brand is, it matters more than ever where you show up.

Notes

1 Thinkbox, Signalling Success, September 2020, www.thinkbox.tv/research/thinkbox-research/signalling-success (archived at https://perma.cc/2E3Q-GGTQ)

2 everyday people, EssenceMediacom UK and everyday people launch updated Signalling Success, January 2024, www.everydaypeopleresearch.com/latestnews/signallingsuccess (archived at https://perma.cc/PVS8-K83S)

3 R Kirk, How to map media quality for physical and mental measures, The Media Leader, January 2024, https://uk.themedialeader.com/how-to-map-media-quality-for-physical-and-mental-measures/ (archived at https://perma.cc/T2KA-ZDBE)

4 Author interview with Sam Smith, Clearcast, May 2025

5 Clearcast, Top #6 Christmas ad watch outs, October 2024, https://clearcast.co.uk/news-and-blog/top-6-christmas-ad-watch-outs/ (archived at https://perma.cc/9QSG-G5BQ)

6 ASA/CAP, TV rulings upheld 2024, July 2025, www.asa.org.uk/codes-and-rulings/rulings.html?q=&sort_order=relevant&custom_date=1&from_date=03%2F01%2F2024&to_date=25%2F12%2F2024&decision=Upheld&decision=Upheld+in+part&media_type=55E98493-727E-4E81-920ECC5CB13DA77D (archived at https://perma.cc/SM5D-DKVG)

7   Thinkbox, Thinkbox Research Archives, www.thinkbox.tv/ (archived at https://perma.cc/ADN9-TSH9)

8   R Shotton, The value of TV: A behavioural science perspective, November 2024, www.thinkbox.tv/research/reports/the-value-of-tv-a-behavioural-science-perspective (archived at https://perma.cc/6Q7E-VWHC)

9   Thinkbox, Adnormal behaviour, November 2022, www.thinkbox.tv/research/thinkbox-research/adnormal-behaviour (archived at https://perma.cc/HG3R-U4RC)

10 Thinkbox, TV is at the heart of effectiveness white paper by Peter Field, March 2024, www.thinkbox.tv/research/reports/tv-is-at-the-heart-of-effectiveness-whitepaper-by-peter-field (archived at https://perma.cc/R9PP-P34W)

11 Cinema Advertising 101, Digital Cinema Media, 2024, www.dcm.co.uk/uploads/documents/Cinema_Advertising_101.pdf (archived at https://perma.cc/K8B4-ZBFK)

12 Radiocentre, Radio for building brand trust, April 2025, www.radiocentre.org/why-use-radio/the-roles-for-radio/radio-for-building-brand-trust/ (archived at https://perma.cc/Q38A-58BX)

13 Radiocentre, Breaking News, June 2024, www.radiocentre.org/policy/breaking-news/ (archived at https://perma.cc/NN4G-PK5X)

14 Radiocentre, Listen Up!, November 2023, www.radiocentre.org/our-research/listen-up/ (archived at https://perma.cc/Q69P-C6GE)

15 F Richter, Podcast ads are poised for growth, Statista, June 2024, www.statista.com/chart/17824/podcast-advertising-revenue-united-states/ (archived at https://perma.cc/H52D-FKY8)

16 Radiocentre, Advertising at the Speed of Sound, March 2025, www.radiocentre.org/advertising-at-the-speed-of-sound/ (archived at https://perma.cc/LE7Y-WB8E)

17 Acast Team, Building brand trust through podcast advertising, April 2025, https://advertise.acast.com/news-and-insights/building-brand-trust-through-podcast-advertising (archived at https://perma.cc/W5T2-KZCM)

18 Spotify Editorial Team, How to build rapport with customers – and earn their trust, September 2024, https://ads.spotify.com/en-GB/news-and-insights/how-to-build-rapport-and-trust/ (archived at https://perma.cc/CM97-4V29)

19 Magnetic, A Matter of Trust, 2017, https://magnetic.media/research/studies/a-matter-of-trust-insight (archived at https://perma.cc/NZR8-B7DB)

20 Good Housekeeping Institute, www.hearst.co.uk/good-housekeeping-institute (archived at https://perma.cc/9AWQ-VU28)

21 JCDecaux (and Clear Channel), The Moment for Trust, 2021, www.jcdecaux.co.uk/leading-insight/latest-research/moment-trust (archived at https://perma.cc/KRV9-6CSA)

22 Outsmart, Why are OOH ads attracting so few complaints? April 2025, www.
    outsmart.org.uk/keep-up-to-date/news/779/why-are-ooh-ads-attracting-so-few-
    complaints (archived at https://perma.cc/PS2F-ZUAR)

23 Marketreach, Build trust, customers keep coming back, www.marketreach.
    co.uk/build-brand-trust-with-mail (archived at https://perma.cc/F9QS-RJ92)

24 Author interview with Heather Dansie, Newsworks, June 2025

25 Newsworks, Trust. A Newsworks report, April 2023, https://newsworks.org.
    uk/research/trust-a-newsworks-report/ (archived at https://perma.cc/43MJ-
    HTYW)

26 Ozone, About Ozone, https://ozoneproject.com/about-us/ (archived at https://
    perma.cc/NLZ5-UAGG)

27 Ipsos Iris, Ozone, 2025, https://ozoneproject.com/ (archived at https://perma.
    cc/3PU9-F2L9)

28 Author interview with Damon Reeve, Ozone, April 2025

11

Trust and brand safety online

Introduction

As advertising has followed people into the online world, big new issues of trust have arisen. The unprecedented opportunities that social media, search, apps, gaming, video sharing platforms and the plethora of online channels have given advertisers, large and (especially) small, have brought with them concerns over consumer and business safety. In the immensity of online space, there are dark places as well as light, whether for individuals or the businesses seeking to communicate with them.

It's not hard to find critics of online advertising. Consumers express concern over the spread of misinformation and hate speech in social media and can be critical of brands that advertise alongside unsuitable content, as well as of the platforms themselves.[1] Plenty also find social media ads repetitive, strident and lacking in creativity – a real turn-off.[2] As we'll see in this chapter, advertisers worry that the placement of their ads next to harmful content can damage their reputation and erode trust, while regulators look for greater protection of children online, including from age-inappropriate advertising, as well as addressing issues over the promotion of high-risk categories like gambling, pharmaceuticals or alcohol, and deceptive practices. Civil society organizations, meanwhile, campaign to restrict such advertising and academics draw attention to emerging problems.[3]

One such example in the UK advertising industry is a membership organization called the Conscious Advertising Network which has a set of guiding principles to build an industry where effective advertising works for everyone.[4]

So serious questions arise for brand owners using online advertising about how to stay trustworthy.

- What ads are 'out there' and how do we know, let alone keep track of them all?

- Who is seeing what – are children receiving and encountering advertising material they should not? Is harm being done to people?
- Where are a brand's ads appearing, and next to what content?
- Is a brand keeping dangerous or damaging company that they don't know about?
- Can the myriads of new, small or young businesses advertising online be expected to know and comply with all the rules?

These questions should concern all who use or work in advertising. After all, the $1 trillion now being spent on ads worldwide is what pays for the social networks and other sites on which billions of people depend for entertainment, connection with others, opinion, advice and news.[5] Success for those running or contributing to the online platforms is based on attracting advertising money. How and where that money is invested should be safe for audiences and advertisers; it should be only in trustworthy places.

So, in this chapter we will look at the work already done and still being done to ensure trustworthy advertising behaviour online. Advertisers, platforms and media owners, regulators and governments have all sought to address public and business concerns and make the online experience a trustful and rewarding one for audiences and brands alike.

For the UK, this involves the Advertising Standards Authority, as the UK's advertising regulator, alongside its rule-making body, CAP; the government's Online Advertising Programme with its pan-industry Taskforce; the IAB with its Gold Standard and other initiatives; industry bodies representing different online advertising stakeholders; and of course at its heart the platforms, particularly the three biggest for advertising – Google, Meta and TikTok; really, a whole ecosystem of protection to engender trust in what has so quickly become the dominant advertising environment for much of the public.

In particular, we're going to take a deep dive into the work Google has done to tackle the issues it faced around brand safety online and the learnings the wider industry can draw from this. Much of this work has informed action being taken around the world, through the work of organizations like EASA and ICAS, to ensure that advertising online can be trusted.

How has the ASA kept online advertising legal, decent, honest and truthful?

Let's start with what is probably the bedrock of trust when it comes to advertising, the Advertising Standards Authority, often referred to as the ASA.[6]

The 63-year-old organization is recognized as a world leader. Well-resourced, carefully structured and consistently supported by the UK ad industry, it added broadcast TV to its scope in 2004 to regulate advertising across the board, a job it was considered to do very well.

Then came the online revolution. Between 2000 and 2020, internet and mobile ad spend grew from 1 per cent to 70 per cent of the UK total, from £150 million to £16 billion – a hundredfold increase.[7] New media, new advertisers, new techniques and technologies all appeared. The ASA system had to respond, and it did.

For one thing, the ASA regulates ads wherever they appear. It makes no difference what medium is involved: all ads should be responsible. So paid-for ads in online media were subject to the rules from the beginning. In 2011, that remit was extended to include companies' claims on their own websites and social media accounts – they might not be 'paid-for', but they were still ads.[8] The same held true for influencers' paid-for communications as they emerged: they were and are ads, so must be labelled to make that clear and come under the ASA's remit.

Secondly, the CAP code, against which the ASA delivers its judgements on online ads, is principle-based. Simply put, ads must not mislead, harm or seriously offend. Flexibility then exists to define just what those terms mean in the context of different audiences, categories or creative executions. James is Chair of CAP and has extensive first-hand experience of the discussions that take place on this.

Content – what's in the ad – and context – where and when it appears – are both considered. Guidance on how to comply with the codes and ensure ads are responsible in content and targeting runs to hundreds of helpful online advice notes, which are constantly evolving and updating according to market developments. Any advertiser, agency or individual influencer can refer to them for help and over a million such pieces of advice and training were accessed in 2024 alone. And on the basis that prevention is better (and cheaper) than treatment, CAP's Copy Advice function gives individual advertisers its informed opinion on any ads they are thinking of running but want reassurance.

So, there is no chapter in the Code headed 'online advertising' because there is no need: the demands of online ad regulation have been addressed as they have arisen within the principles of the Code and by the addition of a few new rules and a lot of new guidance to define and explain any specific requirements.

Examples include online targeting and the protection of children from ads for restricted categories like gambling or alcohol, how influencer ads must make clear their commercial status, what is an ad on a website or organic social media post, and more.

But of course, as James acknowledges, nothing's perfect. Not rules, not enforcement, not all advertisers and channels. Regulating online advertising effectively has proved a constant challenge. Back in 1995, in the earliest days of web-based advertising, the ASA received 45 complaints about it; by 2000, the number had reached 500; in 2018, the online total was 16,000.[9]

Chairman Lord Currie remarked in his foreword to that year's annual report that 'the vast, diverse and unruly nature of the internet demands that regulators of all stripes redouble their capabilities to keep up with the fast-moving content'. Some 90 per cent of the 10,850 ads amended or withdrawn at the ASA's behest in 2018 had appeared online.[10] Commenting on children's exposure to age-restricted ads online, Lord Currie acknowledged that 'parents and policymakers want reassurance on this important matter, which is why we are working proactively rather than waiting for complaints'.

This proactive approach has grown ever since. The ASA's strategy, launched that year, was titled 'More Impact Online', and was followed in 2023 by a new five-year strategy 'AI-assisted collective ad-regulation'.[11] You will recall we covered this, and the ASA's adoption of AI, in detail in Chapter 8.

Regulating online advertising is not easy. 'Vast, diverse and unruly' it remains, if considerably less unruly than it was, despite its continued growth. The ASA has to stay alert to breaches of the rules, as evidenced by the nearly 34,000 ads it had amended or withdrawn in 2024.[12] Some 84 per cent of these were 'unpaid' ads online, i.e. on companies' own websites or social media accounts, and over 90 per cent as a result of proactive work led by its Active Ad Monitoring system, which processed almost 30 million ads.

In the end, the ASA system's work is about trust – 'It's what it's all about', as ASA CEO, Guy Parker told us. 'We want people to believe that the ads they are seeing are worthy of their trust and, of course, we want them to be worthy of their trust.' That means setting and enforcing rules of advertising which keep advertisers honest and their ads truthful, above all by preventing misleading ads from harming consumer confidence in what they see and hear.

As Shahriar Coupal, the long-standing Director of the CAP Committees has written: 'Misleading advertising is bad for business, bad for consumers and bad for the reputation of the advertising industry as a whole.' CAP's new eLearning module, he went on to say, 'underlines our commitment to helping marketers get their ads right – promoting fair competition and consumer trust which in turn is good for business'.

But the ASA can only do what its scope and powers allow. Many members of the public as well as many policymakers still want to see more done, which is where the next set of initiatives involving the industry come in.

The tech sector's engagement: Intermediary & Platform Principles (IPP)

Now that 80 per cent of the investment in advertising in the UK is spent online (in its broadest sense), it is clearly vital to ensure that the ASA can regulate the ads people encounter there as effectively as in any other media. While assessing its ability to do this in the early 2020s, the ASA wanted to enhance two essential components of better regulation: transparency and accountability. Transparency is considered fundamental to public trust in organizations and regulators. Accountability, as a key control mechanism, is integral to any regulatory system and can help address any societal lack of trust in advertising.

Happily, online platforms and others in the UK online advertising supply chain have a good history of engagement and cooperation with the ASA. They help uphold the advertising rules and contribute to the consumer protection the rules require. IPP sees them taking a further voluntary step in that direction.

As the name suggests, the Intermediary & Platform Principles are a set of principles that at present involve some of the largest companies in the digital advertising supply chain, including Adform, Amazon Ads, Google, Meta, Snap Inc, TikTok, Yahoo for Business and X. More online players are expected to join as we write, to make this initiative truly market wide.

The Principles were piloted in 2022–23 to explore how the ASA system might evolve to bring greater transparency and broader accountability to its work online. There are six, as seen in Figure 11.1.

In the ASA's published report on the pilot, it noted that the 10 participating companies had implemented the principles as applicable to them, demonstrably supporting the ASA to raise awareness of its rules and to remove ads online that broke them persistently.[13] It concluded that 'We believe the Pilot has showcased the real-world value of the Principles... to enhance the existing self-regulatory system... in which relevant companies... play a part, and are seen to play a part, in supporting the ASA to help secure responsible advertising online.'

FIGURE 11.1 Intermediary and Platform Principles (IPP)

Intermediary and Platform Principles – in short
As applicable to the services they offer, participating companies will:

1 Raise awareness of the CAP Code on their services

2 Use Ts&Cs to help secure advertisers' compliance with the Code

3 Assist with promoting awareness of the ASA regulatory system

4 Support advertisers to meet obligations with regard to paid age-restricted ads

5 Act swiftly against an advertiser that persistently refuses to remove a non-compliant paid ad

6 Provide relevant information to the ASA to help carry out its investigatory regulatory duties

A full copy of the principles can be found at asa.org.uk/ipp-principles.

So, to help make online ads more trustworthy, some of the biggest companies in the world of advertising have stepped up to add new, voluntary measures to those already required by the UK codes. This shouldn't be underestimated. It is a remarkable world first and a strong indicator of the value of trust in the eyes of these major corporations.

The Online Advertising Taskforce

Another key development in the drive to ensure online advertising can be trusted is a joint government/industry initiative, the Online Advertising Taskforce (OAT).[14]

Established in 2023, the Taskforce, made up of industry organizations and government officials and chaired by a Minister of State, has several working groups addressing the issues identified by government.

Its primary focus has been on tackling illegal advertising and minimizing children being served advertising for products and services illegal to sell to them.

The Taskforce action plan brought together and built on work that was in progress to strengthen evidence, minimize harm and protect consumers and businesses, including promoting and extending industry initiatives which address in-scope harms associated with paid-for online advertising.[15] Improving transparency, accountability and trust in the online advertising supply chain are central to its objectives.

The Internet Advertising Bureau Gold Standard

Beyond its cooperative initiatives with the ASA or the government, the online advertising industry has also created and developed its own policies and tools to enhance trust in its ecosystem from individuals and advertisers alike. The Gold Standard is the leading example.

The Internet Advertising Bureau (IAB) is a global organization whose members are leaders in digital advertising and media. Its mission is to empower the media and marketing industries to thrive in the digital economy.

The IAB UK Gold Standard is a certification for buyers and sellers of digital media to improve the digital advertising experience.[16] It incorporates cross-industry standards and initiatives to address numerous shared challenges within the ecosystem, including tackling ad fraud, improving supply chain transparency and helping to limit carbon emissions.

Some 100 companies in the UK have achieved certification, including direct sellers such as publishers and content owners, media agency buyer-planners, buy side and sell side support and buyer activation service providers.

Q&A WITH JON MEW, CEO OF IAB UK, ABOUT THE GOLD STANDARD[17]

Why is trust in online advertising important?

When we talk about trust, it's often about how consumers feel about our industry and the advertising they see. That's vital and – with 81 per cent of UK ad spend on digital channels and people spending 4 hours, 20 minutes a day online – trust in digital ads is a huge component of trust in advertising overall.[18,19] It's encouraging to see that trust rose in 2024 with younger, digitally native people driving the trend particularly when it comes to online ads, but we're under no illusion that there is still work to be done.[20]

It's also vital that advertisers can trust online advertising. In my view, that comes down to accountability. Just like consumers who have the reassurance of the ASA regulating all ads, advertisers want to know that the ecosystem they are investing in is upholding best practice, utilizing tools to ensure common standards, and taking a responsible and proactive approach to tackle shared challenges. This applies as much to brand safety and scam ads as it does to supply chain transparency and sustainability. It's for this reason that we developed the IAB Gold Standard – to coordinate solutions in these areas and provide a simple way for advertisers to see that their partners are investing in best practice.

What prompted the establishment of the IAB Gold Standard?

The Gold Standard was created in 2017 as a direct result of *The Times*' investigation revealing that advertisers had unwittingly been appearing alongside illegal content online. The industry was swift to react, with P&G's Marc Pritchard delivering a landmark speech at IAB US's ALM where he labelled the digital supply chain 'murky at best, fraudulent at worst'. We knew that we had to act, and the Gold Standard was born – a certification for buyers and sellers of digital media to proactively address shared challenges and improve the digital ad industry for the benefit of everyone.

We started out by prioritizing three core areas – reducing ad fraud, upholding brand safety and improving people's experience of online advertising – and set about incorporating existing tools and initiatives from bodies such as IAB Tech Lab and the Coalition for Better Ads that would raise the bar in these areas and create a common understanding of what 'good' looks like.

In the years since, we have evolved and strengthened the Gold Standard. In addition to the above areas – which have also been developed – we have introduced criteria to bolster transparency, support compliance with ePrivacy law, and limit carbon emissions in the supply chain. And we have expanded the scope of the Gold Standard so that it includes specific frameworks for TV+ and retail media. While the Gold Standard has come a long way, we're not done. The initiative will continue to evolve to ensure that it is keeping pace with shared challenges that are in all our interests to address.

For those new to this, what does it mean if a company has the IAB Gold Standard?

It's simple – a company that is Gold Standard certified is proactively adhering to shared best practice and upholding a responsible approach to its digital advertising. By working with businesses who are Gold Standard certified, advertisers have an easy way of ensuring their partners are using the right tools to address vital issues. That helps to ensure your advertising is safe and effective, while also contributing to the overall long-term health of the advertising industry.

> *What would you like to see happen next, as the UK (and the world's)*
> *advertising industry moves progressively online, to ensure advertising can be*
> *trusted?*
>
> However much uptake, momentum and recognition the Gold Standard gets, it's
> massively important that it keeps pace with digital developments, and this
> becomes more acute with generative AI on the scene. As record spend goes
> into online channels, we at the IAB have a responsibility to galvanize support
> for the Gold Standard and the wider industry has a responsibility to take action.
>
> If you're a supplier, get involved. If you're an advertiser, ask for the Gold
> Standard from your partners. It makes huge business sense to be taking steps
> that actively crack down on ad fraud, support brand safety and improve
> transparency. It also shows policy makers that we're taking the future of our own
> industry seriously. The Gold Standard is an established part of the Online
> Advertising Taskforce's Action Plan, which means the government has recognized
> it as a crucial aspect of effective self-regulation. Let's collectively build on that to
> show that we deserve to be trusted – by advertisers and consumers alike.

Brand safety and the platforms

The major social media platforms, as we have seen, have been at the centre
of the storm over safety online, whether for individuals, especially children,
or advertisers. Over the years, they have worked to raise standards, establish
protection for users and businesses, and balance the demands of creative
expression and freedom of speech with responsibility, security and safety. All
have comprehensive toolkits for advertisers and creators to adopt, standards that they set and enforce, and sophisticated AI-powered processes to
prevent and ban abuses.

Concerns over brand safety and suitability – the first protecting brands
from appearing alongside the most egregious content, the second enabling a
brand to appear amidst content that aligns with its values and objectives –
have been a major issue for advertisers and their agencies, as we have heard.
But that appears true for the public as well as brand owners.

Exploring consumer perception of appropriate
online content and misinformation

IAS (Integral Ad Science) is a technology company that works on behalf of
digital advertisers, agencies and publishers to detect ad fraud, measure the

viewability of ads, report on the suitability of the digital content surrounding ads and support contextual ad targeting. In research published early in 2024, they showed how the US public felt about the issue of brands and the content they find them in.[21]

Key findings include:

- 82% of consumers say it's important to them that the content surrounding online ads is appropriate.

- 75% of consumers say they feel less favourable toward brands that advertise on sites that spread misinformation.

- 51% of consumers say they are likely to stop using a product or service of a brand whose ad appears near inappropriate content.

The IAS study points to a view that consumers deem the amount of online content that is inappropriate is growing – and brands are being held more accountable for ad placement than ever before.

Safety measures being taken by the tech platforms

In response to public and political pressure, the demands of advertisers and of course their own wish to do the right thing, all the major social media platforms have comprehensive policies to protect people and businesses alike.

If we look at two of the biggest – Meta, with Facebook and Instagram, and TikTok as now the UK's most popular platform amongst the young – it is evident that they take the issue very seriously.

Meta emphasizes how its Community Standards that aim to keep people safe also play a role in keeping advertisers from appearing next to harmful content.[22] Their Advertising Standards and Monetisation Policies for both partners and content set controls on the type of advertising content allowed or prohibited.[23] Ads are reviewed against the policies when they are placed. Reporting, authenticity and transparency features exist. At the same time, brand suitability controls enable advertisers to prevent their ads appearing within or alongside content they would rather avoid.

Similarly, TikTok talks about how it, too, invests heavily in ensuring a trustworthy environment for individual users, creators and advertisers.[24] Its Community Guidelines set down the norms and code of conduct required of users to maintain a safe environment, with rules for what is allowed on the platform, rules that are applied in no fewer than 70 languages globally. With the goal of creating a 'safe and entertaining' experience for over a billion people creating and connecting on TikTok, keeping these rules up to date as behaviours and risks evolve is a considerable task.

And, like Meta, TikTok has to maintain brand safety and suitability policies with inventory filters and comment management controls to align content with the inventory tiers of risk or sensitivity levels advertisers have chosen.

Both these giant platforms with their billions of worldwide users and audiences also partner with third-party experts to provide independent assurance to advertisers that their ads are beside safe and suitable content.

But despite all their efforts, social media platforms continue to encounter public criticism, regulatory threats and political attacks for the ads that slip through the net with potential harm to audiences or advertisers. Those 'rogue' ads may be just a tiny proportion of the millions that run every day, but amongst so great a number even that tiny proportion may seem too many.

How YouTube overhauled its approach to brand safety: interview with Dyana Najdi

With all the above in mind, particularly the concerns of the public and policymakers around online advertising and brand safety, we're taking an in-depth look at how Google, owner of YouTube, handled a brand safety crisis back in 2017 which made national and international headlines.

Dyana Najdi was leading Google's video solutions business for EMEA in March 2017, when a number of advertisers found their ads were appearing alongside material not deemed to be brand safe.[25] Bad actors operating across platforms resulted in the media naming some big corporates as inadvertently 'funding terrorism'. 'It was a real moment of reckoning for us,' admits Najdi, but she is proud of the way that the company reacted.

With around 400 hours of content being uploaded to YouTube every minute at the time, bad actors were working around the clock to circumvent Google's policies and controls in attempts to spread harmful content. The company immediately realized, says Najdi, that there was a potential brand safety risk to advertisers and equally as importantly that it could potentially harm the viewing experience for users as well.

That realization proved a real inflection point, launching a whole series of work streams, both to focus on what had happened with the cases highlighted in the press to explain to advertisers exactly what had gone wrong and to gain a much broader understanding of where the gaps were and how to plug them holistically.

Google set up what Najdi describes as war-rooms, bringing together expertise from across the business, all working to try and understand at which point did the system require further measures and what was the level of exposure.

It was evident that the offensive material had received only very few views and was often hard to find, but the working group realized that none of that mattered; even though the numbers were really small, what they learned, Dyana says, 'was it only took one impression to erode trust'.

She spent a lot of time working closely with ISBA, the clients' representative body in the UK, to ensure their community of advertisers remained well informed on Google's response. Furthermore, it was important to ensure stakeholders had the necessary support to implement appropriate safeguards using the existing controls, ensuring they could continue running their media with confidence.

The working group partnered closely with agencies, who played an important role in acting as a communication channel to help Google understand what was top of mind for advertisers and help relay back best practice recommendations. In those early days, Dyana remembers, the Google team was focused not only on determining the scale of the existing problem and what exactly was needed to solve it, but also on how to anticipate and prevent the next potential threat and harmful use case before it had a chance to manifest on the platform. It's this pivot and shift from being reactive that allowed them to get to today's position where Dyana believes trust has been rebuilt. 'That was a really important part of the journey,' she says.

Another aspect was its international nature. Although the furore was loudest in the UK, where the national press had taken up the issue with urgency, the company responded on a global basis.

Indeed, she describes it as one of her proudest moments of working at Google, because the global leadership showed such commitment to making sure that YouTube was 'on the right side of history'. Even though it started in the UK, management treated it as a global problem and all of the controls, and the solutions were globally applicable.

Those controls were first focused on identifying and removing bad content, 'detecting and actioning early', as Dyana put it, to make YouTube safe for viewers and advertisers. This meant investing in third-party partnerships to help build out the platform's suitability controls and to give advertisers the ability to tailor based on their brand preferences, simply and easily across campaigns and accounts. No mean feat when a typical global advertiser might have a whole hierarchy of accounts with dozens of campaigns running at any time.

Dyana described policy as always Google's first line of defence, so to identify the blind spots in their policies where there were nuances in the type of content making its way through their filters they worked with NGOs, government organizations and experts across the fields of child safety and online harms. This helped them understand the latest trends and how they were manifesting online so that these were reflected in their policies and AI models to identify and detect them as well as by human reviewers, making sure they were really investing in that first line of defence.

Google in fact invested in 10,000 human reviewers around the world, beefing up their trust and safety team with a combination of people and machines to interrogate content that was being uploaded and flagged by the system. They also set up a social listening intelligence desk to pounce on any new harmful content as soon as it was apparent.

The second thing that Google did was overhaul the approach on who was able to monetize on the platform. They went from monetization being a right to being a privilege, raising the bar by putting a threshold in place of a minimum of 1,000 subscribers and 4,000 watch hours with a number of abuse indicators, which went a long way to remove channels and videos from being able to monetize.

The third action Dyana recalls was to beef up the tools and the support that YouTube were offering advertisers, both through the controls in the interface for setting up a campaign and in the third-party partnerships that they started to build. So today there is third-party reporting with Integral Ad Science (IAS), Double Verify and Zefr; third parties who are able to review a campaign after it's run and give feedback to the advertiser and to Google in terms of how safe and suitable it was.

Those were the mechanisms initiated as a result of the whole brand safety storm, with the result, Dyana says, 'that we got to 99 per cent brand safety, because nothing is ever 100 per cent guaranteed'; things may slip through the cracks because of the nature of the open web and of having a such a broad video platform. The goal was to make sure that Google was catching those as early as possible and limiting exposure and limiting advertising impact, as evidenced by a quarterly transparency report on how effectively they were doing that. Dyana sees those reports as showing that the company really holds itself accountable so that advertisers could see over time how effectively it was progressing.

The results of Google's rapid and multi-component response to the crisis were exemplified, Dyana relates, through the advertisers that had switched off during that time but then came back onto the platform and, as they came back, evolved from having extremely tight controls in place, which meant that they were only showing up on a very small subset of content, to becoming confident in the systems now in place and relaxing those controls.

Three tiers of control exist: expanded, standard and limited mode. The last has the most stringent application of suitability but carries the penalty of a more restricted reach because the advertiser is bidding on a smaller corpus of content restricted based upon industry aligned risk levels. As advertisers have gained comfort with Google's first-party controls and third-party verification tools, so more and more have moved to the standard or even expanded tier where they have access to a greater breadth of content that meets their suitability guidelines and often delivers the best performance.

Thinking back about her key learnings from this journey, Dyana identifies three. First and foremost, she says was taking accountability.

> We always have to continue to hold ourselves accountable, owning the mistakes and recognizing where the gaps were and continuing to address those, because even when there are shortcomings, even when things go wrong, we have such a strong foundation of trust now with advertisers in the ecosystem that they know that nothing is 100 per cent, but actually we're going to do the right thing... addressing the gap and making sure it doesn't happen again.

Next was something also very important to her: doing what's right, not just what's urgent. Dyana cites YouTube Kids as an example, with investment to make a safer environment for children because it was the right thing to do, not because it was urgent or even a major advertising platform with advertisers switching off; another reason why she remains so proud of YouTube's journey.

The last is the importance of partnership: Dyana acknowledges that they couldn't have made the progress they made without a close relationship and partnership with ISBA, representing UK advertisers. Its Director General at the time, Phil Smith, she says, 'did not make it easy. He really held us accountable. But that partnership was so important because it helped us understand what mattered to the industry, get our voice back into the industry and equally with the agency communities as well and with a number of other trade bodies.'

Accountability, doing what's right and forging partnerships – the three key policies and principles that took YouTube from a place of crisis to a place of trust with advertisers and their audiences.

The 2024 'Why We Watch 2.0' report

Before we leave Google and YouTube, just a mention of their 2024 'Why We Watch 2.0' report and its findings on the relationship between quality and trust. In discussing the value and benefits of high-quality video, the report stresses the emotional as well as technical properties viewers expect.[26] But it also draws attention to what it describes as 'an additional quality signal that is becoming increasingly important: trustworthiness'.

'Across all platforms', the report goes on to explain, '80% of viewers in the UK agree that high quality video content means content that provides accurate and trustworthy information'. As its authors conclude, 'The finding underscores the growing significance of trust in the digital age, where misinformation and disinformation can spread widely.'

Conclusion

The internet and its advertising content may no longer be the 'Wild West' it was accused of being in past years, but as advertisers and industry practitioners we've interviewed have emphasized, care and attention are still critical when placing ads online. Ads play a small part in the waves of criticism that crash against the social media platforms and their content. But it is advertising that pays for that content and attracting advertising revenue that drives the attention-grabbing algorithms to deliver advertisers' audiences. To be trusted, that advertising must be seen to be responsible in terms of what is in it and where it appears.

Although the proportion of 'rogue' or misplaced ads is small, dangers lurk in the immensity of the online advertising ecosystem. The ASA's constant sweeps of different category ads or those delivered to children continue to throw up examples of bad practice, intentional or otherwise.

But action to avoid becoming such an example is straightforward.

The tools exist to ensure a trustworthy experience, whether offered by the platforms themselves, the agencies and intermediaries in the supply chain, or independent auditing and monitoring services. Our advice to advertisers is simple: use them.

Make sure that the firms involved in creating and placing your ads are signed up to the relevant certification schemes, standard-setting bodies and trade bodies which can ensure good conduct.

Use the contracts you have with your partners and suppliers to confirm their adherence to the codes of conduct, transparency and accountability you require. ISBA's Media Services Framework is a comprehensive agreement designed to govern the relationship between advertisers and their media agencies.[27] It sets out the terms for media strategy, planning and buying services to bring clarity and transparency to these relationships and ensure that both parties have a clear understanding of their obligations and expectations. The 2025 framework takes transparency to the next level and addresses agency non-compliance in proprietary media. It also refines the GenAI elements, making them more accessible for advertisers to implement.

Be aware of the rules of advertising as they affect your work – and they will. Take advantage of the free advice and guidance offered online by CAP and the ASA on hundreds of topics, as well as that available from publishers, platforms and trade organizations.

Ensure you and your media supply chain have excluded audiences that should not be exposed to your ads, which may include children or specific vulnerable groups. Think before you buy!

Wherever you work within the online advertising ecosystem, you have a responsibility to make sure that your work can be trusted by the audience that it reaches, and that is not inadvertently funding dangerous or harmful content. This sounds simple, but we recognize its complexity when ads can appear in hundreds, thousands, even millions of online locations, placed there through a complex supply chain.

All the links in that chain – from client to agency to demand and supply-side platforms and other adtech intermediaries – as well as the platforms and publishers, have to get it right.

Settling for anything less than this can harm public trust and confidence in advertising, open it up to further interventions from governments and regulators, and diminish the effectiveness of each and every ad.

Notes

1 T Stewart, Consumers are growing more critical of social media ads, New Digital Age, 2023, https://newdigitalage.co/social-media/social-media-advertising-misinformation-integral-ad-science/ (archived at https://perma.cc/6QN8-YBEJ)

2   Spider AF, Decoding audience behavior: Why are ads so annoying? March 2025, https://spideraf.com/articles/why-are-ads-so-annoying-understanding-the-overload-of-irritating-marketing (archived at https://perma.cc/XXD7-AVA9)

3   Y Ekinci, S Dam and G Buckle, The dark side of social media influencers: A research agenda for analysing deceptive practices and regulatory challenges, *Psychology of Marketing*, January 2025, https://onlinelibrary.wiley.com/doi/10.1002/mar.22173 (archived at https://perma.cc/53D3-EJSA)

4   Conscious Advertising Network, About us, www.consciousadnetwork.com/about-us/ (archived at https://perma.cc/6PS9-ESA8)

5   WARC, Global advertising spend to pass $1 trillion for the first time this year, November 2024, www.warc.com/content/feed/global-advertising-spend-to-pass-1-trillion-for-the-first-time-this-year/en-GB/10119 (archived at https://perma.cc/AM8X-GPCF)

6   ASA/CAP, About ASA and CAP, www.asa.org.uk/about-asa-and-cap.html (archived at https://perma.cc/J7R5-X2BJ)

7   Advertising Association & WARC Expenditure Report, 2020, www.warc.com/about-media/expenditure-report (archived at https://perma.cc/X8YJ-4USU)

8   ASA and CAP Annual Report 2011, www.asa.org.uk/resource/asa-and-cap-annual-report-2011.html (archived at https://perma.cc/QEP2-5JPX)

9   ASA and CAP Annual Reports 2000, 2010, 2018 and 2024, www.asa.org.uk/advice-and-resources/resource-library/annual-reports.html (archived at https://perma.cc/2BYN-A7TV)

10 ASA and CAP Annual Report 2018, www.asa.org.uk/resource/asa-and-cap-annual-report-2018.html (archived at https://perma.cc/DA7X-396H)

11 ASA, More Impact Online, November, 2018, www.asa.org.uk/resource/more-impact-online.html (archived at https://perma.cc/8H29-FAWK)

12 ASA and CAP Annual Report, 2024, www.asa.org.uk/resource/asa-and-cap-annual-report-2024.html (archived at https://perma.cc/XX8Y-8MDW)

13 ASA, Intermediary & Platform Principles Pilot – Final Report, October 2023, www.asa.org.uk/resource/intermediary-and-platform-principles-pilot-final-report.html (archived at https://perma.cc/97RR-3BRS)

14 Online Advertising Taskforce, Gov.UK, www.gov.uk/government/groups/online-advertising-taskforce (archived at https://perma.cc/A2DV-2SKR)

15 Online Advertising: Taskforce Progress Report, Hansard, UK Parliament, December 2024, https://hansard.parliament.uk/commons/2024-12-02/debates/24120221000009/OnlineAdvertisingTaskforceProgressReport (archived at https://perma.cc/N2SU-PJ9W)

16 IAB, The Gold Standard, www.iabuk.com/goldstandard (archived at https://perma.cc/25PH-3U59)

17 Author interview with Jon Mew, IAB UK, March 2025

18 IAB UK / PwC Digital Adspend Study 2023 & AA / WARC Expenditure report 2024, 2023, www.iabuk.com/news-article/digital-adspend-2023-digital-ad-market-grows-11-ps296bn (archived at https://perma.cc/EEK5-FFQ4)

19 Ofcom, Online Nation, 2024, www.ofcom.org.uk/siteassets/resources/ documents/research-and-data/online-research/online-nation/2024/online-nation-2024-report.pdf?v=386238 (archived at https://perma.cc/GY85-YHB5)

20 Advertising Association, Trust in advertising rises in 2024, driven by younger people, January 2025, https://adassoc.org.uk/our-work/trust-in-advertising-rises-in-2024-driven-by-younger-people/ (archived at https://perma.cc/34EJ-N9SE)

21 Integral Ad Sciences (IAS), Research: The state of brand safety, January 2024, https://integralads.com/uk/insider/state-of-brand-safety-research/ (archived at https://perma.cc/YY4Q-MU8D)

22 Meta, Brand safety and suitability, www.facebook.com/business/brand-safety-and-suitability (archived at https://perma.cc/3J4S-M9U6)

23 Meta, Introduction to the Advertising Standards, https://transparency.meta.com/policies/ad-standards (archived at https://perma.cc/DMN3-SPBM)

24 TikTok, Transparency Center, www.tiktok.com/transparency/en (archived at https://perma.cc/2PVH-2UP2)

25 Author interview with Dyana Najdi, Google, May 2025

26 Why We Watch 2.0, Google, 2024, www.thinkwithgoogle.com/_qs/ documents/18431/IT_Why_We_Watch_2.0_-_2024_Digital_Report.pdf (archived at https://perma.cc/ACD8-VES5)

27 ISBA, Media Services Framework, March 2025, www.isba.org.uk/knowledge/ media-services-framework-2025 (archived at https://perma.cc/5S5F-LQ3Y)

12

What happens if we're not trusted?

Introduction

Losing trust has consequences. So does never gaining it. That's true for a person, a government or any organization. For advertising, whether seen in the round as a giant and varied collection of communications or in the form of individual advertisements, the consequences are worth thinking about.

As we see it, there are three key benefits of winning trust in advertising: better results, better regulation, and better talent recruitment and retention. This book concentrates on the first, better results, but when you think about the downsides of a lack of trust in our business or our work, then the other two enter the picture as well. We're also going to look at how advertising played an important role in rebuilding public trust after a collapse experienced by the finance industry during the global banking crash.

Our hope in this chapter is to help explain why you should care about trust in advertising generally, not just trust in the work you make. The consequences of an industry not being trusted have far-reaching implications which can impact everyone who works in it, whether they are directly responsible or not. It is in all our interests for our industry to be trusted.

The risks from regulation

If people don't trust you, but believe others do and are influenced by what you say, they will seek to limit your freedom of speech. They may even try to ban you from speaking. The same is true of advertising: if it's not trusted, it's vulnerable to attack by legislators and regulators.

You don't have to live under an autocratic government to experience limits on your freedom of expression; we have laws in the UK against speech that stirs up violence, unlawful behaviour, discrimination or harassment, for example. Images considered defamatory, pornographic or harmful can also break the law. Similar rules exist even in the US, where the First Amendment famously protects free speech, but not at all costs to society.

Earnest debates take place in the media about where or when the limits should apply, to what and to whom. Recently, the rise of social media with its angry or provocative comments, often uncontrolled by editors or fact-checkers, has made the issue higher profile than ever. Campaigners and politicians argue the case for reining in the 'free speech' exercised online and the UK's Online Safety Act does just that in cases of evident harm, but more libertarian voices here and in the US want to release the brakes on any personal or political comment.[1]

Advertising, which is a form of commercial speech and therefore rather less fully protected by law than, say, editorial, has for many years operated under considerable constraints as to what can be said and shown. As well as the law of the land, in the UK we have the CAP Code of advertising rules, administered by the Advertising Standards Authority. But to those who are suspicious of the power and role of ads, there should always be more regulation. And the more powerful advertising seems to be, the greater the perceived need to restrict it.

What do politicians think about advertising?

Credos has regularly run surveys of the UK Member of Parliament's attitudes towards advertising.[2] In January 2024, it commissioned YouGov to ask a sample of them about trust and regulation. The results were stark, with party affiliations revealing big differences in the responses of MPs from the two biggest political parties.

Asked whether they were trusting of the ad industry, 77 per cent of Conservative MPs said yes, they were, either very or fairly; only 32 per cent of Labour MPs felt that way.

What about ad regulation, was there too much, too little? Just 8 per cent of Conservatives thought there was too little; 63 per cent of Labour members thought there was.

So, should there be more government regulation of advertising? Yes, there should, said 71 per cent of the Labour MPs; only 10 per cent of Conservatives agreed.

FIGURE 12.1 MP Trust in the advertising industry

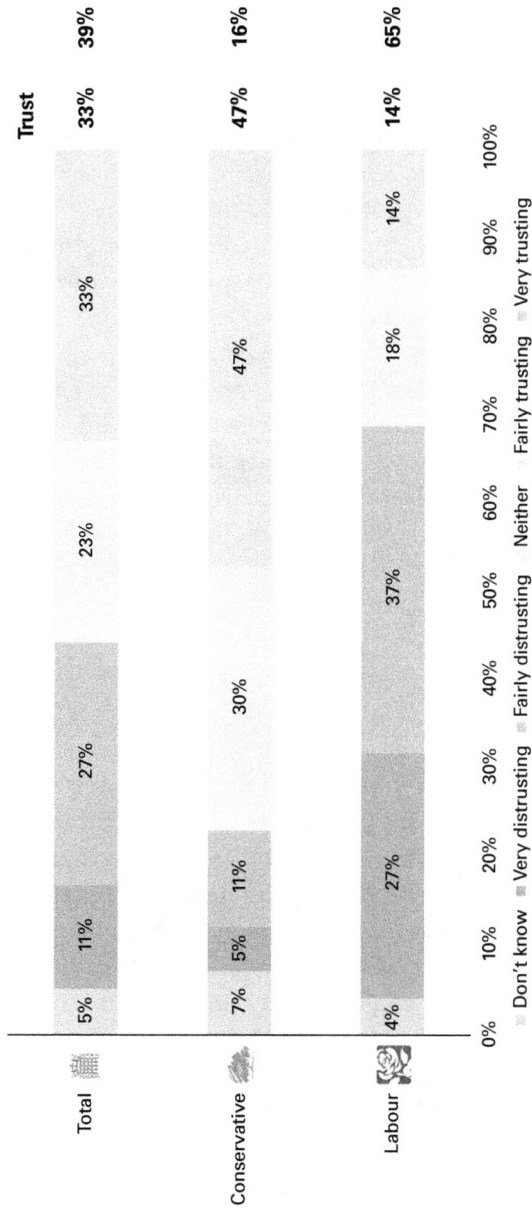

Trust

	Very distrusting	Fairly distrusting	Neither	Fairly trusting	Very trusting	
Total	5%	11%	27%	23%	33%	33% 39%
Conservative	7%	5% 11%	30%	47%		47% 16%
Labour	4%	27%	37%	18%	14%	14% 65%

Don't know · Very distrusting · Fairly distrusting · Neither · Fairly trusting · Very trusting

SOURCE Credos

FIGURE 12.2 MP views on advertising industry regulation

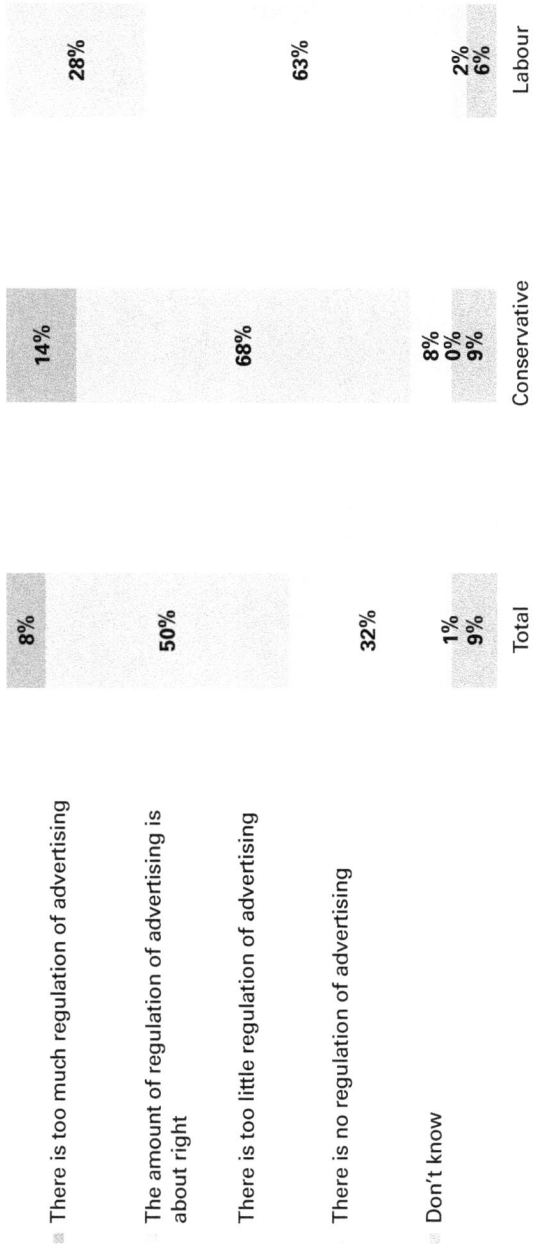

There is too much regulation of advertising

The amount of regulation of advertising is about right

There is too little regulation of advertising

There is no regulation of advertising

Don't know

	Total	Conservative	Labour
There is too much regulation of advertising	8%	14%	28%
The amount of regulation of advertising is about right	50%	68%	63%
There is too little regulation of advertising	32%		
There is no regulation of advertising	1%	8% 0%	2%
Don't know	9%	9%	6%

SOURCE Credos

FIGURE 12.3 MP views on more government regulation of advertising

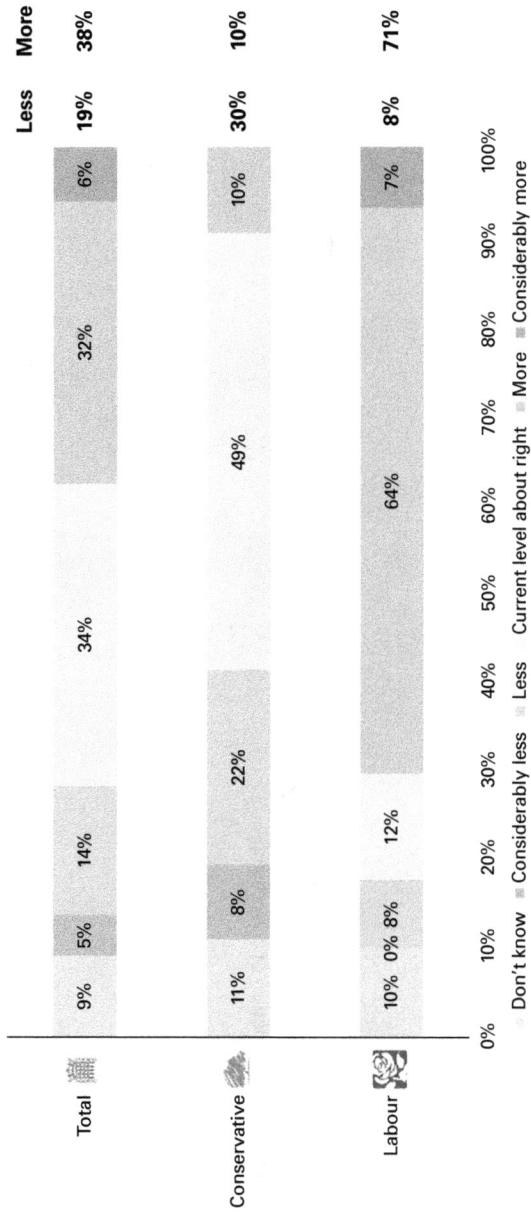

	Don't know	Considerably less	Less	Current level about right	More	Considerably more		Less	More
Total	9%	5%	14%	34%	32%	6%		19%	38%
Conservative	11%	8%	22%	49%		10%		30%	10%
Labour	10%	0% 8%	12%	64%	7%			8%	71%

SOURCE Credos

The Conservatives, of course, have long been seen as the more pro-business party, with Labour more interventionist. The striking result of the Credos survey showed just how clearly a lack of trust in the advertising industry was reflected in a desire to impose greater restrictions on it. The Conservatives were in power at the time of the survey; Labour are as we write. The new Labour government professes to be pro-business and pro-growth, but how does that fit with the desire to regulate advertising more?

Watch this space…

A politician's view

We got a first-hand view of an MP's – and minister's – perspective on the issue by talking to parliamentarian and past Secretary of State for Culture, Media & Sport (DCMS) as well as Education, Baroness Nicky Morgan, who is now chair of the Advertising Standards Authority.[3]

She started by sharing her view that advertising is a window into our society and that when society is wrestling with what to do about something, its advertising is inevitably in the crosshairs. She said that, while serving as DCMS Secretary of State, advertising was rarely the focus of discussion, but it constantly popped up in all sorts of conversations, whether as part of the creative industries, tackling online fraud, helping to fund the media or in discussions about online safety and the tech platforms more generally.

Over time, she told us, she had seen the need for regulatory intervention into industries and sectors as diverse as financial services, telecoms and schools. She explained that when it came to the advertising industry, her view was that government tended to be relatively neutral. Any DCMS Minister might dread being asked to comment about an ad that had been in the news for controversial reasons, but advertising was not one of the 'bombs likely to go off in a Secretary of State's face!'. The tipping point for some category of advertising can occur when the industry is 'in trouble' because it seems to be acting contrary to government policy or it has become unexpectedly newsworthy, or possibly a combination of the two. We will delve deeper into how this has happened to the category of high fat, salt and sugar (HFSS) food advertising later in this chapter.

Baroness Morgan reminded us that politics is always about timing and an industry can find itself heading for statutory regulation when it is seen to be getting more than one important thing wrong. For example, financial services were regulated when concern grew at the heart of government over both irresponsible practices and a lack of consumer protection, so the resulting regulation sought to reduce risk and remove bad actors. She observed that when the banks came to the support of their customers during the Covid-19 pandemic, government's approval of the sector revived. Her advice to an industry keen to avoid regulatory intervention is to go with the grain of government policy, be a useful sounding board on policy considerations and treat your customers fairly and responsibly.

Turning to the advertising industry, she said that her time leading DCMS became dominated by conversations about people's online experience, with issues on the agenda like privacy, scam and fraudulent advertising, and online harms. Noting the rapid shift in the shape and structure of the UK advertising industry towards online predominance, Lady Morgan doubted that the industry had realized early on just how quickly it was happening and what its implications might be, any more than government had.

To the point, she asked whether advertising is really one industry that can speak with one voice anymore? She pointed to the contrast between media owners like the broadcasters, who rarely cause problems, and the tech platforms on which advertising and influencer content often attract attention over the safety standards that intrinsically link to trust. Her point was that trust in the advertising sector will only be ensured when all participants take it seriously. That, she said, included the proper funding of advertising's co-regulatory system with the necessary processes and principles in place all along the ad-supply chain to ensure the highest standards are met. She urged that the responsibility for this must be accepted in the boardrooms of all the businesses in the advertising ecosystem.

Lady Morgan reflected that, while in government, her focus as far as advertising was concerned was on what she perceived as the greatest pollutant of the industry, scams and frauds. Now, at the ASA, the question was more about things that could cause the greatest potential harm, for example in public health or medicines, and how the industry can ensure it is fully responsible in these areas. Hence the consistent focus on obesity levels, alcohol and gambling. Looking forward, she highlighted how shifts in society could present new challenges for the industry. For example, if weight-loss drugs become an everyday product on the shelves, how will advertising respond? Or if a ban on smartphones for under-16s became a popular policy decision, would a call to disallow their advertising soon follow? Even if outright bans lacked support, she mused, 'crackdowns' often resonated well with politicians and public.

All of this is wrapped up in the government's, and, perhaps more broadly, society's trust in the work of the advertising industry. It operates within a constantly moving social context. The importance of supporting the work of the ASA and efforts to set and enforce standards must not be underestimated.

The hot issues for advertising regulation and trust

As Baroness Morgan observed, politicians are not interested in restricting all advertising for the sake of it, but just particular aspects. These tend to be of two types: product categories that are seen to carry risks for the public, especially to their health; and media platforms considered less than perfect in ensuring that their audiences, particularly children, only see the ads that they should.

High risk content

Advertising the first type, those products like alcohol or gambling which can cause harm to some through irresponsible or addictive use, is not trusted because its critics see it as magnifying their risk. In their eyes it may be the products that are the problem, but advertising cannot be trusted to responsibly curtail the risk they carry to some people. They argue that it not only encourages consumers to try or buy more of the product, but it gives social licence, the gloss of public approbation, to them. It must be restricted.

So campaigning groups in the UK like Alcohol Change UK, the Obesity Health Alliance or Lords for Gambling Reform lobby government to 'clamp down' on advertising. Left alone, they may say, the industry with its competitive urges and lust for growth will not do enough. Here's a sense of what they are saying…

> What needs to change. Alcohol marketing is everywhere… we need to put in place some sensible restrictions on the ways that alcohol can be promoted. We are calling for a thorough overhaul of the way alcohol marketing is regulated…
>
> *Alcohol Change UK, June 2024*[4]

> Due to the multiple formats, complexity, and fast changing nature of the digital marketing environment along with the issues in regulating this environment, ending all digital junk food marketing with a total online ban is the most effective way to protect children and would also benefit adults' health.
>
> *An End to Junk Food Marketing Online: Policy Position, Obesity Health Alliance 2020*[5]

Without further action, we will continue to be bombarded with gambling adverts on TV, radio, billboards (including round sports grounds, in match day programmes and even on the shirt sleeves of premiership players) as well as online…

And we are particularly concerned about the impact that this has on children…

We believe further reforms are needed…

Other countries are taking action to ban or restrict gambling advertising. The majority of the British public want us to do the same. We believe more should be done in this country.

Peers for Gambling Reform, Recommendations, 2024[6]

To some extent they are, of course, right. Left alone without sensible regulation, some advertisers will inevitably behave irresponsibly at the expense of those – and they will be a large majority – who restrain their marketing. But nearly all countries, including the UK, have existing and ever-evolving rules and regulations that already ensure advertising, especially of high-risk categories, is regulated. The CAP Codes have scores of such rules and hundreds of guidance notes to help advertisers and their agencies avoid mishaps. The industry complies with the rules because of its collective commitment to trustworthy communications, a commitment it makes in exchange for appropriate freedoms to compete and innovate through advertising and for the level competitive playing field that judicious regulation brings.

Nonetheless, the politicians and campaigners arguing for greater restrictions will often enjoy considerable public support. Banning the advertising of popular but potentially harmful products can sound attractive and perhaps 'the right thing to do'.

Reports on two YouGov surveys in 2021 illustrate this. The first, reported in the *Guardian* found that 77 per cent of adults supported a ban on gambling ads on radio and TV before 9pm, with a similar number in favour of the same curbs applying to social media and online[7]; the second, reported in The Grocer in the same month, showed 57 per cent of adults favoured an online ban on HFSS foods and 58 per cent a 9pm TV 'watershed'.[8]

As we have seen in Chapter 4, people who are concerned about social issues like alcohol abuse or gambling addiction will naturally find ads for those products a problem and their very existence a sign of an untrustworthy industry.

Obesity and advertising restrictions

It can be very tempting for governments to see advertising regulation or bans as an inexpensive, popular and (for them) risk-free way to be seen to act on thorny issues. One is diet and a current example of how distrust of advertising's role and effect can provoke restrictive action is the UK's Less Healthy Foods legislation.

Obesity is a very real problem in modern society, with complex root causes, whether psychological, physiological, familial, societal or commercial. It costs the UK dearly in terms of the demands it puts on the National Health Service and social care, its impact on employment and the economy, and the personal suffering it causes. Frontier Economics have put the total cost at some £98 billion, or 4 per cent of UK GDP, with some two-thirds of that falling to individuals and one-third to government and business.[9] Successive governments have attempted to reverse the seemingly inexorable increase in average weight, but without success. Inevitably, banning the advertising of products that can be judged to contribute to the problem has always been on the list of attractive remedies.

Foods and drinks high in fat, sugar or salt (HFSS) have been severely restricted in the content and targeting of their advertising through the CAP Codes and their enforcement by the ASA for years. But after his brush with death during the Covid crisis, then-Prime Minister Boris Johnson determined that further limits on HFSS ads were warranted for the sake of the nation's health, especially children's. The medical community, well-supported campaigning groups and many in the general public were behind him – after all, who would not want 'junk food adverts' to be kept away from children?

After an extended and tortuous passage of debate and amendment, new restrictions on the advertising of 'less healthy foods' were passed into law and, after some delay, are due to come into effect as this book is being written. No such products will be allowed in any TV ads before 9pm and not at all online, except from small businesses.

Advertisers from the food, restaurant, delivery service and retail sectors, as well as key media owners, see the new restrictions as onerous, unwieldy and potentially damaging to their companies, but if a government decides that the industry cannot be trusted to turn away from advertising it considers harmful in some way, the consequence can be just that.

The bigger question for the industry in the coming years is what else might be viewed as 'high risk content' and whether the industry can be trusted to advertise it.

High risk context

The other way a lack of trust brings on restrictions is when the context, rather than the content, of the advertising is suspect. As the media landscape has changed, so has the focus of suspicion and the scope of regulation. Once it was printed 'fliers' or 'handbills', in the 20th century broadcast TV, and most recently the so-called 'Wild West' of internet advertising. Each powerful new advertising medium sparks the call for new regulation to prevent abuses of its power and now is the turn, in particular, of social media.

We have seen from Credos' long-term tracking data in Chapter 3 how advertising in some media is trusted more than in others. Young people may feel comfortable in the online world they have grown up with, but older generations are less confident of the 'new media' and their trustworthiness. This lack of confidence translates into pressure to regulate online media more strictly.

In the UK, we see this from lobby groups concerned to protect young or otherwise vulnerable groups from, for instance, advertising that presents unattainable or unhealthy body images as desirable or online ads targeted at adults which nonetheless are accessed by children. If the media are not considered to be policing themselves adequately in areas outside the scope of the ASA or other regulators, then the result can be legislative intervention.

The government responded to these pressures with its Online Advertising Programme. A consultation was launched in March 2022 and in her foreword then-Minister of State Julia Lopez wrote that while the rapid growth of online advertising had brought significant benefits, it came with risks and potentially damaging consequences.[10] She went on to explain how the Online Advertising Programme will look at ways to address this by building on the existing self-regulatory framework.

Mentioning its fit with the then imminent Online Safety Bill and the government's initiatives on competition and data protection issues across the online landscape, the minister's introduction continued that the Online Advertising Programme will have a remit to protect people and businesses from harm.

This threat of new law to regulate online ads further than they had been led to industry initiatives to stave off such intervention and the evolution of the government's Online Advertising Taskforce to develop effective industry-led policies to achieve its objectives. But it has showed again how a lack of public and political trust in advertising can provoke moves to impose restrictions.

And it's not just politicians who regulate

But Parliament is not the only organization with the power to bear down on advertising if it thinks it must. Ofcom has long been the UK's broadcast regulator, with a statutory responsibility for advertising that it delegates to the ASA. Now Ofcom has new regulatory powers in the online space, including over aspects of the advertising that funds most online services.

Its Chair, Lord Grade, spoke at the Advertising Association's LEAD Conference in January 2024, where he highlighted how important it was for advertisers, their agencies and their media partners to consider the impact of online harms on their reputations and to make trust a priority.[11] To this powerful regulator, the relationship between online content, his primary concern, and the brands using it to reach their audiences was clear.

Lord Grade's remarks were aimed at the advertisers and their agencies whose use of online media might run the danger of jeopardizing their brand's safety. How? By appearing alongside harmful content and so being seen both to fund it and approve of it. Not a 'safe' place for a brand to be. Not a place that would reinforce trust in the brand but indeed could do the very opposite.

REAL-WORLD EXAMPLE
Gambling advertising

In some cases, the industry whose products are considered to create some risk of harm is persuaded to fund independent bodies that can work to mitigate or help remedy any such harms. For gambling that is Gamble Aware, complementing the industry's statutory regulator, the Gambling Commission.[12]

Working to create a society free from gambling harms, Gamble Aware is an independent charity that commissions gambling harms education, prevention, early intervention and treatment. Its 2024 annual report shows that Gamble Aware devoted some £15 million to education and prevention, including behaviour change campaigns using advertising to raise awareness of the risks of gambling, reduce stigma, encourage the use of preventative tools and increase engagement with support and services.

It may seem contradictory to spend money attracting people to gambling services and then spend more money to help people stop gambling, but of course the large majority of individuals do not develop problem gambling behaviour and competing for their custom is legitimate. All gambling ads carry a link to Gamble Aware to nudge anyone whom the ad might affect negatively toward their services: 'Be Gamble Aware.org' appears on all UK ad formats.

Is this enough for gambling advertising to be trusted? Perhaps not. The ASA has consistently clamped down on irresponsible gambling ads, but their overall volume is unregulated and powerful lobbying for a full ban on advertising by betting companies continues. We know that some categories of advertising are simply less trusted than others because of the nature of the product or service being sold, so perhaps the notion of all ads being trusted is a stretch too far? Certainly not by everyone: the roughly half of the adult population who never gamble are a lot less willing to approve of its advertising than those who do like a bet. It's an interesting exercise to think what more might a sector like this do, and what would be needed to encourage further action other than the threat of regulatory intervention.

Lessons from the finance industry

Let's look at an industry that experienced a collapse in public trust which led to regulatory intervention, and how advertising played an important role in rebuilding trust in its brands.

Following the 2008/09 financial crisis, banks faced challenges, including failures, government bailouts, mergers and increased regulation aimed at preventing future crises. They also faced a challenge of trust – from governments, civil society and their customers. The banks were blamed for the crisis, which had not only cost their many shareholders money, but required enormous loans from the taxpayer to keep them solvent. Stricter rules on lending, risk and liquidity all played their part in restoring confidence in the financial system, but rebuilding trust in bank brands took time and effort. Five years on, the *Guardian* reported a survey from Which showing that trust in banks had hit an all-time low, with 71 per cent of UK adults saying that they did not think the banks had learned their lesson.[13]

Even 10 years on from the crisis, YouGov Omnibus research commissioned on behalf of Positive Money indicated that trust in banks remained low.[14]

The study revealed that two-thirds of British adults did not trust banks to work in the best interest of society, as opposed to the 20 per cent that thought they did. Looking to the future, 63 per cent worried that banks might cause another financial crisis in the future, with only 27 per cent not worried.

But that has changed. Credos has measured trust in banking, alongside that in several sectors including advertising, for 15 years.[15] The recovery from the post-GFC period is clear to see.

FIGURE 12.4 Trust in banking industry

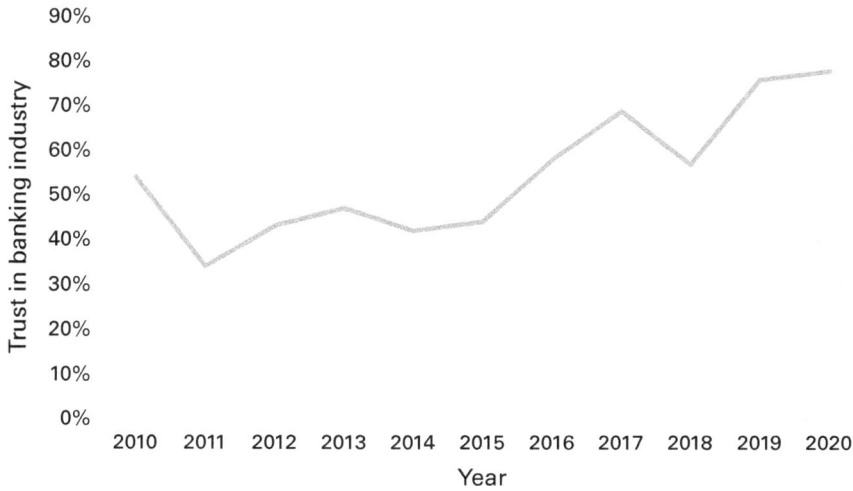

SOURCE Credos

And globally the big financial services players have seen a similar recovery, according to the FutureBrand Index 2025 study.[16] It reports that, over the last decade, financial services brands have seen the biggest improvements in overall reputation of all the 100 top brands that they track. Their average scores on all combined 'experience and purpose' dimensions rose from 19 per cent in 2014 to 32 per cent in 2024.

As the banking industry put its house in order with new regulatory disciplines and an all-out effort to improve service and improvements stimulated by the entry of new 'challenger banks' like Monzo, Revolut and Starling, so customer trust revived.

The stories of how individual bank brands used their communications and advertising to support their efforts to restore consumer trust are illuminating. These all come from the IPA's unmatched Effectiveness Awards case history bank.

Barclays: Purpose Pays (2018)[17]

Trust in banks, described in this case as 'the foundation stone of the whole banking system', had been dramatically shaken by the 2008/09 financial crisis. According to the Edelman Trust Barometer quoted, public belief in banks' integrity halved in the US and UK, falling from 69 per cent to 29 per cent from

2008 to 2010 in the former, and from 41 per cent to 22 per cent in the latter. Indeed, in the UK it was still bumping along at just 21 per cent in 2012 and Edelman's global survey showed that by 2013 banks and financial services were the least trusted sectors of the fifteen tracked. On top of that, Barclays had been hit in 2012 by the Libor-fixing scandal, so that trust in the brand 'plummeted to a historic low'.

Barclays knew that this was bad for business, as their brand-drivers analysis showed trust as a top driver of brand consideration, in turn a critical driver of long-term sales. A cultural transformation was needed and was led from the top, integrating purpose and values in a new code of conduct for all Barclays' people, aligning their behaviour and rewards. New communications campaigns were launched with the brand's stated purpose of 'helping people achieve their ambitions the right way' at their heart.

This meant moving from product-focused advertising to using marketing to rebuild trust by showing what Barclays was doing to help people move forward in a digital world. Over the years 2014–17 the series of campaigns featured the Digital Eagles, Barclays staff helping the unconfident learn digital skills; presented Life Skills for the 21st century workforce; created the Code Playground to help children learn to code; and culminated in Digital Safety, advising and assisting the public on how to protect themselves from online fraud. They all shared three campaign strands: trust, education and action.

Using a broad range of media including TV, VOD, social, press, online, their websites and plenty of PR, the campaigns generated a massive response. Digital Safety proved particularly strong – described as 'impactful, practical, helpful, sometimes funny, sometimes a little bit shocking' it sounds like the epitome of the creatively engaging ads that earlier chapters in this book have advocated.

And the results? The case study shows that the primary metric the advertising was designed to improve, that Barclays was 'more trustworthy than others', increased dramatically. It rose by 42 per cent from 2014 to 2017, alongside other key drivers of consideration. The bank's brand image modelling indicated that trust in the brand recovered by 60 per cent and its econometric modelling attributed over £150 million in sales increase to the campaign, at a very healthy ROI.

Altogether, this trust-boosting purpose campaign delivered direct sales impact and indirect sales effects on enhanced consideration that considerably out-performed the previous product-focused advertising. And this along with its impact on colleague empowerment and its positive societal benefits. Certainly, for Barclays, purpose – and trust – paid back.

Lloyds Bank: The Power of Pure Brand (2020)[18]

Faced with the same need to rebuild trust after the Global Financial Crisis, Lloyds' revival and consistently compelling dramatization of its famous Black Horse emblem made for a powerful brand-led campaign over the years 2015–19. The horse, symbolic of a caring, supportive companion, 'By Your Side', generated strong branded ad recall, unleashing the power of high spontaneous awareness and brand saliency for Lloyds, which in turn drove impressive business outcomes. Famous, emotional advertising centred on a symbol of trustworthy companionship throughout customers' lives.

Views from the Finance Industry 2025

To help inform our understanding of how trust matters to the finance industry, and how advertising has been deployed to help support the rebuilding of trust in banking brands, we interviewed leading marketers from the UK financial services sector.

First up, Marg Jobling, CMO, NatWest Group, and her colleague Petra Cameron, Director of Brand Partnerships and Programmes.

TRUST IS OUR CORNERSTONE

Brands are like people, and so, trust is the cornerstone of relationships between brands and their customers, says Jobling.[19] She and Cameron clearly care about the reputation of the Group and the level of customer trust in its brands. You must be worrying about trust all the time, Jobling says: we look at it, we track it, because these days, brands have nowhere to hide. What you say and what you do must be completely aligned and your system must work in its entirety, otherwise you risk mistrust which can be damaging to your brand and business. She reflected on her experiences in marketing and how, in the past, it was easier for a marketer to govern the message and the context. Now, it is harder to tell precisely where the advertising campaign is going to show up, because of the nature of programmatic advertising. Her advice is that you must be certain that any brand promise you make 'on air' has to be matched by the service and the products that you provide. For a responsible business, this means everything you do as an employer and everything you do in your supply chain has to be aligned with your business strategy. Advertising is a part of that, 'the illumination of what you stand for'.

Jobling broke down the marketing team's approach to building trust in three ways:

1 Make sure we know what we are advertising is what the customer wants and is of the highest standard – this is all about competence.

2 Make sure we show up where our customers are and be mindful that as a group of brands connecting with 19 million customers across British society this includes always being politically agnostic – this is all about being on people's side and avoiding conflict where necessary.

3 Make sure we are always representative and relevant to the real-life experiences of our customers – this is all about showing understanding and, where possible, giving something positive back.

Jobling acknowledges the challenges above, in particular around the second point and the challenge of context when running advertising campaigns that number into thousands of different placements. This is something we explored in Chapters 9 and 10 – the challenge of handling where you show up.

Jobling's view is that trust must be consistently high for finance brands for mistakes to be forgiven and forgotten. This was particularly acute for the Royal Bank of Scotland brand which had a dramatic fall in trust, following its collapse and the rescue by the UK government during the global banking crash, and it has taken a long time for that trust to be regained. Jobling and Cameron noted that in their experience of managing the two brands since then, an issue that affects both the RBS and the NatWest brand, such as a tech outage, would have a greater and longer-lasting impact on RBS.

The NatWest Group team started to use influencers in 2016, initially as a test with RBS, and they now use them across a range of different service and product campaigns. Jobling describes a shift from tactical use to strategic use over the past decade, with a notable acceleration in the past three years to account for some 3 per cent of media spend by 2024, a number that the team expects to keep growing. They frame the role of influencers for NatWest Group's advertising and marketing campaigns in three categories:

1 The company's own 'coalition' of content creators, employees tasked with making content that tells stories of how products and services connect with everyday life.

2 The influencers that come as part of major sponsorship deals made by the brand, such as the athletes who are part of Team GB and Paralympics GB, where the access is carefully managed but the reach is larger.

3 Content creators who have built their own communities, where the goal is to secure implicit endorsement of the brands.

Jobling described that endorsement as 'creativity reborn', representing borrowed credibility for specific audiences about the bank's capabilities. In other words, customer engagement re-created in a world where linear TV no longer performs its old role for younger adults and TikTok has become the number one search engine for under-16s.

In that context, she noted the challenge of the rise of social media – the battle to tell stories through entertaining content in just a few seconds. However, Jobling points out that in marketing, you must fish where the fish are, and increasingly, social media is now where people are. Setting guard-rails for programmatic buying and demonstrating responsible media selection was just part of a bigger picture aligning all aspects of NatWest Group's communications with its business behaviours.

Jobling and Cameron continue to worry about trust, and the future of being trusted, with the advent of new technology such as AI. The application of AI means we can greatly personalize our advertising to customers, they said, but at the same time, we have to ensure our customers are not victims of a scam such as impersonation of the bank. They ask, how do you know NatWest is NatWest and how do we make sure everything we do holds true to that?

The future of bank marketing, with all its complexities, will be fascinating to see, but we can be sure that trust, Jobling's 'cornerstone' of the relationship with her customers, will retain its centrality.

THREE KEY TAKEAWAYS

1 Trust is completely dependent upon total alignment between what you say your brand is and what your brand does; how customers experience it.

2 Influencers include your own staff, who can play a strategic role for your brand alongside celebrities, and content creators.

3 Remember, trust is an investment in your brand to help you through difficult times.

HIGH-QUALITY PRODUCTION IS INTEGRAL TO TRUST

'Definitely in our sector,' says Richard Warren, Director of Brands, Marketing & Corporate Affairs at Nationwide, 'trust is incredibly important'.[20] It is an imperative for Nationwide, which benefits, he says, from being so trusted, engendering loyalty and protecting margins, for instance by preventing other banks' better short-term interest rates from pulling away Nationwide customers.

Despite that, Nationwide do not use trust as a metric per se but favour a basket of metrics that add up to being seen as a trusted brand: 'have heard good things about', 'leading the way' and 'provides long-term value' amongst them. He describes a blunt metric of 'trust' as too crude a measure, when it is an umbrella term for several dimensions of consumer belief.

When it comes to advertising, trust becomes 'much trickier' in Richard's eyes, as applying a rational lens to something that doesn't necessarily work rationally can be counterproductive. The media context, though, is 'super-important' for him, with Nationwide choosing to focus on those media that achieve a trust threshold and to curate their media choices with care. This curation takes two forms: using online channels including newsbrands, Meta and TikTok, for instance, but no 'run-of-web' options; and curating the advertising experience to avoid click-driven, cluttered and confused screen environments where the ad may interfere with the reading experience.

Moreover, on the importance of his audience's advertising experience, Warren extolls the value of high production values. 'We believe that production quality is a proxy for trust,' he says. Far from being 'non-working media expenditure' as it has been described, he sees a healthy production budget as essential – 'People can see the money... and if you can see the money, you are more likely to trust the advertising... That suffers when consumers can see that less money has been spent on it.'

This faith in quality has been borne out by the success of Nationwide's recent A Good Way To Bank campaign starring Dominic West and focusing on the benefits of banking with a modern mutual society rather than his 'greedy' A.N.Y. bank.[21] Warren comments on the implicit message of trustworthiness that comes from the venal banker's young daughter, who naturally sees that a member-owned mutual is going to benefit its customers as against a shareholder-driven alternative: 'The trust is coming from the contrast between her and her father,' he explains.

The advertising, says Warren, has been very well-received 'and it's been developed to maximize trust'. That trust is, of course, assured at the level of the honesty of any claims made by Nationwide's adherence to the UK advertising codes, via the ASA and Clearcast for TV, but also reinforced by the bank's own internal procedures. He reminded us that UK banks have to demonstrate to their regulator, the FCA, that they have robust processes in place; their advertising must, for instance, be easily understood and truthful. But it is the bigger mantle of trust that Nationwide benefits from in its business that is so important to Warren to sustain, and advertising clearly plays a big part in that.

THREE KEY TAKEAWAYS

1   Trust builds loyalty, which can help protect against competitor brands poaching your customers.

2   Trust is built through that combination of media choice and careful curation, creative storytelling and production quality.

3   Remember that being a trusted brand is important to those who regulate your industry – is your brand a trusted operator in your sector?

Trust and talent, now and future

One of the very best things about advertising is that it is a people business. It relies on people understanding people and communicating effectively with them in order to be successful.

So, we're going to look finally at trust and its connection to talent. We're going to consider the importance of a trusted advertising industry to the people who work in it. We are also going to look at the work of an industry initiative to help attract future talent.

Working in a trusted industry

What might a lack of trust mean to people when choosing which industry to work in?

Talented people have a choice of careers and in what they do professionally. This is particularly true for those at the beginning of their working lives. Being in the business ourselves, we'd like talented young people to consider advertising as their choice of career. But we worry that if they think it's an untrustworthy occupation, they are less likely even to consider it.

When entering the workforce, Gen Z more than previous generations look for employers who stand for something worthwhile, who are inclusive, offer flexibility and can be trusted. Of the institutions measured in the Edelman Trust Barometer 2024, 'my employer' was the only one still trusted by most UK adults at 77 per cent, compared to business at 48 per cent, NGOs at 47 per cent, media with 31 per cent and government with 30 per cent.[22] With trust in other institutions faltering, especially amongst the young, employers need to prove trustworthy.

In 2023, the Credos Trust Tracker asked people about working in advertising.[23] Trust made a big difference to their consideration of doing so. Amongst 18–34 year-olds, 70 per cent of those expressing trust in the advertising industry said they would consider working in the business; only 38 per cent of those distrustful of the industry were prepared to do so.

Among that same 'ad-trusting' group of young people, the reasons for considering a job in the industry included the pay, the learning opportunity and a good work/life balance, each scoring about 30 per cent; 'joining a well-regarded industry' came in not far behind at 22 per cent.

The Advertising Association's 2025 'All In' survey of attitudes to their employment amongst people working across the UK industry threw up some interesting findings on the issue. Some 14,000 respondents chose to participate, making it the biggest survey of its kind we are aware of, and they were asked whether they felt that advertising was a trustworthy industry to work in: 40 per cent said they agreed that it was, 24 per cent disagreed and 36 per cent gave a 'neither' response.[24] While 40 per cent might seem rather low, the 36 per cent voicing a 'neither' opinion could be hazarded to respond that way on the reasonable basis that 'sometimes – or in some places – it is and sometimes it isn't'.

It's usually true that people in a business are more conscious of its flaws than those outside it – they care a lot more about it!

Helping young people consider advertising as a career

We wrote about Media Smart back in Chapter 4 and the work led by its Executive Director, Rachel Barber-Mack, to help young people (and those that look after for them – parents, carers, teachers) to understand all types of media and how to identify and read advertising.

A recently added dimension to Media Smart's work is to showcase to young people what job opportunities are offered across the industry, with the ambition to inspire them into future careers in advertising and media whatever their background.

Omnicom Media Group's EMEA CEO, Dan Clays, who chairs Media Smart, has helped the two organizations join forces through dedicated career workshops which provide an introduction to the advertising and media industries, allowing young people to think about the different roles available to them and offering client briefs from giffgaff and Channel 4 (with a sustainability focus) for students to work through and pitch their ideas back to the class.

Since 2024, the career workshops have reached 24,000 students with their online resources for teachers, while 55 OMG UK volunteers have also been trained to deliver inspiring careers sessions themselves, with a road-show to local state schools across the country commencing in autumn 2025.[25] The workshops underscore the idea that the better young people understand advertising, the more likely they are to trust it.

Media Smart's work is backed by people and organizations in the advertising industry taking more responsibility for 7–25 year olds' understanding of ads. By doing so, we can help ensure they are critically aware of what content and advertising they encounter can be trusted and how to differentiate the good from the bad. Increased support for initiatives like Media Smart by our sector means the full benefits and value of creating trustworthy advertising can be realised now and in the future.

Conclusion

Ultimately, if the advertising industry isn't trusted by those outside it who make the law, there will be restrictions placed upon the work we can and cannot make, whether we like it or not. And whether our own self- and co-regulatory system led by the ASA is doing a good job or not. Particularly, if we, as practitioners, do not understand, respect and follow the rules.

Advertising's critics are many and various. Wherever a product is associated with a problem in society, be it food, alcohol, fossil fuels or gambling products, advertising is likely to be a very visible aspect of its presence in our lives. Shooting the messenger often looks an eminently sensible (and inexpensive) way to make the problem go away. This may be simplistic, and not all critics are that naïve, but 'the solution' will involve advertising restrictions. So it is vital that the behaviour of advertisers and the nature of their advertising is responsible, ethical and trustworthy. Or the messenger will indeed be shot.

We have seen the implications of what working in an industry that has lost society's trust means, and the hard work involved to rebuild it. It took more than a decade for the banking industry to rebuild trust. But it is possible, and this is integrally linked to the industry behaving (and indeed, advertising) in a trustworthy fashion.

In a way, our industry has a responsibility to all industries to ensure we are trusted, because they look to us to communicate how they can be trusted.

It's a case of the more work we make that is trustworthy, the more trusted we will be.

And if we are to retain talent and attract the very best talent for the future, making sure we do everything we can to be trustworthy is central to the responsibilities of everyone working in the industry, particularly those in leadership positions.

After all, the fundamental value of what we offer won't be possible to deliver if trust is lost in advertising itself.

Notes

1   UK Government, Online Safety Act: Explainer, 2023 (updated April 2025), www.gov.uk/government/publications/online-safety-act-explainer/online-safety-act-explainer (archived at https://perma.cc/R7QA-QYM7)

2   Credos & YouGov, UK MP Trust Tracker, Credos archives, 2024

3   Author interview with The Rt Hon Baroness Nicky Morgan, March 2025

4   Alcohol Change UK, Alcohol marketing, https://alcoholchange.org.uk/policy/policy-insights/making-sure-alcohol-is-marketed-responsibly (archived at https://perma.cc/R7QA-QYM7)

5   Obesity Health Alliance, An end to junk food marketing online: Policy Position, 2020, https://obesityhealthalliance.org.uk/policy-positions-briefings/ (archived at https://perma.cc/3PSU-E2AK)

6   Peers for Gambling Reform, Recommendations, 2024, https://peersforgamblingreform.org/recommendations/

7   R Davies, Majority of public support total ban on UK gambling adverts, poll finds, The Guardian, June 2021, www.theguardian.com/society/2021/jun/16/majority-of-public-support-total-ban-on-uk-gambling-adverts-poll-finds (archived at https://perma.cc/55YT-G6J8)

8   I Quinn, Majority of Brits support total ban on online junk food advertising, The Grocer, June 2021, www.thegrocer.co.uk/news/majority-of-brits-support-total-ban-on-online-junk-food-advertising/656693.article (archived at https://perma.cc/TJ62-EYAR)

9   Frontier Economics for the Tony Blair Institute, The rising cost of obesity in the UK,November 2023, www.frontier-economics.com/uk/en/news-and-insights/news/news-article-i20358-the-rising-cost-of-obesity-in-the-uk/ (archived at https://perma.cc/WTW6-W926)

10   DCMS, Julia Lopez MP Minister of State for Media, Data and Digital Infrastructure, Online Advertising Programme, GOV.UK, March 2022 (updated July 2023), www.gov.uk/government/consultations/online-advertising-programme-consultation/online-advertising-programme-consultation (archived at https://perma.cc/L7XS-SJV5)

11   Lord Grade speech at LEAD 2024, Advertisers need to stay alert to the impact of online harms, Ofcom, February 2024, www.ofcom.org.uk/online-safety/illegal-and-harmful-content/lord-grade-speech-to-advertising-association-february2024/ (archived at https://perma.cc/28VC-J84L)

12   GambleAware, About us, www.gambleaware.org/what-we-do/about-us/ (archived at https://perma.cc/UV2S-FQVE)

13   The Guardian, Financial crisis, five years on: trust in banking hits new low, August 2012, www.theguardian.com/business/2012/aug/09/financial-crisis-anniversary-trust-in-banks (archived at https://perma.cc/KW42-ZP66)

14   M Palframan, YouGov Omnibus for Positive Money, Ten years after the financial crisis – two thirds of British people don't trust banks, August 2018, https://yougov.co.uk/economy/articles/21435-ten-years-after-financial-crisis-two-thirds-britis (archived at https://perma.cc/G8DR-V5RT)

15   Credos Banking Industry Tracker, Credos archives, March 2025

16   FutureBrand Index Sector Study, Financial Services 2025: Trust as the New Currency, March 2025, www.futurebrand.com/futurebrand-index/futurebrand-index-financial-services-2025 (archived at https://perma.cc/7K7K-U4R7)

17   Institute of Practitioners in Advertising, Barclays: Purpose Pays, IPA Effectiveness Case Study Bank,2018, https://ipa.co.uk/knowledge/case-studies/purpose-pays/ (archived at https://perma.cc/9JTD-FX9T)

18   Institute of Practitioners in Advertising, Lloyds Bank: The power of pure brand, IPA Effectiveness Case Study Bank, 2020, https://ipa.co.uk/knowledge/case-studies/lloyds-bankthe-power-of-pure-brand/ (archived at https://perma.cc/Q5XV-WGCJ)

19   Author interview with Marg Jobling and Petra Cameron, Nat West Group, March 2025

20   Author interview with Richard Warren, Director of Brands, Marketing & Experience, Nationwide, January 2025

21   Nationwide, The Boss is back: Nationwide returns with fourth spot, September 2024, www.nationwidemediacentre.co.uk/news/the-boss-is-back-nationwide-returns-with-fourth-spot (archived at https://perma.cc/T8D7-QV98)

22 Edelman, 2024 Edelman Trust Barometer 2024: A new polarization in the workplace, www.edelman.com/trust/2024/trust-barometer/special-report-trust-at-work (archived at https://perma.cc/J2XF-59CN)

23 Trust Tracker, Credos, Credos thinktank, 2023

24 Advertising Association, All In Census, May 2025, https://advertisingallin.co.uk/all-in-census-data/ (archived at https://perma.cc/NUM3-WPSP)

25 Career Workshops, MediaSmart, https://mediasmart.uk.com/career-workshops/ (archived at https://perma.cc/N3ZS-YTS6)

13

What does good look like?

Introduction

We have argued that trust is essential to relationships, including those we have with brands and companies. We have heard how much marketers care about trust in their brands, and how valuable trust can be in contributing to a brand's success. We have demonstrated how central good advertising can be to that contribution. But how do you actually win in the market by using advertising to help build a trusting relationship with your customers? This chapter examines some great examples of effective campaigns that have leveraged trust to deliver success. It shows what good looks like when it comes to real life experiences.

To set the scene, we asked Laurence Green, Director of Effectiveness at the Institute of Practitioners in Advertising (IPA) and a noted author on advertising to give us his personal perspective.

A CONFIDENT RELATIONSHIP WITH THE UNKNOWN[1]

By Laurence Green

Consumer trust in advertising – or, perhaps more correctly, audience trust in advertising – is a critical but elusive cornerstone of our industry practice.

Critical because trust underpins our audience's general faith in and favourability towards the advertising that they encounter and now encounter on an unprecedented (and unprecedentedly invasive) scale.

Critical also because trust seems to underpin the specific performance of, and returns from, advertising at a campaign or advertiser level.

Elusive because – although we can robustly map the correlation between trusted communication, trusted media and marketplace effectiveness – the precise mechanism by which trust confers commercial advantage has gone relatively unexplored, until now.

In short, we know that trust 'works', but not necessarily how it works.

The IPA – and by extension, the UK – is uniquely well-positioned to underscore the contribution of trust to effective commercial communication, thanks to the 'treasure house of learning' accumulated since 1980 by way of its biennial Effectiveness Awards and a Databank that now comprises two thousand case studies.

Thanks to that Databank, we know there has been a long-term shift in the significance of brand trust amongst our Awards entrants. Twenty years ago, trust was the sixth most important brand metric in terms of correlation to very large business effects (such as sales, market share or profit). Today it is the second most highly correlated.

Recent examples of specifics naturally abound, and are perhaps instructive.

Until 2021, Xero, the New Zealand-based business accounting software company, had failed to make sustained headway in the UK against bigger rivals such as Quickbooks and Sage. New advertising fronted by Rhys Darby – of cult Kiwi comedy *Flight of the Conchords* – was then backed with sustained investment. Its aim was to make Xero stand out through humorous and empathetic identification with sole traders and other business owners. The communication massively outstripped the targets set for it, increasing trust by 11 percentage points and significantly closing Xero's consideration gap with its competitors. In a declining category, Xero grew market share by 8 percentage points and revenues quarter after quarter by double-digit rates. Between 2021 and early 2024, the campaign returned an estimated £2.11 in short-term gross profit for every £1 invested in it.

Already the UK market leader in eye tests, Specsavers was hampered from further growth by the fact one in three Britons wearing glasses had considered and rejected the brand. However, research established that when non-customers learned about the little-known Specsavers Home Visits service, they were more likely to see the company as trustworthy and caring and to reconsider using it. After advertising Home Visits with the 'I Don't Go to Specsavers... They come to me' campaign, perceptions of the brand's trust and care credentials – and its overall consideration score – hit record highs. The campaign convinced more than half a million brand rejectors to visit Specsavers for an eye test and delivered almost £20 million of incremental profit in just under two years.

Among other recent IPA Effectiveness Award-winners, Tesco Mobile, Nurofen and McDonalds have also documented the link between growth in brand trust and improved commercial performance.

But perhaps the more general unlock for anyone aspiring to more effective brand communication – and contemplating trust's role in it all – springs from the Advertising Association's own annual barometer.

As reported elsewhere in this book, distrust in advertising springs from highly plausible sources: from bombardment and excessive frequency through to problematic categories such as gambling. One might expect therefore that the drivers of trust would simply be their opposite.

In fact, the single biggest driver of advertising trust is enjoyment, or creative quality. The more enjoyable advertising is, the more it is trusted.

At first, this seems anomalous: enjoyment sounds frivolous whereas trust is a serious matter, no? But that, of course, is to place our definition of trust above our audience's more loosely held version, one that is perhaps closer to Rachel Botsman's 'confident relationship with the unknown'.

Although this data is gathered by the AA at a general level, the IPA's own campaign-level data would seem to bear this correlation (and indeed causation) out. Enjoyable advertising begets trust.

The implication for advertising practitioners is straightforward: if your audience enjoys your advertising, you will enjoy the superior returns of the trusted advertiser. Trust needn't be set as an additional objective, let alone be considered a competing one.

Creative quality is our industry's version of the marble halls lavishly erected by the first wave of banks. However illogical, they both create a confident relationship with the unknown.

The IPA Effectiveness Awards

At Laurence's invitation, we have explored the 'treasure house of learning' he looks after, the IPA Effectiveness Awards Databank, to plunder some compelling stories of advertising campaigns that have delivered results through building brand trust.

But first a word on the awards.

Since their launch in 1980, the IPA Effectiveness Awards (originally Advertising Effectiveness Awards) have been considered the most demanding and rigorous tests of the contribution of advertising to commercial success.[2] Or for governments, NGOs, charities and the like, non-commercial success against their own objectives. The cases presented must demonstrate to the satisfaction of some very experienced and expert judges from the industry (and outside) that the advertising made a measurable – usually meaning profitable, but other objectives can be equally valid – and positive difference to the performance of a brand, company or organization.

In the ad agency world, these awards are generally seen as the most prestigious and meaningful of all the different ones a campaign or agency can win. James, Matt notes wryly, thinks this because he was a Grand Prix-winning writer and later judge of the awards back in the day. But he agrees that, especially from the perspective of marketers and brand owners, business effectiveness and ultimately financial contribution trump any other measure of a campaign's real quality.

Typically, then, the case histories have to isolate the effects of advertising on a brand's commercial performance from all the factors that might make a difference. This is often achieved through econometric analysis, but before and after or regional with/without analyses can play their part, alongside a plethora of measures of consumer attitudes, beliefs and behaviours.

For our purposes, looking at the role of trust in some stand-out campaigns, we will not go through all of that. Summaries of the key points germane to our theme will do. But we urge anyone interested in advertising and using it successfully to access the published IPA cases. Of the 2,000 case histories in the database, there will be plenty relevant to your business.

Out of them, we have selected just a handful for this chapter. Stories from the financial services sector are elsewhere in the book – in Chapter 12, in fact – as they illustrate how a whole industry rebuilt trust after the Banking Crisis of 2008/09. And Green has already drawn attention to two very recent winners, Specsavers and Xero, in his earlier contribution. Further, because times change and relevance can be seen to diminish over the years, we've stuck to cases published in this decade. Finally, although you could argue that all successful brand and advertising stories will have trust at their core and, as Green pointed out earlier, trust as a metric corresponds highly with large business effects across the cases, we have restricted our selection to cases in which trust plays a named part.

We have still been spoilt for choice, so a variety of sectors and approaches have been chosen here, although some common themes do seem to emerge, as you'll see.

REAL-WORLD EXAMPLE

McDonald's: How we got customers Lovin' It and kept them Lovin' It, no matter what[3]

(Note. Italics denote text from the IPA Effectiveness paper.)

This 2022 study by Tom Sussman of Leo Burnett and others tells, to quote its introduction, how *McDonald's used brand-building to rekindle the love and trust of the public in the UK and drive 15 years of almost continuous growth.*

McDonald's had previously lost the love and trust of the British public, leading to low brand measure scores, fewer visits to restaurants and stagnated sales.

McDonald's ensured that the campaign sparked real emotion in the audience, connected with the universal experiences of everyday British life and thought about the culture that surrounds the brand.

Over the years, McDonald's campaigns... have generated an increase in affinity and trust score... an increase in all core brand metrics and increased market share.

This is the story of how McDonald's unique approach to brand building helped to not just initiate but also continue an extraordinary 15 years of commercial growth, despite a catastrophic PR crisis, the fragmentation of the IEO ('Informal Eating Out') category and the unprecedented disruption of Covid-19.

And how this contributed £4.6bn of additional net revenue to the McDonald's business – making this the most effective case-study for any restaurant brand in IPA history.

Throughout this multi-year, multi-stage paper, the authors come back to the brand values of trust and love, which correlate quite closely as we have seen elsewhere, as *the two brand metrics proven to be most strongly correlated with McDonald's customer visits.* In the first chapter of the story, from a low for both in 2005, the authors write that *It was clear that if we wanted to return McDonald's to growth, we'd have to rebuild Love & Trust. And we'd need to do this by reconnecting the McDonald's brand with the heart of the nation.* Thus, the brand-building approach they adopted, founded on a new 'Pillar Model' which *fundamentally refocused the business's investment in communications. Until then McDonald's had exclusively invested in two strands of promotional advertising: 'Value' and 'Variety'. However, this new Pillar Model added two new streams of emotional brand-building: Favourites (i.e. Love) and Trust.*

The first chapter ('Reconnection') relates how this brand-building approach using emotionally rich creative advertising succeeded in returning McDonald's customer visits and sales revenue to growth, despite no further expansion of the estate, with the revival of those critical love and trust scores.

Between 2003 and 2006, Love and Trust had both declined by 20%+. But, as the campaigns went live, this trend was reversed... this new brand strength translated into improved pulling power, with customer visits also returning to growth.

The importance of love and trust to McDonald's sustained success continues through the next two chapters of the case, Expansion and Leadership, when the brand fought first a proliferation of new competitors and then the Covid-19 crisis to keep customer visits and revenues growing. And the importance of advertising to bolster those brand-building properties, as well as all the evolving aspects of McDonald's value and quality offerings, is front and centre. In the first phase, the trust pillar was restored with *advertising to reconnect McDonald's with the hearts of the nation*; in the second, to drive trust and food quality scores *we pushed the 'Confidently Humble' tone to give it a newly confrontational edge...to confront negative myths surrounding the quality of our food...[and] ...enlighten people with stories about our food and behaviour*; and in the third, the campaign helped McDonald's win back after the Covid shut-down by 'Going Big' and *claiming emotional leadership of the category.*

This commitment to brand-building advertising meant serious investment, with multi-media campaigns throughout the years that grew in size and (like the McDonald's menu) variety. The initial focus on 'event TV' evolved into a broader 'total AV' approach, with an ever-increasing exploitation of digital media and app-based experience, together with media, music and influencer partnerships. Of the four pillars, Love and Trust received an increased share of total spend, levelling out at around 40 per cent. As described in the paper, the three media strategies for the three phases of brand-building and business-winning activity were 'Emotion at Scale', 'Breadth with Brains' and 'Big or Bust'. They paid back. Even as annual spend increased over the 15 years from £30 million to £150 million, ROI grew to, and remained at, over £4 per £1 spent.

Award-winning creative work characterized the whole period, as McDonald's emotionally frank and true-to-life stories resonated with the British public.

It's an outstanding example of a brand that recognized the value of consumer trust as a foundational pillar of success, treated it as a priority in its marketing and communications, and could demonstrate that building that trust (with record scores at the end of the period and an increased advantage over McDonald's competitive set) contributed materially to commercial performance. Hand in hand with the value of love, often supporting messages of competence or quality, and always seen as a metric to take seriously, brand trust grew through 'Confidently Humble' advertising that was 'relatable... emotional and frankly... British'. Advertising that kept McDonald's customers 'Lovin' It, No Matter What'.

REAL-WORLD EXAMPLE
Nurofen: 'It's all in your head' – how Nurofen tackled a hidden health crisis to regain category leadership[4]

(Note. Italics denote text from the IPA Effectiveness paper.)

Nurofen's 2024 paper by Joss Major of McCann London and others, on how the brand *regained society's trust, re-established itself as a leader, and achieved an impressive ROI*, echoes McDonald's in some ways.

It, too, had experienced a diminishing level of consumer trust over some years as generic ibuprofen products had eroded its market share. Perceptions of value and actual value sales had declined. Scores for as 'a brand I can trust', the third most important driver of consideration after 'a brand for me' and 'suitable for the pain I suffer', alongside 'allows me to get on with my life', had fallen. Unfounded scare stories about ibuprofen during the Covid-19 crisis further knocked consumer confidence, notably amongst those who had heard the negative 'news'.

The brand had to fight back. It did so by getting to the emotional heart of the problem of pain, and *elevating empathy while others focused on efficacy*. The advertising moved 'from Pills to People'.

To quote the paper: *In 2020, with the objective of rebuilding brand relevance and stemming decline, we set out to re-establish Nurofen as a leader in pain management.*

The campaign had two distinct phases: first, 'Leave the pain to us' from 2020–2022, which put the emotional impact of pain front and centre, and then, building on its success, 'See My Pain', focusing on women's health and the 'Gender Pain Gap' .

The two phases of advertising turned round perceptions and performance. Levels of trust, relevance and value perceptions all improved. Indeed, trust scores went up by 6 per cent overall and 11 per cent amongst those recalling the campaign. The result of strengthened consumer perceptions? *After years of people losing confidence in Nurofen, the brand has emphatically regained its status as a leader in pain management.* A sales decline averaging some 5 per cent a year from 2016 to 2019 was reversed, with sales growing by over 4 per cent per annum from 2020 to 2023.

As with McDonald's, advertising that found new insights into the drivers of its category, that expressed these in empathetic and compelling human stories, and through sustained investment in brand values, all helped Nurofen to turn round perceptions and build the foundational trust so important to long-term success.

REAL-WORLD EXAMPLE

Tesco: From running shops to serving customers, a turnaround story[5]

(Note. Italics denote text from the IPA Effectiveness paper.)

Tesco's 2020 case, written by Simon Gregory, BBH and James Parnum, MediaCom with others, is a turnaround tale of how the supermarket chain gained back consumer trust in the UK from 2015 to 2019 with a strategy that put helpfulness at the heart of its messaging. By rebuilding the brand-consumer relationship through a host of well-communicated initiatives that served customers better, Tesco was able by the end of 2019 to post its highest Trust, Quality and Value scores in over nine years and a profit of £2.21 billion.

The authors relate how, after nearly two decades of solid growth and leadership, Tesco was facing some big challenges by 2015. New competitors in the form of discount chains, new shopping behaviours amongst the public and 'internal headwinds' signalling organizational problems all combined to knock both brand health and financial performance. Perceptions of Quality and Value for Money – the two critical drivers of choice – had fallen heavily since 2009. Scores for Reputation, described as a proxy for trust, and Recommendation were both falling, too.

A plan for recovery was made. *As part of a total business turnaround, rebuilding the Tesco brand became a priority area, with marketing recognized as the key lever that could re-engage customers. Marketing had three clear tasks: rebuild trust, repair quality perception (focusing on food) and restore value perceptions.*

This was led from the top. Dave Lewis had arrived from Unilever as Tesco's first CEO from outside the business and he set about revitalizing the ethos of the company, emphasizing transparency, acts over words, and *From running shops to serving customers.*

The advertising task within the overall marketing strategy for Tesco's recovery, to rebuild trust by putting 'serving customers' back at the heart of the Tesco business, 'Serving Britain's Shoppers a Little Better Every Day' had a number of dimensions.

A new media strategy was one, re-balancing investment towards campaigns with long-term objectives as opposed to a previous focus on the short term, regaining a leading share-of-voice in the category and re-weighting the media mix toward digital channels. Taking advantage of Tesco's size featured, too, maximizing its extensive 'owned channels' of its stores, employees, vehicles, Clubcard members, magazines and websites to integrate owned, earned and then paid media to develop stronger through-the-line plans.

A new creative approach was another, putting customers and Tesco colleagues front and centre in campaigns that headlined 'helpfulness'. *Branding, cut-through and likeability instantly improved with the new focus on helpfulness*, the paper reports.

The second leg of the marketing strategy, repairing Tesco's food credentials, was brought to life in a series of 'Love Food Stories' showing how Tesco cared about the food its customers created.

The third leg, restoring value perceptions by simplifying and rebuilding Tesco's value offering around serving customers had its advertising strands, too. 'Weekly Little Helps' communicated the emotion-driven feeling of value that research showed as so important to customers and how Tesco could help people achieve that feeling by answering their needs. Long-term partnerships with major press media gave Tesco unique, impactful spaces to carry these value messages, in combination with targeted digital media.

Tesco's centenary in 2019 was used to celebrate value with '100 Years of Great Value' and 'Prices That Take You Back', while major TV programme and channel tie-ins at Christmas 2018 and 2019 added a 'winning hearts and minds' dimension to the value story.

And what was the result of this massive repositioning and marketing revolution? To quote the paper, *Over the five years of Tesco's recovery plan Reputation (as a proxy for Trust), Quality and Value all experienced improvements on a scale previously unseen in the category.*

Trust was rebuilt and restored, with Reputation rebounding from -6% to +14% and reducing the competitor gap to only 2.5 points. Quality and value perceptions similarly bounced back, and customers came back with more people choosing Tesco more often. Crucially, like-for-like sales increased by 28 per cent between 2014 and 2019 and in April 2019, the business posted its highest profits in five years reflecting 16 consecutive quarters of growth. The three legs of the strategy had delivered with brand health measures and financial performance recovering together.

The paper goes on to isolate the impact of marketing and advertising on the turnaround. That analysis concludes that *since 2015, an improved brand has grown revenue and marketing has driven 45 per cent of this revenue growth, equating to £1.8bn.* Considering both short-term and long-term sales effects, the authors calculate that *between 2015 and 2019 this equates to £4.3bn incremental revenue with every £1 invested in marketing returning £13.65.*

First among the learnings that the paper draws from the whole story is that *central to this recovery was the reparation of the relationship between customer and brand. For a brand to succeed customers must trust that the seemingly simple colours, logos and language stand for a consistent delivery of what's promised... Restoring Every Little Helps to a promise rather than an end line required a fundamental reparation of customer trust.*

Again, we see a case history that underlines the core value of trust, the dangers of losing it and the rewards from winning it, as well as how entwined it is with other brand values such as liking, reputation and helpfulness. Again, we see that building or restoring trust amongst the public and other stakeholders requires insightful consideration of your customers, present and potential, to understand their attitudes and motivations, and putting them first. We also see that sustained advertising effort and resource are needed to achieve solid results that endure. And again, we see that creative thinking as well as meticulous execution pay dividends.

What the public thinks: Marketing Week's 'The Works'

The IPA Awards may be the most prestigious prizes for long-form essays demonstrating the commercial effectiveness of ad campaigns, but another perspective on success is offered by Marketing Week's monthly 'The Works'.[6]

This partnership between the Advertising Association, Kantar and Marketing Week celebrates advertising campaigns that generate the most positive public response, sharing what marketers can learn from them. A regular feature champions the power of creativity; we know this is the number one driver of trust in ads.

Lynne Deason, Head of Creative Excellence at Kantar, has been integral to The Works since its inception. She provided this overarching review of learnings so far which reinforce many of the lessons we have highlighted about the connection between great creative work, trust, media context and effectiveness.

ANALYSIS OF THE WORKS, LYNNE DEASON, KANTAR

Our analysis reviews 149 ads that have gone through testing, all of them selected as great examples of creativity in different media, so all of them ads we should expect to perform well. We're going to look at the potency of the 35 winning ads versus the other 114 ads researched, which for ease we will refer to as 'winners' and 'others'. Figures shown are averages unless specified otherwise. As shown in Figure 13.1, the commercial potential of the winners massively outperforms the average achieved by the others – both in the short and long term. The winners sit in the top third of UK ads for short-term sales, whilst the others fall toward the bottom third. The long-term potential of the ads follows a similar pattern: winners land in the top 31 per cent of ads, others fall in the bottom 37 per cent of UK ads.

Kantar also asks people for their perspective on how credible what is being put across about the brand by the ad is. We can use this as a surrogate for whether they trust what's being put across or not. When we compare the difference between winners and others, credibility lands in second place for having the greatest difference (alongside branding and long-term brand-building potential). As you can see in Figure 13.2 it's also one of the measures that winners are particularly strong at.

FIGURE 13.1 Kantar, winners of The Works analysis, 2025

The Winners of The Works are hugely effective ads

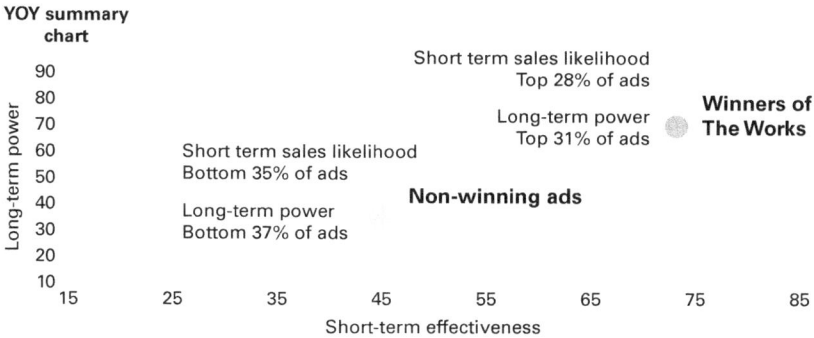

YOY summary
chart

Short term sales likelihood
Top 28% of ads

Long-term power
Top 31% of ads

**Winners of
The Works**

Short term sales likelihood
Bottom 35% of ads

Long-term power
Bottom 37% of ads

Non-winning ads

Long-term power (y-axis: 10, 20, 30, 40, 50, 60, 70, 80, 90)

Short-term effectiveness (x-axis: 15, 25, 35, 45, 55, 65, 75, 85)

FIGURE 13.2 Kantar, winning factors analysis, 2025

**Winners are enjoyable, interesting ads that make people feel good.
Music and humour (where used) fuel emotional engagement.**

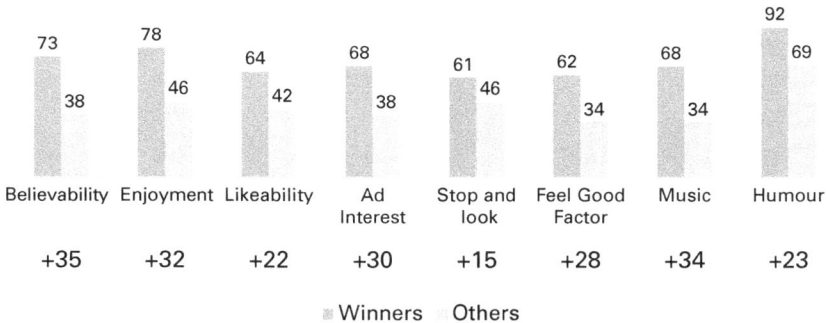

	Believability	Enjoyment	Likeability	Ad Interest	Stop and look	Feel Good Factor	Music	Humour
Winners	73	78	64	68	61	62	68	92
Others	38	46	42	38	46	34	34	69
	+35	+32	+22	+30	+15	+28	+34	+23

▪ Winners ▫ Others

The winners of The Works are a very enjoyable set of ads, landing in the top 23 per cent of all UK ads, whilst the others are close to the average. Emotional resonance is a hallmark of winning campaigns featured in The Works. Winners evoked powerful emotive reactions – joy, nostalgia, empathy, surprise, sadness and laughter – and landed on average in the top 9 per cent of UK ads for humour. Music was also hugely effective at eliciting a powerful emotional response to the winning ads.

Few ads lead to a direct sale in the moment of exposure. To have any possibility of influencing future sales, your advertising needs to build predisposition to choose your brand over alternatives. People want to know which brand an ad is for, they get frustrated if it isn't clear, we see the winners standing in the top 20 per cent of all ads in the UK for branding, whilst others are in the bottom 45 per cent of ads.

But great creative is only half the battle. The other half is context. Ads that are tailored to the medium and the moment perform better. They avoid the disconnect – and scrolling thumbs that kick into action – that happens when an ad feels like an intrusion, when it feels like an unwelcome interruption rather than an enjoyable part of it.

Whether it's a print ad that speaks to a magazine's readership or a digital ad that plays to platform strengths, contextual relevance ensures the message lands where and how it matters most.

Over time, a set of consistent themes has emerged from these top performing campaigns. These are not just trends; they are principles that can guide marketers and their agency partners in creating advertising that connects, converts, and endures.

A key insight from the comparison of winning ads versus others, which fits with Kantar's Creative Effectiveness expertise, is that confusion kills effectiveness. One of the measures in LINK+ asks people to say how easy they found it to follow what was happening in the ad, from very easy to very hard. Winners land in the top 36 per cent of all ads for being easy to follow; others by contrast land in the bottom 32 per cent of all ads in the UK! This is one of the top five measures in terms of the scale of the difference between the two sets of ads. Although the difference isn't as large, we can see further evidence of this on people's faces. People's brows are furrowing more when watching the 'other' ads. This measure is the only place where we see a big difference in the opposite direction, i.e. where others have a higher score than winners.

FIGURE 13.3 Kantar, winning factors analysis 2, 2025

Winners connect powerfully with the brand–brand cues play a strong role but brand fit, focus and uniqueness are also critical.

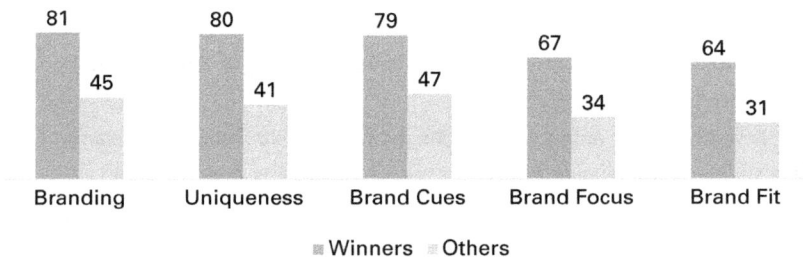

	Branding	Uniqueness	Brand Cues	Brand Focus	Brand Fit
Winners	81	80	79	67	64
Others	45	41	47	34	31

■ Winners ■ Others

And what has this got to do with trust? Just that those enduring principles of what makes an ad possess powerful popular appeal chime with all we have seen in earlier chapters about what makes a trusted ad. Emotional resonance, enjoyment, likeability; brand cues, focus and fit – in content and context.

Advertising and government

Commercial organizations are not the only ones for whom trust is vital and advertising a contributor to building and keeping it. Charities and NGOs seeking donations need to show that their use of the money raised will really go to help the cause they champion, that they can be trusted to spend people's gifts wisely. Government often has a case to make, too, and UK governments have a strong history of using advertising to communicate policies that citizens need to understand or respond to – think drink-driving, vaccinations or crime prevention.

Sometimes, trust in government is key to that public response, but as we have seen earlier in the book, trust in governments around the world has been falling. What can they do? Quite a lot, it seems, as Simon Baugh, Chief Executive of UK Government Communications, and Conrad Bird CBE, Director, Campaigns & Marketing, Cabinet Office, explained to Matt and James in this fascinating insight into how a 21st-century government able to use the tools of 21st-century marcoms can approach the big task of rebuilding trust in government:

HOW GOVERNMENT COMMUNICATORS CAN CLOSE THE TRUST DEFICIT AND SHOW PUBLIC INSTITUTIONS AS A FORCE FOR GOOD[7]

By Simon Baugh and Conrad Bird

Britain faces a crisis of confidence in its political system. According to the 2023 OECD Trust in Government Survey, only 27 per cent of the UK population trust their national government – significantly below the OECD average of 39 per cent. More than half of Britons said they did not trust the national government.

This alarming statistic carries real-world consequences that extend far beyond political popularity. When citizens trust government, they are more likely to abide by laws, pay taxes and participate in the democratic process. Higher trust in government was associated with higher adoption of health behaviours, such as during the Covid-19 pandemic.

Without trust, government functions less effectively and society becomes more vulnerable to threats ranging from pandemics to hostile states. The challenge is substantial but not insurmountable. Building trust begins with being trustworthy – delivering on promises and acting with integrity. It also requires rethinking how government listens to and engages with the public.

The government recognized this challenge in its manifesto. The Prime Minister told Civil Service leaders this year: 'We are working in an era of mistrust... Our job is to re-earn that trust. We shouldn't accept that there is nothing we can do about it.'

THE TRUST DEFICIT: UNDERSTANDING THE CHALLENGE
Behavioural science research identifies three key drivers of public trust:

1 Competence: people having faith in government's ability and judgement.

2 Benevolence: people believing that government cares about them and acts in their interests rather than its own.

3 Integrity: our words match our actions and people's experience of interacting with government matches promises made.

Crucially, trust is about more than delivery. Changing the public's experience is not enough. People often don't notice when conditions improve – for example, they consistently overestimate crime rates. Building trust therefore involves not just improved service delivery but also bridging perception gaps. Which is where communications can play a key role.

Government can help rebuild public trust through more effective communication strategies, harnessing new technology and reconnecting with citizens where they are – not where government has assumed them to be.

THE COMMUNICATION CHALLENGE
Three factors make the government's communication challenge particularly acute.

First, media fragmentation means fewer people receive information through traditional channels. The public increasingly consumes information from diverse sources, including social media platforms that operate according to different rules. Social media outperforms the BBC as the main source of daily news for those under 45, and this generational difference extends to levels of trust. Those over 45 have low levels of trust in news they glean from social media, but the reverse is true for those under 45. Young people in the UK trust online creators more than politicians to tell them the truth about news.

Second, misinformation and disinformation travel rapidly through online networks. According to YouGov, 72 per cent of Britons worry about false information on social media, and 34 per cent admit they sometimes believe fake news, only to discover later it was incorrect. This erodes the foundation of shared facts upon which democratic discourse depends.

Third, in a tight fiscal environment, government spending on public information has declined dramatically. Once one of Britain's biggest advertisers, government now accounts for less than 1 per cent of UK media spend.

This combination creates a perfect storm for declining trust in government institutions and is a powerful case for change, which the government communication service is embracing.

A MODERN APPROACH TO BUILDING TRUST

New technology enables an increasingly sophisticated understanding of public needs and concerns. If government communicates on issues the public doesn't care about, or on platforms they don't use, resources are wasted 'shouting into the void'.

Government communicators have developed an overarching audience segmentation, based on citizens' levels of trust, that will underpin all government communications. This will ensure messages reach the right audiences through the right channels on issues that matter to them. And we are using AI to test messages, hold conversations with AI focus groups and to develop communications specifically tailored to audience segments based on their concerns, preferences and media habits.

The newly established New Media Unit in the Cabinet Office is a fundamental rethink of how government should communicate. It aims to tell a long-term story of delivery. Reflecting changed media consumption habits, it integrates specialist skills in data, paid media, partnerships and creative content. Operating on platforms the public actually use, including TikTok, its goal is to build trust by demonstrating that government can be a force for good in people's lives.

The Unit recognizes two critical insights. First, people in the UK are more likely to trust other people than any government institution. Government messengers are among the least trusted voices – so it needs stronger partnerships with those who are trusted to help tell the government's story. If people hear positive messages about government from people like themselves, trust will increase. The best content will be that which is co-created with influential voices so that it resonates authentically. A practical early example was a collaboration with the parenting influencer Mother Pukka to help parents access new breakfast clubs. Similar content appearing on government channels met with sceptical comments or worse, whereas authentic content from a deeply trusted voice resulted in genuine conversations about how to access new services.

Second, hyper-local content builds trust and confidence more effectively than national statistics. Promising 'new community diagnostic centres' feels like just another political pledge. However, introducing people to their new local diagnostic centre – explaining opening hours, booking procedures and sharing patient testimonials – feels real, helpful and authentic.

For government communication to be trusted, it must be inherently trustworthy. The Government Communication Service and its media partner OmniGOV @ MG OMD have developed the SAFE Framework – a toolkit for communicators to assess digital environments and introduce minimum required standards and a risk-based approach to government advertising. SAFE principles cover a rigorous assessment of Safety and Suitability, Advertising Context, Freedom of Speech and Ethics and Enforcement.

In short, trust will grow if the government demonstrates it can be a force for good in people's lives. This means telling a consistent story of delivery that is relevant, local and authentic; addressing issues the public genuinely cares about; and communicating on platforms they use.

For government communicators, this means embracing new communication approaches while upholding the highest standards of public service. It means working collaboratively across departmental boundaries to present a coherent government narrative. And it means constantly challenging ourselves to see our work through the eyes of those we serve.

Trust isn't built overnight, but with concerted effort and modern approaches to communications, Britain can begin to close the trust deficit and build institutions the public believe in once again.

This look at what the UK Government's Communications Service is doing carries lessons for marketers of every background. Acknowledging the problem of a trust deficit and the potential benefits of addressing it; absorbing the lessons of behavioural science to guide a response; appreciating the key role communications can play; using sophisticated audience segmentation and AI-assisted messaging research; realizing the authenticity-advantage to be gained from employing social media creators and hyper-local targeting; committing to the highest standards of digital channel selection and ethical content – all harnessed to the genuinely important task of rebuilding trust in government and in its vital public communications. As a public communications professional himself, Matt was impressed, to say the least!

Building on this, what else can we do, as advertising and marketing professionals, to make sure the work of our industry can be trusted?

Allwyn's The National Lottery story

Finally, we're going to take a look at an example of a brand that sits at the sweet spot of positive economic and social contribution, and how trust (including its advertising) is central to its success.

'Trust is an absolutely critical component of any brand, whether it's one raising over £30 million a week for good causes or if it's a shampoo. A consumer needs to believe in the benefit the brand is offering them.' So says Steve Parkinson, Brand and Marketing Director of the UK's National Lottery owner, Allwyn. But he explains that in The National Lottery's case, that benefit isn't just the chance to win big prizes.

> The National Lottery was invented with the singular objective of raising life-changing sums of money to fuel arts, heritage, sport and community projects. In a consumer landscape where so many brands are now looking to convey a social purpose, we recognize the value in leveraging the authentic first-person testimony of those impacted by The National Lottery and finding ways to curate this message… that will drive the trust and affinity they have with it. We ultimately are not looking for those storytellers to endorse the brand but instead to champion the impact our players have had through the funds they have raised – which in turn ladders back to brand sentiment.

Parkinson went on to give us the examples of Sir Anthony Gormley talking about his iconic Angel of the North sculpture, actress Vicky McClure's story of founding Our Dementia Choir and sporting heroes speaking about The National Lottery's transformative effect on Team GB's success in the Olympic and Paralympic Games.

> Trust is built through the storytelling or showcasing of the vast range of good causes that have benefited through lottery funding – the Olympics and Paralympics being one of the biggest proof points.

> Advertising is how we build and maintain a brand's mental availability – how we show up within an ad should build on a consumer's positive associations of

the brand. For The National Lottery, we must demonstrate that we turn people into millionaires and that 'It could be you'.

To explain, 'It could be you' is a famous strapline from The National Lottery's past that Allwyn are reviving because it – like many such brand slogans or catchphrases that the public have come to know and love over the years – retains warm and positive associations and is, as Parkinson says, 'ultimately the most truthful line'.

He was also keen to stress the significance of using a wide span of different touchpoints across owned, paid and earned media. 'Using the right media and content channels is also important to re-enforce the trust of your brands,' he says. 'Thinkbox research has shown time and again that advertising on TV builds trust, and we know Radio carries a high degree of trust. Likewise, the growth of influencers and podcasts has shown how using voices and platforms which your target consumers trust, can further build brand trust.'

At a time when people are looking to businesses to help make things better (remember that Edelman research?), Allwyn, the operator of the UK's National Lottery, is a clear example of a company using advertising to build people's trust in how what it is doing offers a positive economic and social benefit.

Conclusion

So, what have we got out of examining some highly successful approaches to deploying advertising to enhance brand trust?

First, that what good looks like for trust-building ad campaigns is what it looks like for good marketing and good advertising in general. Don't promise what you can't – or even might not – deliver. Competence has to be real; advertising has to be honest. Accept accountability. Demonstrate transparency. Justify people's trust.

And on a lighter note, make ads that people love! Likeability, enjoyment, relevance to my needs and my life are all qualities of good ads that translate into trust. Humour, music, character, surprise and quality storytelling can all play a part in engaging, disarming and winning over an audience. As The Works winners have shown, creativity has power in establishing credibility.

Second, if trust is an issue for your brand, company or category, look seriously at what that really means. Why is there a problem? What can you do about it? How can you communicate that you are trustworthy, directly or (more probably) indirectly? Is that different for different people or segments, so that your ads or their targeting must reflect those differences?

Third, remember that trust is not one-dimensional. Competence, benevolence and integrity, as cited by the Government Communications Service, all play their part in making a brand trusted: doing the thing right for your customers, doing the right thing by them, and insisting on best practice in how you develop and deliver your communications. As well as doing what's expected of it, a brand that shows it is making things better for people, as The National Lottery does, will enrich its reputation.

Fourth, that focus on context as well as content. Where and when you are seen or heard, amongst what company and amidst what other content all add up to a statement of your own brand standing and your view of your audience. Choosing the right touchpoints, from the reassurance of 'big media' to the hyper-local voices of respected individuals, can make all the difference to how your messages are received.

Fifth, stay with the programme. Trust isn't built overnight. The McDonald's, Nurofen and Tesco cases all feature long-term campaigns. But in each case, building trust went hand in hand with building business success; the commitment was worth it.

Those are at least some of the lessons we can take from the best of the best, who recognized the foundational value of trust (that 'critical but elusive' factor in success, as Laurence Green described it) to their businesses and the importance of communicating it. They are not easy lessons to execute, but the remarkable success that has come from following them in the cases we have studied suggest that it's certainly worth trying!

Notes

1 Laurence Green, IPA, A confident relationship with the unknown, April 2025
2 IPA Effectiveness Awards 2025, Institute of Practitioners in Advertising, https://ipa.co.uk/awards-events/effectiveness-awards (archived at https://perma.cc/2S55-EYCB)
3 IPA, McDonald's: How we got customers Lovin' It and kept them Lovin' It, no matter what, 2022, https://ipa.co.uk/knowledge/case-studies/mcdonalds-how-we-got-customers-lovin-it-and-kept-them-lovin-it-no-matter-what (archived at https://perma.cc/4VL4-B2N8)
4 IPA, Nurofen: 'It's all in your head' – how Nurofen tackled a hidden health crisis to regain category leadership, 2024, https://ipa.co.uk/knowledge/case-studies/its-all-in-your-head-how-nurofen-tackled-a-hidden-health-crisis-to-regain-category-leadership (archived at https://perma.cc/85F9-TGAK)

5 IPA, From running shops to serving customers: The Tesco turnaround story, 2020, https://ipa.co.uk/knowledge/case-studies/from-running-shops-to-serving-customers-the-tesco-turnaround-story (archived at https://perma.cc/FK7D-LUQK)

6 The Works, Advertising Association, Kantar and Marketing Week, July 2025, https://adassoc.org.uk/our-work-category/the-works/ (archived at https://perma.cc/774S-ARRN)

7 Simon Baugh and Conrad Bird, How government communicators can close the trust deficit and show public institutions as a force for good, July 2025

14

Improving trust – a silver bullet?

Introduction

Is there one simple way that advertising can rebuild trust in its work, the profession and the industry? This is a question that we have seen asked time and again by leaders of the advertising industry as they look at the long-term decline of trust and seek ways to tackle it. An often-used phrase is that we need to get better at 'advertising advertising'. But how easy is that, and what might it look like?

What it should not look like, those considering it felt, was an overt appeal from the 'advertising industry' to be trusted. When someone you don't know – and in advertising's case, someone you may already be sceptical about – just says 'trust me', alarm bells naturally ring. Why are they worried that you will not? The risk of doing so is raised, doubts surfaced. No, people deserve to be given good reason to think advertising trustworthy and that should come from a source with integrity. In the UK, we had such a source and a good story of reassurance about advertising to tell in the form of the Advertising Standards Authority, and its work.

In this chapter, we will have a look at a recent initiative to raise public awareness of the role that the ASA, our national ad-regulator, has in setting and enforcing standards for all ads to ensure they are legal, decent, honest and truthful. It has shown encouraging signs of success. While not a magic silver bullet, what we are learning here might just be something that the advertising industry worldwide, wherever such regulators exist, should adopt more broadly: make it known that there is 'a bobby on the beat', a body that monitors advertising, that you can complain to if you believe an ad is wrong, and that will take action against advertisers who don't play by the rules.

About the Advertising Standards
Authority – legal, decent, honest and truthful

We have already met the Advertising Standards Authority (ASA) in this book – the one-stop shop for advertising complaints with its 30,000 complaints a year and its AI-enabled scanning of millions of ads a month.[1]

But we haven't really examined the effectiveness of the ASA's work yet. Generally speaking, UK advertising sticks to the rules. The ASA's compliance surveys show more than 97 per cent of ads are in line with the Advertising Codes and those in breach are almost always amended or withdrawn swiftly without needing to resort to legal action.[2]

If ads are judged by the ASA to have broken the rules, inadvertently or on purpose, their offence is publicized. Every week, the UK media run stories on ads that have been 'banned' and this public calling-out has a powerful impact on the companies concerned if they are, as is almost always the case, responsibly minded and reputation-aware. Not just big companies shun such embarrassment: individual influencers, for instance, whose celebrity and trust amongst their followers matters, can feel the sting of an ASA judgement against them in the adverse publicity that results.

Nor do the advertisers, although held primarily responsible by the ASA's rules, bear the pain alone. Agencies and media or platform owners may well be named, too, and expected to play their part in redressing any issues.

Furthermore, the ASA can impose sanctions to bring problem advertisers into line. For example, advertisers who regularly break the rules can be denied access to advertising media space. Significantly, less than 1 per cent of advertisers ignore an ASA judgement if made against one of their ads, and those few intransigents can be referred to statutory authorities with more punitive legal powers.

So, we have a pretty effective regulatory system, it seems. And as we've seen earlier, the public have indicated they are more likely to trust advertising if they know it is effectively regulated, and that any offending ads are swiftly dealt with. But when the AA's Trust Group began to consider the question, they also saw that not everyone knew much, if anything, about the ASA. If the levels of awareness of the organization and its role were higher, Credos asked, could that have a positive effect on trust levels in advertising?

We were aware that in its early days the ASA did advertise widely, thanks to space donated by the media, and had consistently maintained a public presence in subsequent decades. But activity had fallen away, and our research indicated that knowledge and understanding of the ASA were low amongst the public. Importantly, that the ASA's work was not confined to traditional media but covered ads online, too, really needed to be communicated, as the public tended to believe that online space was a 'Wild West' even if that was not so.

The case was made through the AA that it was time for the industry to marshal the resources needed for a new drive to bolster trust in advertising by boosting awareness of the ASA's role. Not 'advertising advertising' directly but giving people further reason to believe in its integrity on the basis that lawbreakers were rare, were found out when they did emerge and were prevented from re-offending.

A test campaign in Scotland

In September 2020, a new ASA advertising campaign[3] was launched in a Scottish 'test market' to promote its role in helping to keep all ads 'legal, decent, honest and truthful'. It featured creative work by the Leith agency which took famous campaigns for brands and gave them a fresh interpretation to remind the public that all ads are fully regulated. Straplines such as Churchill's 'OOoh Yes', Mastercard's 'Priceless' and Marmite's 'Love it or hate it' featured in donated advertising inventory across TV, radio, print, outdoor, social and online display in activity planned by Mediacom.

Stephen Woodford, Chief Executive of the Advertising Association, said of the launch:

> We know that strong awareness of the ASA as an effective regulator of
> advertising content correlates with public trust in advertising and this campaign
> demonstrates the breadth of the ASA's remit across all media. We all have an
> interest in rebuilding public trust in advertising and I'm sure this campaign will
> play a key role in moving us forward in the right, positive direction.

A year later, and the results were in...

The post-campaign research revealed 33 per cent of Scottish adults recalled seeing or hearing the ads from the campaign.[4] Recognition of the ASA's logo was up and, importantly, trust in the ASA was a third higher among those who saw or heard the ad campaign. Perhaps most significantly though, the results showed that awareness of the ASA's advertising was reflected in greater trust in the ad industry. Those who said they had seen/

heard the ads proved two-thirds more likely to trust the ad industry than those who didn't – and 50 per cent more likely to trust most ads. The case for ASA advertising looked solid and the industry was convinced to go national with its funding and support.

Scaling the ASA's awareness campaign across the UK

In October 2022, in the ASA's 60th anniversary year, the UK advertising industry launched its biggest-ever awareness campaign for its regulator.[5] The goal was to build on that original objective – to raise the ASA's profile and remind the public and businesses alike that UK ads across all media are regulated and that there's a body to maintain standards and step in when needed.

The campaign was lent the support of brands including Tesco, Marmite, IRN-BRU, Lloyds, and Churchill all starring in creative executions across TV, print, online, cinema and OOH channels for a three-month period. Media owners from all sectors gave inventory in a show of solidarity with the campaign.

So, what was the impact?

The findings, published in May 2023, showed the campaign not only drove trust in the ASA but that those who saw or heard the ASA's ads were over 80 per cent more likely to trust the ad industry, and over 50 per cent more likely to trust most ads than those who didn't.[6]

Alessandra Bellini, Chief Customer Officer, Tesco and AA President, said at the time:

> We are delighted that our 'Every Little Helps' strapline is featured alongside other great brands in the ASA's advertising campaign. It's great to see such strong results, with increased public trust and confidence that advertising is well-regulated. Our customers' trust in the Tesco brand and communications is very important to us and that is why we wanted to support this campaign, in partnership with the ASA, to reinforce the credibility of the advertising industry.

The research results also revealed that when people were asked about trust in ads by media channels, there were higher levels of trust across all media. For example, trust in online ads climbed from 16 per cent to 32 per cent while trust in TV rose from 36 per cent to 51 per cent.

Increased support from advertisers and media? Simples!

A further wave of the campaign followed in 2023, and as signs of success grew from some fairly modest levels of exposure, media and platform owners committed to greater support in late 2024.[7] Creative executions were refreshed and, this time round, Compare the Market's much-loved 'Simples' strapline and Meerkat imagery also featured in press and OOH advertising, as the ASA set out to remind the public that they ensure ads remain legal, decent, honest and truthful.

In addition to extensive support from media owners and tech companies, the campaign ran on podcasts for the first time. It was significant, with the growing popularity of podcasts, to remind people that ASA regulation spans all media.

Research into the campaign's impact showed 36 per cent of UK adults recalled seeing or hearing the ASA ads.[8] Awareness of the ASA reached 60 per cent amongst that ad-aware population and recognition of its logo reached its highest ever level. They also showed uplifts in the important understanding that the ASA covered social media and website ads (at 56 per cent and 62 per cent respectively) and in trust in the ASA, too (at 66 per cent). That these scores were markedly higher amongst those who said they had seen or heard the ads served to underline the campaign's effect.

But most significantly for the campaign's many backers, people who said that they had encountered the ASA ads were more than twice as likely to trust the ad industry than those who did not. In the same vein, positive attitudes towards advertising were significantly stronger among those who said they had seen or heard ads for the ASA: 43 per cent who had seen or heard them said they 'tend to trust most ads' versus 24 per cent who had not seen the ads.

This effect held true across media types, with the ad-aware expressing much higher degrees of trust in media of all sorts, especially online. This was no doubt in part because younger people, generally more favourable towards online advertising, proved the most responsive to the ASA campaign, registering higher levels of awareness and positive opinion. But the strength of the relationship between recall of the ads and those positive and more trustful attitudes was striking.

Certainly, the forecast link between trust in the ASA and in the ad industry was fulfilled. Trust in the latter reached 36 per cent amongst respondents trusting the ASA as against 25 per cent amongst all adults; trust in ads rose to 43 per cent and 31 per cent respectively for the same groups. The 'bobby on the beat' was indeed reassuring.

Conclusion

What have we learned here? Perhaps that while there are many different creative ways to '*advertise* advertising', a campaign that builds awareness of the UK advertising's effective regulatory system can have a positive effect on whether people trust advertising or not.

The reassurance that advertisers don't and can't get away with abusing their freedom to communicate competitively, and that standards exist and are enforced across the board, gives a solid reason to be more trusting of ads.

It is no mean feat to persuade advertisers to lend their brands to an advertising campaign which essentially says that if a brand doesn't follow the rules, it will be told off and the advertising taken down. But it worked.

Nor is it easy to ask media owners of any kind to donate advertising inventory, given this is essentially their own money they are giving up for the benefit of advertisers. But trust in their channels was enhanced.

Nor is it easy to secure ad credits from the big global tech companies that carry millions of ads regulated by the ASA and often seem at the eye of the storm when it comes to criticism of the current advertising environment. Yet trust in online advertising was markedly lifted by the campaign.

Bear in mind, the greater the trust, the greater the greater the effectiveness and everyone wins here – not just the public, but the advertiser too.

In a competitive media market where trust can give an edge, a pan-industry campaign that rises above the battle to achieve something for the whole industry is a big ask. Media owners and others may feel justified in demanding their competitors to do more or give more if they feel the balance of funding is unfair. But it was achieved in the UK and the benefits accruing to the ASA, as a crucial regulator respected by the industry, and to the world of advertising as seen by its audience, the public, more than justified the effort.

When it comes to people's trust in advertising it's clear that not only does the industry need an effective regulatory system, it needs everyone to be aware that it exists and that it works well.

We hope that the ad industry will do even more in the coming years to support and promote the ASA and its work. It's important to give people the firm belief that the industry not only has rules that nearly all advertisers abide by nearly all the time but can be trusted to do something about it should an advertiser break them, whoever that advertiser is and wherever their ads appear.

Notes

1 ASA, Our history, www.asa.org.uk/about-asa-and-cap/our-history.html (archived at https://perma.cc/V5E6-LBPX)

2 ASA, Our history, UK ad compliance rate, www.asa.org.uk/about-asa-and-cap/our-history.html (archived at https://perma.cc/V5E6-LBPX)

3 Advertising Association, ASA launches Scottish campaign, September 2020, https://adassoc.org.uk/our-work/asa-launches-scottish-campaign/ (archived at https://perma.cc/MCC7-7M64)

4 Advertising Association, New Credos research shows signs of improvement in public trust in advertising, October 2021, https://adassoc.org.uk/our-work/new-credos-research-trust/ (archived at https://perma.cc/8GBP-U8Q9)

5 Advertising Association, ASA launches UK-wide ad campaign, October 2022, https://adassoc.org.uk/our-work/asa-launches-uk-wide-ad-campaign/ (archived at https://perma.cc/MPK4-DSL3)

6 Advertising Association, Research shows ASA's biggest ever ad campaign boosted public trust of advertising, May 2023, https://adassoc.org.uk/our-work/research-shows-asas-biggest-ever-ad-campaign-boosted-public-trust-of-advertising/ (archived at https://perma.cc/5LXQ-G4YX)

7 Advertising Association, ASA partners with Compare the Market and Acast for latest ad awareness campaign, September 2024, https://adassoc.org.uk/our-work/asa-partners-with-compare-the-market-and-acast-for-latest-ad-awareness-campaign/ (archived at https://perma.cc/7CQT-DPH7)

8 ASA Ad Campaign 2024: Wave 7 results (unpublished and by permission), December 2024

15

Summary, reflections and action

There's a tremendous amount of interest in what 'trust' is and why it is important in business as well as life. The work by the Edelman Trust Barometer team, alongside that of experts in the field like Rachel Botsman, helps explain why, and paints a picture of the changing structure of trust in the 21st century.

Established institutions, whether in government and politics, civil society or the news media, are having to contend with the ways trust is now won (and lost) through the social networks and tech platforms which people access worldwide. With traditional sources of trusted authority losing credibility and traction, there appears to be an expectation that business will step forward to help solve the problems of 21st-century society.

But businesses are certainly not all trusted, either. They have to earn trust through behaviour and communications that are trustworthy, helpful and consistent. And the same goes for their advertising. Especially if it is to play the key role it can in building successful, durable brands.

The value of trust

Trust matters increasingly to the bottom line. The FT, in partnership with the IPA, published Bridging The Trust Gap, at Cannes Lions 2025, reminding us that trust as a metric in advertising now lies second only to quality in importance amongst factors driving market share, profit and customer acquisition.[1] It highlighted that while the majority of business sectors are trusted more than governments, they (including finance, food, energy, travel and retail) were nonetheless perceived on balance as more untrustworthy than trustworthy. This gap between desire (what people want from companies) and expectation (what they think will be delivered) presents a huge opportunity for brands to build trust.

But trust matters more than just in generating profit.

As we've seen, it matters to any person or organization seeking support for what they are trying to achieve. That includes governments, NGOs, public service organizations and public figures. Trust in your brand (wherever it operates) is essential for competitive advantage. Your advertising can play an integral role in building and maintaining that trust.

A changing world

It is as true today as it was a century ago that the effectiveness of your advertising relies on audiences trusting what it says. What have changed are the ways you can now use advertising to convey trusted messages through its content, context and, crucially, who delivers that message on your behalf. These factors are all under your control. You can't make people trust you, but trustworthy advertising grounded in truth and honesty will help.

As an industry, we know a great deal about people's trust in advertising – the things that help them to trust it and the things that might damage their trust in it.

We know, for instance, that some people are innately more trustful than others. Aspects of character and belief affect how much individuals trust advertising. Some accept the roles of business and marketing in society whereas others are hostile to them. Negative views towards specific product categories also shape views on advertising. Age and experience of different media can also determine levels of personal trust, while fear or experience of scam ads may pollute people's trust of all advertising. These are factors beyond the control of any individual advertiser but are important to recognize and understand.

The do's and don'ts

When it comes to how your advertising builds trust or damages it, there are clear do's and don'ts.

We know advertising that is enjoyable, engaging and authentic, provides useful information, makes a positive social contribution or offers a rewarding value exchange can be well received. More, it offers positive returns on the trust that is a foundation of effectiveness. Likeability carries over from advertising to brand, and we are more likely to trust people we like, although there is a difference between being liked and being trusted. We have covered some great advertising campaigns in this book that successfully built trust with people as a result of engaging, relevant, creative entertainment, using humour, music, emotion and loveable characters.

Likewise, we know that bombarding people with your advertising, repeatedly targeting them with the same message or intruding on their space or time all have damaging effects on trust levels. We also know that some people will perceive advertising as 'irresponsible' by virtue of what it is promoting, to whom and how, which to them has a negative impact, not just on the brand or advertising category in question but on 'advertising' more generally. It is important then to be extra careful if your brand is from one of the 'sensitive' categories.

The fast-emerging role of influencers (including content creators) in advertising is intrinsically linked to the shift in trust that we are witnessing towards individuals rather than organizations. People are investing their trust in the influencers they identify with and creators they admire. Brands are recognizing this and exploring ways to be part of those intimate, personal conversations.

If the influencer advertising sector does grow in line with projections, scrutiny of its disclosure and content will grow. Agreed standards, shaped by industry bodies with the support of specialists in the field, will help this up-and-coming sector establish itself as a robust channel for trusted advertising.

The same is true for the use of AI – Generative, Predictive, Agentic and more – in advertising. People will increasingly make decisions based on advertising driven or created by AI and trust AI to decide for them on all kinds of purchases and transactions. Work is underway to set the standards for the responsible use of AI to improve people's experience of advertising.

So, building trust through your advertising isn't just about what you say in your ads. It's also about how and where your advertising appears and the response this prompts from your audience. It's essential to consider what impact this will have on trust levels in your brand, which requires a combination of informed insights – about your audience and about the different opportunities offered by the range of media partners available to you. It's your (the advertiser's) responsibility to check what these partners, from media owners to tech platforms to individual influencers, do to ensure the content and advertising they carry can be trusted, and to make your choices on that basis as much as on any other.

This consideration is particularly true when advertising online. It is essential that the rules are understood, that the tools offered by tech platforms to ensure brand safety and suitability are used correctly, that partners up and down your supply chain operate in line with what the industry deems best practice, and that your advertising isn't mistakenly funding dangerous or harmful content.

We have seen the importance of being clear about what it is that you want to be trusted for. Trust grows with consistency. The best advertising builds trust over time, providing a bedrock of resilience that allows a brand to recover from any mistakes made.

We also know that we can't just tell people that advertising can be trusted; we have to show them how we, as an industry, make sure the work they see meets adequate standards to ensure they can have confidence in it.

The role of the self-regulatory body in your market (like the ASA in the UK) is fundamental, and it is in your interest, short and long term, to make sure you, your business and your advertising partners support it. The alternative? People will actively avoid your work, and regulators will place restrictions on what advertising is allowed, which may have broader repercussions about what you can, and can't say, about your brand.

Finally, before we give our checklist of recommended actions, some personal reflections on what we have learnt while writing this book.

From James:

'Trust me, I'm in advertising'. That was the tongue-in-cheek challenge that opened this book. But it's a real challenge. We have seen that advertisers and the advertising industry can't assume that people will trust them or their work as perhaps they once did. The public show a natural and justifiable scepticism about both the claims and motives of advertising. Indeed, the redistribution of trust across society we have seen in the 21st century has made building trust in advertising more of a challenge than ever. The impact of online advertising, and in particular the role of social media, has been profound in changing the dynamics of communication and credibility.

Yet almost 100 people in the business were happy – no, keen – to talk to us for the book. Brand owners, researchers, media owners, creative and media agency leaders, influencers and commentators, all sharing the belief that trust in advertising matters, that winning it is important and legitimate, and that it can be won to positive effect for business and society.

But what did they mean by trusted advertising? In essence, two things. First, credible and trustworthy ads that can successfully convey a message. If people simply cannot believe an ad to be telling the truth, it falls at the first hurdle. They can and will happily ignore it. Its value is nugatory. It reflects badly on both advertiser brand and advertising in general: a few bad apples rot the whole barrel.

For the hundred years of the Advertising Association's existence, stamping out such dishonest or misleading ads has been a constant effort, spearheaded over the last 60 years by the ASA to enforce standards of truthfulness and transparency, as we have seen. That work has to go on, with the full support and engagement of the industry, because, human nature and commercial competition being what they are, we must expect lapses, corner-cutting, even occasional downright lying, and we must deal with them. Advertising has plenty of critics quick to pounce on perceived abuses of its freedom to communicate; only by being trustworthy can the industry justify its role and revenues.

Second, trusted advertising meant a lot more to our contributors than merely telling the truth. It meant advertising that enhances brand or company reputations and generates preference and competitive advantage. This is of enormous value to advertisers, as our interviews and case histories have shown. And it gives all sorts of opportunities for practitioners to use their skills and resources to deliver success to their clients.

Communicating not just a brand's competence, its ability to deliver on a promise, but its integrity and benevolence, the qualities of character and purpose that build a durable relationship with customers, should engage all the elements of great creative content and right media context that we have discussed. Creative work that respects your audience by understanding them, engaging them and rewarding their attention. Media selection that reinforces your brand's stature and integrity. The sum of these parts is success, with performance that not only delivers results but adds to your brand's value into the future by giving it that priceless asset, the trust of your customer.

It has been a fascinating journey of discovery for us, trying to describe the anatomy of trusted advertising and to produce, through the work and help of so many expert practitioners, some guidance on how to achieve it. We hope you have found it illuminating; now it's over to you to use it to make ever better, more trustworthy and trust-enhancing advertising.

From Matt:

I studied media and business at university in the early 1990s. 'Trust' didn't really figure, particularly not when it came to advertising and marketing. There were rules, sure, but my recollection is that trust in ads was generally a given. Fast forward three decades and that's changed, so much so, it seems that for many (certainly, the majority), a view on advertising starts from a point of distrust. This shift is not just a challenge to advertising alone; it impacts upon many areas of our society. But it also appears that the value of being trusted, whether economic, social or political, is more important than ever.

I believe people trust as much as they always have but who, what, how and why people trust has changed. Technology has had a major impact on this, as has a combination of life-shaping events in the 21st century. However, the same issues of dishonesty in advertising – dodgy medical cures, get-rich-quick scams – are as prevalent today as they were 100 years ago. This dishonesty needs 'policing' by the likes of the ASA. Probably always will.

There is much debate within advertising over which is more important, the content or the context. To my mind, both are critical. Creating and producing the messages that communicate what your brand stands for requires a brilliantly thought-through and executed approach, one that can be trusted to be legal, decent, honest and truthful, but also entertaining, offering a useful value exchange, and one that is responsible, socially aware and respects the needs of your target audience. At the same time, your choice of messenger is many, complex and nuanced. It requires a high degree of expertise about the choices you have and understanding of how your target audience will respond, depending on your selection of who you choose to keep company with.

Despite many leading figures in our industry making the time to speak to us for this book, I think our industry can still do more to make trust a central tenet of its advertising campaign objectives, strategy and measurement. Quite simply, my call to action now is put trust on the ad plan.

What are you going to do to make sure the end result of your campaign includes greater trust in your brand, greater trust in the sector you operate in and greater trust in advertising generally? If it doesn't, why are you doing it? These questions apply as much to leaders of political brands, public sector organizations and NGOs as to commercial brands.

Finally, it's now apparent to me that nobody trusts anything in the same way or for the same reasons; why we trust is personal to each and every one of us. But we all need to be able to trust the things that are important to us in our lives. I think a useful next step would be for someone to develop a trust diagnostic tool for brands – one that helps establish how much trust there is in your sector, how much trust there is in your brand versus your competitive set, and one that describes the differing levels of trust in your target audience, from the person who's coming into contact with you for the first time, to the long-term, brand-loyal person, with a clear definition of what they need from your brand. If I cared deeply about the brand I was responsible for, this is what I would do next. I believe the person, organization or even nation with the strongest levels of trust wins. If I don't trust you, why should I listen to you? Furthermore, why should I believe you and act in the way you're asking me to if I don't trust you?

I challenge the notion advertising is just about selling things. Even if that's your main goal, you'll lose that sale if I trust your competitor more when it comes to factors like price, service or quality. But I think 21st-century advertising is about problem-solving through creativity. Many of the societal challenges we face in building a sustainable and inclusive future for everyone can be solved by creativity.

Success (or your ability to deliver that brilliant solution that makes a positive difference) ultimately depends on how much I trust you.

Trust matters to everyone working in advertising

As Paul Bainsfair, IPA Director General, observed at LEAD 2025, trust is like blood pressure.[2] It's invisible and silent, but it's vital for the health of advertising, and we must all keep an eye on it.

We have been confident enough in these conclusions to give you, the marketer or agency, a set of actions to ensure you can achieve the very best for your brand through trusted advertising.

If we can help you put trust at the heart of your work, and that work is responsible and made with good intentions, then the benefits flow to you and your brand, and maybe the economy and society more widely.

Here are our recommendations to you.

10 steps to trusted advertising

1 Remember, trust is one of your brand's most valuable assets – you have a responsibility to monitor its status and progress.

2 The dynamics of trust in the 21st century are changing – you cannot control trust in your brand, so be a proactive part of the conversation.

3 There are rules set by the industry and its regulators to ensure your work is legal, decent, honest and truthful – know, understand and comply with them.

4 Different people will have different levels of trust in you, your competitors and your sector – consider ways you can better understand this.

5 Be clear about what you want to be trusted for – make sure the promise in your advertising is matched by people's experience.

6 To gain trust, it helps a lot to be liked, but there is still a difference between being liked and being trusted – think about why your audience may like your brand and why they may trust it.

7 Great content enhances trust – use the armoury of creative techniques, including humour, emotion, music, storytelling to engage with your customers and strengthen their connection to your brand

8 The context your advertising appears in can affect people's trust in your brand – put your money where your trust is.

9 It is vital for trust levels in advertising generally that the commercial relationship between a brand and content or advocate is clear and transparent – don't be tempted to conceal it!

10 Your advertising supply chain is your responsibility – make sure your service providers live up to the standards of trustworthiness that your brand needs.

Notes

1 New IPA/FT global study reveals trust is the second most powerful business driver, The IPA, July 2025, https://ipa.co.uk/news/bridging-the-trust-gap/ (archived at https://perma.cc/D62K-XA6X)

2 Advertising Association, LEAD 2025 Digest, February 2025, https://adassoc. org.uk/our-work/the-lead-digest-key-takeaways/ (archived at https://perma.cc/ X66H-84X9)

INDEX

Looking for another book?

Explore our award-winning
books from global business
experts in Marketing and Sales

Scan the code to browse

www.koganpage.com/marketing

More books on Marketing and Sales from Kogan Page

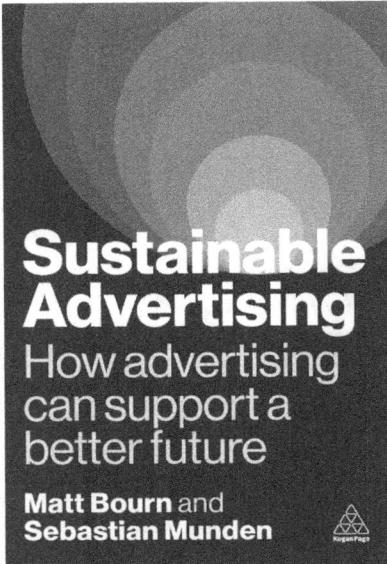

Sustainable Advertising
How advertising can support a better future
Matt Bourn and **Sebastian Munden**

ISBN: 9781398613836

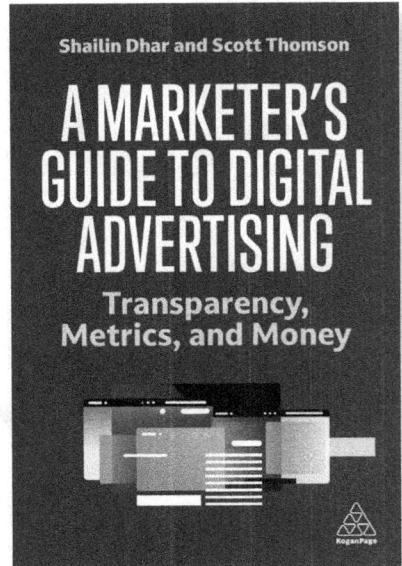

Shailin Dhar and Scott Thomson
A MARKETER'S GUIDE TO DIGITAL ADVERTISING
Transparency, Metrics, and Money

ISBN: 9781398609662

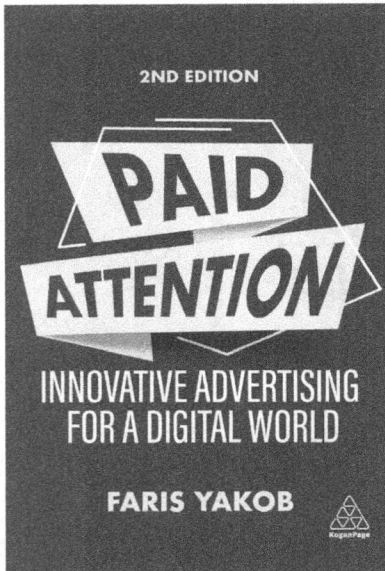

2ND EDITION
PAID ATTENTION
INNOVATIVE ADVERTISING FOR A DIGITAL WORLD
FARIS YAKOB

ISBN: 9781398602502

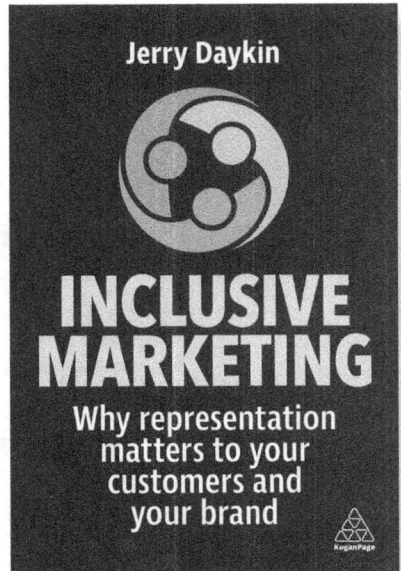

Jerry Daykin
INCLUSIVE MARKETING
Why representation matters to your customers and your brand

ISBN: 9781398607316

www.koganpage.com

KoganPage